The Impact of Regulatory Law on American Criminal Justice

The Impact of Regulatory Law on American Criminal Justice

Are There Too Many Laws?

Vincent Del Castillo

Carolina Academic Press

Durham, North Carolina

Library of Congress Cataloging-in-Publication Data

Del Castillo, Vincent.
 The impact of regulatory law on American criminal justice : are
there too many laws? / Vincent Del Castillo.
    p. cm.
 Includes bibliographical references and index.
 ISBN 978-1-61163-064-0 (alk. paper)
 1. Criminal justice, Administration of--United States. 2. Crimi-
nal law--United States. 3. Criminal procedure--United States. I.
Title.
 HV9950.D455 2012
 364.973--dc23   2012019502

CAROLINA ACADEMIC PRESS
700 Kent Street
Durham, North Carolina 27701
Telephone (919) 489-7486
Fax (919) 493-5668
www.cap-press.com

To my wife, Mary Alice, for her support and for attending to many of the details of our daily lives. Also, to my daughters, Doris and Rose, and their children, Berke, Sasha, Heloise and Alexandra, who all bring joy to my life. Finally, in loving memory of John Del Castillo.

I would also like to dedicate this book to my mentors and long-time friends, Charles Lindner, Charles Brennan and Sydney Cooper.

Contents

Preface   xv
   Book Structure   xvi

Part One • The Problem   3

Chapter One • Introduction   5
   Law, Criminal Behavior and the Criminal Justice System   5
      What is Law?   5
      Kinds of Law   7
      Who Enacts Law?   7
      Criminal Behavior   8
      The Criminal Justice System   9
      The Rule of Law   10
   The Crisis   10
      What is the problem?   11
      How did this crisis evolve?   13
      Community Standards   17
      The Federalism of Criminal Law   20
   Societal Effects   21
      Protection of Life and Property   22
      Public Health   22
      Rule of Law   23
   Discussion Questions   24
   Notes   25
   Bibliography   26

Chapter Two • Prohibition   29
   Introduction   29
      Background   30

The Prohibition Era: Passage of the Volstead Act   32
   Prohibition Enforcement   32
   Enforcement, Politics and Corruption   36
   Organized Crime   38
Summary   40
Commentary   40
Discussion Questions   42
Notes   43
Bibliography   44

Chapter Three • Illegal Drugs   47
Introduction   47
   Background   48
War on Drugs   52
Narcoterrorism and Transnational Organized Crime   55
Summary   56
Commentary   57
Discussion Questions   61
Notes   62
Bibliography   63

Chapter Four • Gun and Prostitution Laws   65
Introduction   65
Gun Laws   65
   History   66
Defensive Gun Use   69
State Comparisons of Violent Crime   70
Summary   71
Commentary   71
Prostitution   72
   Introduction   72
   Background   73
Prostitution Today   74
   Prostitution Enforcement   76
   Alternatives to Enforcement   79
Summary   79
Commentary   80

Discussion Questions   81
Notes   81
Bibliography   83

Chapter Five • Vehicle and Traffic Laws   87
Introduction   87
    History   87
Traffic Laws and Violations   88
    Traffic Enforcement   90
    Automated Enforcement   93
    Scofflaws   93
    Summary   93
Commentary   94
Discussion Questions   98
Notes   99
Bibliography   99

Part Two • Impact on the Criminal Justice System   101
The Criminal Justice System   102
The Criminal Justice System Flow Chart   104

Chapter Six • The Police   107
Introduction   107
The Police Role in Society   107
    Law Enforcement   107
    Protection of Life and Property   108
    Order Maintenance   108
    Crime Fighting   109
    Providing Services   109
Law Enforcement: A Brief History   109
    The Political Era (1850s to 1900)   110
    The Reform Era   111
    The Community Era   113
Attitudes Towards Regulatory Laws   114
Enforcing Regulatory Laws   115
    Police Discretion   116
    Enforcement Activity Quotas   117

Racial Profiling 118
Police Corruption 120
Summary 124
Commentary 125
Discussion Questions 128
Notes 129
Bibliography 130

Chapter Seven · The Courts 133
Introduction 133
Historical Perspective 133
The Criminal Court 134
Prosecuting Attorney 134
Prosecutorial Discretion 135
Defense Attorney 136
Judges 137
The Jury 138
Selection of Jurors 139
The Criminal Trial 139
Alternatives to Trial 142
Plea Bargaining 142
Summary 145
Commentary 146
Discussion Questions 147
Notes 148
Bibliography 148

Chapter Eight · Corrections 151
Introduction 151
History 151
Colonial Period (1600s to 1790s) 152
Penitentiary Period (1790s to 1860s) 152
Reformatory Period (1870s-1890s) 153
Progressive Period (1890s-1930s) 153
Medical Period (1930s — 1960s) 154
Community Period (1960s-1970s) 154
Crime Control Period (1970s to Present) 155

Contemporary Corrections   155
　　Prisons and Jails   156
　　Prison Gangs   158
　　Infectious Diseases   159
　　Probation and Parole   160
　　Recidivism   161
　Summary   162
　Commentary   163
　Discussion Questions   165
　Notes   165
　Bibliography   167

Part Three • Consequences for Society   171

Chapter Nine • The Social Contract and the Rule of Law 173
　Introduction   173
　The Social Contract   173
　Causes of Criminal Behavior   175
　　Classical Theory   176
　　Deterministic Theories   176
　　Labeling Theory   177
　Criminal Justice and the Social Contract   179
　The Rule of Law   180
　　Laws Based on Popular Consent   182
　　A Functional Judicial System   183
　　Professional Law Enforcement   184
　　Does the Government Subordinate Itself to the Law?   185
　　Encouraging Criminal Behavior   185
　　Public Perceptions of the Criminal Justice System   186
　Summary   187
　Commentary   189
　Discussion Questions   192
　Notes   193
　Bibliography   194

Chapter Ten • Race Relations   197
　Introduction   197

Background 197
Race and Class 199
Police Deployment 200
Arrests for Regulatory Law Violations 201
Racial Profiling 202
Stop and Frisk 203
Minority Officers 205
Summary 206
Commentary 207
Discussion Questions 208
Notes 209
Bibliography 210

Chapter Eleven • Societal Consequences 213
Introduction 213
The Facilitation of Crime 213
Eroding the Rule of Law 216
Incarceration 218
Perpetuating an Underclass 219
Infectious Diseases 220
Minority Relations 221
Misdirection of Criminal Justice Resources 222
National and Local Economy 223
Summary 224
Commentary 225
Discussion Questions 226
Notes 227
Bibliography 228

Chapter Twelve • Summary and Conclusions 231
Introduction 231
Prohibition 233
Illegal Drugs 233
Gun Control 235
Prostitution 235
Vehicle and Traffic 236
Police 237

Courts 238
Corrections 238
Social Contract and the Rule of Law 239
Race Relations 240
Societal Consequences 240
Conclusion 241
Discussion Questions 242

Index 245

Preface

The Impact of Regulatory Law on Criminal Justice was written to present an overview of the systemic problems associated with the enforcement of regulatory laws. Regulatory laws are those criminal laws that prohibit socially unacceptable behavior such as the possession, sale and use of certain drugs, prostitution, gambling, traffic violations and so on.

This project began several years ago as a textbook for a 400 level seminar course in police problems. As a preliminary step, over one hundred police chiefs from across the country were asked to provide a list of about five of their most serious problems. Nearly all of the responses rated police/community relations problems highest on their lists. Those problems included racial profiling and a negative police image, particularly in minority communities.

Further examination revealed that many of the community relation problems were related to the enforcement of regulatory laws. It also became apparent that the enforcement of regulatory laws placed a heavy burden not only on the police, but also on the resources of the entire criminal justice system, resulting in a system that cannot function as it was intended. Because of over-legislation, it is argued that there are too many laws for the criminal justice system to adequately enforce and process. Law enforcement, traditionally considered an action taken by the police is also a *process*, one that begins with an arrest by the police and continues through the adjudication and correctional phase and ultimately ends with re-entry into society.

Because of inadequate resources, those arrested by police routinely have their charges and sentences reduced through plea negotiations, resulting in early release back into society, and more often than not, a continuation of criminal activities ending with another arrest by police: the often-cited *revolving door of justice*. The complexities of this problem require an examination of the impact of regulatory law enforcement on the police within the context of the entire criminal justice system.

Although police acknowledge that they cannot enforce all laws, they still make more arrests than the courts can adjudicate without heavy reliance on plea negotiations. Additionally, corrections lack sufficient facilities to house all those convicted of crimes. Nevertheless, as a nation we still incarcerate a higher proportion of our population than any other country in the world.

Book Structure

Each chapter in the text addresses one aspect of the overall theme, beginning with background material and, where applicable, a historical timeline of events leading up to the present. The chapters end with a review and a commentary that seeks to provide additional insight into that chapter's contribution to the book's theme. This is followed by a list of discussion questions related to topics covered within that chapter.

Part One contains an introductory overview of the entire textbook as well as a review of some of the more familiar regulatory laws. Part Two examines the effects of regulatory law on the three major components of the criminal justice system: the police, courts and corrections. Part Three shows the impact of regulatory law on society in terms of the social contract, the rule of law, police/race relations and society in general. The final chapter provides a summary of the entire text.

The Impact of Regulatory Law on American Criminal Justice

PART ONE

The Problem

Government has a responsibility to protect the life and property of its citizens from victimization. This is accomplished through a code of criminal law enforced by a criminal justice system. In addition to laws that protect citizens, the government also enacts laws that criminalize certain behaviors that are deemed to be inconsistent with the best interests of society. These are called regulatory laws and it is these laws and their effect on the criminal justice system and society that will be the subject of this book.

Is our criminal justice system broken? Police readily admit that they don't have enough officers to fully enforce all laws. Yet, they are able to make more arrests than the courts can adequately adjudicate. Additionally, the judicial process is so overwhelmed that it must rely on plea negotiations in order to circumvent the lengthy trial process, thus reducing criminal charges and/or terms of incarceration. Nevertheless, more people are convicted than the correctional facilities can house. Despite that, our nation incarcerates a higher proportion of its population than any other country. Finally, because of plea-bargaining, early release of prisoners due to prison overcrowding and the police practice of ignoring certain incidents of lawlessness, it is no wonder that the public holds our criminal justice system in low esteem.

Why does this situation exist? Are there too many laws or is our criminal justice system simply lacking the resources necessary to deal effectively with the laws we have? It's like the question of the glass being half full or half empty; it all depends on one's perspective.

The proceeding chapters will endeavor to answer these questions. The chapters in Part One will study the problem in greater detail and will examine some examples of regulatory law. Part Two will consider the effects that regulatory laws have on the criminal justice system and Part Three will review the impact of this problem on society.

CHAPTER ONE

Introduction

Are there too many criminal laws in the United States? Have these laws created a crisis in our criminal justice system and our society? The criminal laws referred to are not those intended to protect life and property but rather the regulatory laws that prohibit behavior that would otherwise be permissible.

This chapter provides an overview of the law, criminal behavior and the criminal justice system. It will also detail the current crisis and its negative social impact. Some common sense principles are proposed to address the issue. Chapters Two, Three, Four and Five will show the evolutionary process leading up to perhaps the most familiar regulatory laws: those dealing with prohibition of alcohol, illegal drugs, gun control, prostitution and vehicular traffic. Chapters Six, Seven and Eight will examine the effects of regulatory laws on the major components of the criminal justice system: the police, courts and corrections. The next three chapters will show the impact of regulatory laws on society and the last chapter will summarize the major issues presented throughout the book.

Law, Criminal Behavior and the Criminal Justice System

What is Law?

There is currently no consensus amongst scholars as to what law is. Scholars have described law as socially approved use of force, rules enforced by legal institutions and rules of conduct made obligatory by some sanction imposed by a controlling authority. According to Bastiat, law " ... is the collective organiza-

tion of the individual right to lawful defense."[1] A simple definition from a lay perspective is that laws are rules of conduct that
have been codified and carry with them standardized consequences for their violation.

Rules are common to all social groups and human interactions.
Put two or more people together and they will soon produce rules
that regulate their behavior. Those rules are seldom written or spo-
ken but understood nevertheless. For example, we expect others
to refrain from striking us in anger or revealing secrets that we have
confided in them and we expect people to keep their word. When
those rules are violated, sanctions usually result. Those sanctions
may range from a verbal reprimand to shunning, severed relationships or even violence.

Larger social groups formalize those rules. If we join a team,
club or become employed by a corporation, we will find ourselves
subject to a formal set of rules with specific, formal sanctions if
those rules are violated. Governments express rules through laws
that affect a range of civil, governmental and criminal circumstances. Evidence of laws has been found in virtually every society
since the beginning of recorded history. Moreover, anthropologists
report that even primitive tribes certainly had rules, rites and rit-
uals that governed behavior.

One of the earliest examples of written law is the Code of
Hammurabi, the king of Babylon. Discovered in 1901, Hammurabi's Code of nearly 300 laws is contained on a stone slab
dated at about 2000 B.C. These laws deal with a wide range of
social activities and responsibilities. They include laws regarding
marital relations; buying, selling or renting property or livestock;
house and ship builders' accountability for structural integrity,
as well as responsibilities for accidental damage, deaths or injuries. Hammurabi's code also contains laws regarding criminal
conduct including murder, rape, robbery and larceny. Hammurabi's Code was based on objectives and principles contained
in its preamble. Of particular interest is the intent of the law to,
" ... bring about the rule of righteousness in the land, to destroy
the wicked and the evil-doers; so that the strong should not harm
the weak ..."[2]

Kinds of Law

There are two major types of laws: civil and criminal. Civil laws refer primarily to responsibilities of individuals to others. Legal standards affecting contracts, marriage and liability for damage to property or personal injury are some examples of civil law. Violations of these laws usually require restitution or compensation rather than punishment.

Criminal laws define prohibited acts committed against the state that are punishable by fine and/or imprisonment. Criminal laws are divided into *malum in se* and *malum prohibitum*. According to *State v. Horton*, 139 N.C. 588, 51 S.E. 945, 946 (1905), *Malum in se* refers to behavior that is "naturally evil as adjudged by the sense of a civilized community."[3] Such behaviors include murder, robbery, and generally any activity that inflicts intentional harm to persons or intentional damage to their property. *Malum prohibitum* refers to offenses that are wrong only because a statute makes it so. "Public welfare offenses" are a subset of *malum prohibitum* offenses as they are typically regulatory in nature and often "result in no direct or immediate injury to person or property but merely create the danger or probability of it which the law seeks to minimize."[4] Traffic violations, and laws that regulate gun possession, prostitution and gambling are examples of *malum prohibitum* offences. *Malum prohibitum* laws are also referred to as regulatory laws. Criminal laws serve two primary purposes: first, to provide clearly identified limits on behavior and second, to punish or sanction those who violate those laws. The issue of punishment raises some interesting issues.

Who Enacts Law?

Most laws are enacted by federal or state legislatures; however, they can also be enacted at other levels of government including cities, towns and villages. An established hierarchy of authority resolves conflicts between laws. The United States Constitution is the highest authority in the country and no law can conflict with the Constitution. Next in line are treaties with foreign governments, followed by acts of the United States Congress, state constitutions, state laws and case law, which are precedent setting court rulings.

Criminal Behavior

We immediately think in terms of criminals when we think of law violators and indeed the definition of a criminal is simply a person who commits a crime. However, most people admit to having done something in their lives, usually in their teen years, for which they could have been arrested. Does it then follow that the vast majority of Americans are criminals? We don't think of ourselves as criminals because we don't murder people or commit burglaries or robberies, but how many of us violate traffic laws? Yes, you can be arrested for a traffic offense. The U.S. Supreme Court upheld the arrest of a woman in Texas for not wearing a seat belt while driving.[5] But, we need to draw a distinction between those who are criminals in the traditional sense of the word and the rest of the population. As will be explained later, many average law-abiding citizens are drawn into violations of laws because of the manner in which those laws are enacted and inconsistencies in the way they are enforced.

For centuries criminologists have tried to understand and explain the criminal mind, the result of which was the formulation of countless theories. The oldest of these theories is the Classical Theory of Criminality, commonly known as Choice Theory, that was developed by Cesare Beccaria in the late 1700s. This theory posits that people choose to commit crimes through a rational decision-making process.[6] According to the theory, people weigh the possible gains and consequences of the act and choose to either commit the crime or not.[7]

There are also a number of deterministic theories. Those theories can be grouped into three broad categories: biological, psychological and sociological. Each of these theories examines the underlying factors that predispose a person to criminal behavior. Biological theories of criminality generally focus on physiological characteristics such as hereditary, genetic predisposition to violence, diet and, in rare cases, brain tumors. Psychological theories are based primarily on the work of Sigmund Freud and focus on the critical first six years of life when such traits as personality, conscience and values are imprinted. Sociological theories argue that such forces as affiliations, peer pressure, neighborhood and life style are major determinants in criminality. There are also numerous additional explanations based on combinations of the theories just mentioned.

The Criminal Justice System

Criminal laws are enforced and processed by the police, courts and corrections, collectively referred to as the criminal justice system. Police agencies are responsible for a number of social roles including: investigating crimes and arresting offenders; protecting life and property through uniformed patrols; promoting highway and street safety through traffic control; maintaining public order; assisting communities in promoting public safety and crime prevention programs; providing emergency services; and a host of other specialized services.

The U.S. judicial system is the arena for the adversarial process of justice. During criminal trials, prosecutors present evidence supporting an accusation of guilt of a defendant and defense attorneys attempt to rebut that evidence and may present evidence to contradict the prosecution's case. Judges supervise the trials and ensure that all evidence and procedures are consistent with applicable laws and procedure. Upon findings of guilt, judges pronounce sentences consistent with legal guidelines.

Correctional agencies are responsible for carrying out court sentences. Jails are used for detention of individuals awaiting trial and for individuals sentenced to less than one year of incarceration. Individuals sentenced to one year or more are usually housed in prisons. Corrections also include the supervision of individuals who are not incarcerated. Individuals sentenced to situations other than incarceration such as house arrest and probation are required to report to probation officers. Parole officers are responsible for supervising those who have been paroled from prison prior to the end of a sentence of incarceration.

The Rule of Law

Central to the concept of law in a free society is the principle of the Rule of Law that holds that no person is above the law and that the law should be applied equally to all persons. The 14th Amendment to the U.S. Constitution takes this ideal further by declaring unconstitutional any unreasonable distinctions made between different people in the application of the law. This principle of fairness provides that the law should be applied objectively and evenly. Law is not an instrument or weapon to be used with malice against some, but rather, with equality toward all. The government is not exempt from the rule of law. When laws are violated, the government is obligated to take those actions proscribed by those laws.

The Crisis

The most apparent impact of the crisis we face is found in the criminal justice system. The system does not have the resources or capacity to adequately enforce all criminal laws or adequately process the volume of people who violate the law. Police cannot fully enforce all laws; consequently, many laws are openly violated and some laws are ignored entirely. Police compensate for this by using measures such as selective enforcement and police discretion to prioritize offenses. Police departments as well as individual officers must decide which offenses will be enforced and which will not, and who will be selected for enforcement and who will not. Although some discretion is essential in policing, the overreliance on individual decision making results in disparate standards in the application of the law. Our American concept of justice holds that all are equally subject to the same law and that no one should be held to a law from which others are de facto exempt. Lack of confidence in the integrity of the police and their ability to maintain order as well as public bitterness associated with accusations of racial profiling are but some of the consequences of the uneven application of the law.

Courts and prosecutors cannot adequately accommodate even the limited number of arrests made by the police. The vast majority of all arrests are plea-bargained and in large cities the rate of plea-bargaining exceeds 90%. Many repeat offenders as well as probation and parole violators are commonly released or given light sentences only to return to habitual criminal behavior. Judges and prosecutors decline to prosecute certain types of criminal behavior, leaving police to either ignore future similar violations, or to lose valuable police patrol time effecting arrests of individuals who are certain to be released: a process that has commonly been referred to as *revolving door justice*. Having to virtually ignore certain violations of law further exacerbates the negative effects on the police image, particularly by individuals who are offended by those violations. Finally, there are not enough prisons to accommodate those who are found guilty of crimes. Violent felons are routinely given early release, not because they are ready to be reintegrated into society, but instead simply to reduce the number of inmates to a level consistent with court-imposed prison capacity standards. Also, numerous alternatives to incarceration programs are abused in an attempt to supervise those who should have been imprisoned, leaving probation and parole officers burdened with unmanageably large caseloads.

What is the problem?

These are just some of the more apparent effects of the crisis. So, what is the underlying problem? Some might suggest that prison overcrowding is the problem that impacts the rest of the system. There is some logic to this proposition because the lack of prison space forces the courts to be more lenient in their sentencing policies which in turn results in less incarceration time for repeat offenders, creating more criminals for police to handle, and thereby more arrests which in turn lead to overcrowded court calendars and overcrowded prisons. A vicious cycle that, it would appear, could be solved by more prisons.

Others might argue that the problem begins with light sentences by lenient judges which encourage crime, leading to more arrests, heavier court calendars, overcrowded prisons, early release, increased recidivism and so on. Still others would contend that the criminal justice system is only equipped to deal with criminals but not the causes of crime and until we address the underlying causes of criminality, we will be frustrated in our attempts to control crime through coercive methods. Although there is some validity to all these theories, they focus primarily on the symptoms of the problem but fail to identify the underlying cause; that is, the tendency on the part of legislators to over-legislate, to create more laws than can be adequately enforced and processed by the criminal justice system. Laws have been increasing in volume over the past century and have reached and even exceeded an unsustainable level, resulting in severe damage to our system of justice. The specific effects on the criminal justice system will be discussed in greater detail in Part Two.

An alternative or competing explanation is that there are not too many laws but rather that the volume of laws is appropriate and there are simply not enough resources to enforce those laws and process the offenders. This explanation, although compelling, overlooks the fact that the United States already incarcerates a higher proportion of its citizens than any other country in the world. According to the Bureau of Justice Statistics (BJS), from 1980 to 2009 the U.S. prison and jail population quadrupled in size, from about 500,000 to more than 2.2 million (2011).[8] (The two million figure somewhat understates the problem. Total incarceration is a function of the capacity of prisons. Many of those under other forms of correctional supervision and alternative to incarceration programs would, if space were available, also be incarcerated).[9] Consequently, a large proportion of our citizens have criminal records, which contributes to a variety of social problems including poverty, broken homes, children without positive role models, homelessness, continued criminality, and a host of related social ills. Perhaps the greatest impact and the most insidious social problem is the growing level of disrespect for the rule of law and our system of justice.

How did this crisis evolve?

We are a nation of laws. We have elected representatives at the national, state and local level of government whose primary purpose is to represent their constituency in the proper governance of our country. They are given the authority to enact laws when necessary to accomplish their governmental purpose. Unfortunately, many people, legislators in particular, believe that if they are against something, it should be against the law or if they are for something, law should mandate it. Also, because law is the most visible aspect of their job, legislators too often enact laws for self-serving purposes. They identify with and point to those laws during re-election campaigns to show that they are tough on crime or support other popular causes. As it applies to regulatory law, they rarely, if ever, allocate sufficient resources to enforce those laws nor do they consult with law enforcement and the judiciary to determine if those laws are enforceable or if enforcement will require additional resources. Legislators also enact mandatory sentencing rules for certain crimes without regard for the capacity of the correctional facilities to handle an increase in inmates.

Since the inception of the United States, legislators have amassed an enormous body of law, while repealing few laws. Further, the rate of criminal legislation has steadily increased over the past century and today we have laws that affect virtually every aspect of society. In fact, as this book was in its early stages, New York became the first state in the nation to enact a law forbidding the use of hand held phones while driving and the United States Congress is currently exploring legislation that would require every state in the country to enact similar laws.

The need for law in society is indisputable and it can also be argued that the need for new laws is dictated by new technologies and the desire for harmonious coexistence, especially in a complex, densely populated social structure. Further, the need for public order requires the enactment of specific prohibitions. However, laws are not without cost. Laws must be enforced, those who are accused of violating those laws are entitled to constitutionally guaranteed due process protections, including the right to counsel, jury trials, appeals, and if convicted, to publicly funded correctional institutions.

Many laws, particularly unpopular laws, have had severe and unintended, but predictable, consequences. Prohibition is perhaps the most notable failure of an unpopular law. Although it was enacted to reduce drinking and crime, it actually had the opposite effect, resulting in more alcohol consumption and giving birth to the concept of organized crime. Likewise, the laws against drugs did not reduce the use of illegal drugs but resulted in international drug cartels and a drug culture that permeates every aspect of our culture. Drug prohibition laws have also had far-reaching international consequences as well. Corrupt governments as well as national and international terrorism can be directly attributed to the enormous profits from the illegal drug trade within the United States, the most lucrative drug market. Repeated political promises for a war on drugs are consistently followed by timid, half-hearted efforts that only appear to wage a serious campaign against the problem.

Laws are repeatedly enacted with little or no regard to how they will be enforced, prosecuted, or punished, thereby leaving the public with often very costly, broken and misleading promises. Questions as to a law's effectiveness in achieving its intended goal are almost never asked. But, when it becomes apparent that laws have not prevented high-profile tragedies, such as the murders at Columbine High School, the invariable solution is the enactment of additional laws, even though existing laws were not sufficiently enforced.

The process by which regulatory laws have evolved and how they negatively impact society is rather complex but with the analyses contained in the following chapters, the underlying causes will become evident. Logical principles for a common sense approach to criminal law legislation can be recommended. The first two principles are: 1) *The enactment of a law requires a commitment to provide the resources and the will to enforce that law,* and 2) *If a law fails to achieve its intended purpose or if there are legitimate reasons why it should not be enforced as written then it should be revised or repealed.*

Too often the enactment of a law is seen as an end unto itself, a public statement of sorts that declares certain behavior as being unacceptable. Whether that law is enforceable or not is of secondary concern. Also, laws frequently outlive their relevance and are ignored by police and the public. This leads to confusion for all concerned and has a deleterious effect on the rule of law. Admittedly a strong statement, but one that the following brief examples will support:

First, except for some high-profile cases, the crime of prostitution is virtually ignored by law enforcement and by the courts. Even when so-called round-ups of street prostitutes do occur they rarely result in jail sentences. Prostitutes are either given suspended sentences, probation or, even worse, fines, thereby reducing the criminal justice system to a partner in the illegal proceeds.

The second example involves traffic laws, particularly highway speed limits. Anyone who has driven on our parkways and highways has witnessed or even driven at speeds well in excess of the speed limit only to be passed by others driving at even greater speeds. The appearance of a police vehicle, particularly when a car has been stopped, may induce only a temporary reduction in speed that will quickly abate when the police are out of sight. In fact, police vehicles often ride along with the speeding traffic, resulting in tacit approval of the unlawful speeds.

The final example is a well-known and controversial contemporary issue, that of illegal immigration. Over the past decades literally millions of people have entered and continue to enter and remain in this country illegally. Yet the federal government has virtually ignored these law violations. Many individuals knowingly and openly employ these individuals — also a violation of the law. The impact on society is considerable in terms of lost jobs and increases in the costs of medical, educational, and other social programs without the compensatory revenues from Medicare and Social Security taxes that go unpaid by the illegal workers and their employers.

The argument that illegal aliens only take jobs that Americans would not want is spurious. Employers pay these workers less than minimum wages and avoid workers compensation, and unemployment insurance payments as well as social security and other taxes. Because of their reduced labor costs they can submit lower bids for landscaping, industrial cleaning and other similar labor-intensive contracts. Competing companies are left to either commit similar violations to remain competitive or go out of business.[10]

When illegal aliens are discovered entering this country they are often given the equivalent of a summons to appear for a hearing. They almost never appear for the initial or subsequent hearings. According to Seper (2004):

> " ... more than 375,000 known illegal aliens have been ordered deported, but have disappeared pending immigration hearings" (p.1).[11] Unlike the undocumented worker stereotype, many actively pursue criminal activities.[12] Even subsequent arrests for serious crimes rarely result in deportation.[13]
>
> About 80,000 illegal criminal aliens, including convicted murderers, rapists, drug dealers and child molesters who served prison time and were released, are loose on the streets of America, hiding from federal immigration authorities ... many state and local police agencies who make contact with the aliens either never learn of their immigration status or never advise the federal government of their release ... [14]

Also according to Seper (2004):

> Making matters more difficult for federal authorities are several municipalities that have passed ordinances prohibiting their employees, including police officers, from enforcing federal immigration laws.[15] Known as "sanctuary laws," the ordinances are in place in varying degree in major cities such as Los Angeles, San Francisco and Houston (p.1).[16]

By enacting laws that hide the identity of illegal aliens these municipalities subvert the intent of the federal law and are themselves in violation of federal legislation. In addition to the economic costs involved, the lack of resources, and equally important, the lack of will of the federal government to enforce these laws also tends to weaken the rule of law. If there are compelling reasons why the law should not be enforced then as the aforementioned principles state, revise or repeal the law. However, if the law is valid then appropriate sufficient resources so that it can be adequately enforced.

Repeated amnesty programs only serve to reward this illegal behavior and encourage others to enter this country unlawfully rather than to immigrate through the conventional legitimate channels. This is particularly troublesome when one considers the number of aliens who attempt to enter the United States legally. They patiently wait for permission to do something that others take upon themselves to do with apparent immunity. Reasons for the failure of immigration law can be found in the first principle, providing the resources and will to enforce the law. Lack of will in this instance can be attributed to political concerns, particularly the desire of members of both major political parties to gain support within the Hispanic population, or at least, not to lose support.

Community Standards

National laws also fail to achieve compliance because they do not have broad-based support, as America is not a homogeneous society. There are regional, racial, ethnic, and religious differences in attitudes towards life and standards of behavior. In a free society, law enforcement relies on voluntary compliance with the law. The criminal justice system does not have the resources to adequately enforce a law if a substantial number of people decide to violate that law. Take highway speed limits again, for example. Motorists commonly exceed highway speed limits by twenty miles per hour or higher. Because of sheer numbers, police must exercise discretion and only cite a small percentage of highway speeders. This issue will be explored in depth in Chapter Five.

The lack of broad-based support is most applicable to laws enacted at the federal or state levels of government. Even if a law is supported by a majority of the public, 50% to 60% for example, this still leaves a substantial proportion of the population, nearly

100 million people, who may not support the law. This is of particular concern when those who oppose the law represent geographic pockets of a state or the nation. This brings us to the third principle: *In order to gain maximum support and be most reflective of community standards, regulatory laws should be enacted at the lowest level of government that is practical.*

One purpose of regulatory law is to ensure that people do not violate socially acceptable standards or engage in behavior that interferes with others or threaten the fabric of society. This is particularly important when people live in close proximity, such as in densely populated urban areas. Community standards are a guideline used by the courts to determine if behavior is patently offensive to prevailing standards in a given geographic area.

The term "community" does not easily lend itself to specific definition, as it is difficult to find consensus among social scientists and legal scholars as to what the term means. Although seemingly straightforward, in legal practice the term "community" is vague and largely without specific meaning. For example, in *HAMLING v. UNITED STATES* (1974) the U.S. Supreme Court held that as a Constitutional matter community standards did not mean that any precise geographic area is required. In fact, national community standards were not constitutionally improper. However, because of the diverse meanings, for the purpose at hand, the conceptualization of community will contain certain basic components, such as a collection of people in a specific geographic area with a sense of belonging or community spirit. Community members may also have common interests in terms of income, religion, social status, race and/or ethnicity. Communities may also be geographically separated from other areas such as islands, small villages, tourist locations, college towns, neighborhoods of larger cities, etc. Further, community standards will be considered those standards of morally acceptable (or unacceptable) behavior of community members or those who find themselves in the community.

As a practical matter, the closer a law is enacted to a local community, the greater the consensus of that community to the purpose and appropriateness of a law and the more they would be willing to support, commit resources to and voluntarily comply with that law. Conversely, because America is not a homogeneous society but rather a socially diverse patchwork of cultural regions, each dominated by ideological, religious, ethnic and lifestyle differences, the likelihood of broad consensus is minimal. Equally important, if a local law is not consistent with community standards those who enacted the law could be pressured to repeal or change the law or be voted out of office.

Successful enforcement of laws depends to a great extent on community support for those laws. The larger the proportion of the population who agree with the law and are willing to comply with that law, the fewer police and criminal justice resources will be needed to enforce that law and process its violators. Conversely, anarchy occurs when there is total disregard for the law, rebellion well beyond the ability and resources of the criminal justice system to suppress. This is particularly relevant to regulatory laws that involve behavior that is deemed to be socially or morally unacceptable. The question is, who finds the behavior unacceptable? If it is not those who are directly affected by that behavior then the relevance of the law is brought into question. In order to ensure that community standards are reflected in regulatory laws, the laws should be enacted at a governmental level closest to the community or communities that subscribe to those standards.

For example, if the vast majority of a town so resent and are offended by second hand smoke that they propose to ban smoking in all public places in that town then it follows that there will be a high degree of voluntary compliance with the ban and the citizens will not only support enforcement but will favor committing the necessary police and criminal justice resources to enforcing the ban. However, suppose that same ban were applied nationally. All that is needed to pass a law is a majority of each of the houses of congress and the approval of the President. Although the process is democratically sound, there could be twenty or more states whose citizens opposed the ban and their congressional representatives accordingly voted against the law. What would happen in those states? There would undoubtedly be large geographic areas, perhaps entire states, whose citizens would rebel against the ban and local police would be reluctant to enforce the law. This was particularly evident during the Prohibition Era. A number of states prohibited manufacture and sale of alcoholic beverages for years prior to national prohibition, some for as long as eighty years. Yet, when all the other states were included in the law it created a large-scale rebellion in addition to the emergence of organized crime. Prohibition will be examined more closely in Chapter Two.

The Federalism of Criminal Law

National surveys on attitudes regarding controversial issues routinely show few positions with overwhelming consensus. Therefore, regulatory laws enacted at the national level are at an even greater risk of being difficult if not impossible to enforce. Nevertheless, over the past century, there has been a steady increase in national criminal law.

From the ratification of the Constitution there was a distinct separation of state and federal governments' responsibility for criminal law enforcement, particularly with respect to laws dealing with crimes against individuals such as murder, rape and assault. The states had primary responsibility for enacting and enforcing criminal law. The federal government enforced crimes that were outside the responsibility of the states and dealt primarily with offenses against the federal government, such as misuse of the mails, crimes involving interstate commerce, bribery of federal officials, perjury in federal courts and treason. It was not until the early 1900s, with prohibition of narcotics and alcohol, that federal crimes began to cover activity that dealt with subjects clearly within the authority of the states' police powers. This expansion was based on Congressional power to regulate interstate commerce.

Criminal laws, including regulatory laws, were also included in an increasing number of federal programs. In the 1960s and 1970s, national concern focused on drugs, fear of crime, urban violence, civil rights and other social problems. The federal government responded with a significant increase in federal legislation criminalizing behavior heretofore relegated to state criminal codes. Soaring crime rates of the 1980s and 1990s, especially drug-related crimes and gun violence, provided even greater impetus for additional federal sanctions, also previously left to state jurisdiction. The federalization of criminal law, particularly the number of federal crimes enacted each year, has become an issue of such concern as to be the subject of a study by a Task Force of the American Bar Association.

Among the findings of the Task Force report (1998) were:

> So large is the present body of federal criminal law that there is no conveniently accessible, complete list of federal crimes ... Criminal sanctions are dispersed in places other than the statutory codes ... and therefore cannot be located simply by reading statutes. A large number of sanctions are dispersed throughout the thousands of administrative "regulations" promulgated by various governmental agencies under Congressional statutory authorization. Nearly 10,000 regulations mention some sort of sanction, many clearly criminal in nature ... Whatever the exact number of crimes that comprise today's "federal criminal law," it is clear that the amount of individual citizen behavior now potentially subject to federal criminal control has increased in astonishing proportions in the last few decades.[17]

The Task Force (1998) also found that, " ... the Congressional appetite for new crimes regardless of their merit is not only misguided and ineffectual, but as serious adverse consequences ..." (p. 41).[18] The federalization of criminal law, especially laws that could be prosecuted by the states, diverts federal authorities and resources from constitutionally mandated responsibilities, particularly those involving border protection.

Societal Effects

In addition to the direct effects on the criminal justice system, the volume of regulatory laws has taken an enormous toll on our society. Three examples are cited here while later chapters will deal with these issues in greater detail.

Protection of Life and Property

As a result of overtaxed judicial resources, the courts and prosecutors have relied heavily on plea bargaining to expedite criminal cases. People accused of violent felonies often plead guilty to reduced charges and are sentenced to terms far less than the law would provide for if they had been convicted of the original offense. By pleading guilty to lesser, unrelated charges, these pleas also serve to side-step mandatory sentences for crimes such as firearm and drug possession. Further, the lack of sufficient correctional facilities to house prisoners has resulted in policies granting early release from prison, thereby reducing even further the amount of time these felons should have served for their crimes. When one considers the high rate of recidivism, it is no wonder that we hear daily of people committing horrendous crimes including kidnapping, rape and murder only to discover that they have been arrested multiple times within the past few years for similar crimes. Eliminating plea-bargains for violent felons and keeping them incarcerated for the full term of their sentence is an effective form of crime prevention. Yet, it is impossible to calculate the amount of violent crime that the public is subjected to because people who should be incarcerated are permitted to roam free and continue to prey on the innocent.

Public Health

Many prisoners suffer from a variety of communicable diseases, including Tuberculosis. While incarcerated they are provided with a regimen of treatment that is often incomplete at the time of their early release. Because treatment is rarely continued after release, these diseases that have become resistant to traditional medications have found their way into the general population. Another example involves selective enforcement and prosecution of prostitutes. Street prostitutes are allowed to operate with little interference while the criminal justice system seems to focus primarily on high-profile cases. Yet, street prostitutes are typically underage drug addicted girls and boys who are infected with a host of sexually transmitted diseases, including HIV, and have been a major conduit for these diseases entering the general population.

Rule of Law

Perhaps the most serious governmental offense has been its violation of the Rule of Law; no one is above the law and everyone is equally subject to the same law. The image of justice being blind is intended to illustrate this concept of objectivity in the enforcement and application of the law and is at the core of our form of government. However, practices such as selective enforcement, and overreliance on personal discretion on the part of law enforcement and in the judicial process has lead to a growing disrespect for the law and the impression that some people can openly violate the law with no apparent consequences while others are held strictly liable to the law's full effect. Whether this is actually the case or not is of little consequence. Peoples' attitudes are formed by their beliefs and when the public perceives an uneven or unfair application of the law, whether true or not, consequences in terms of lowered esteem for the criminal justice process will still result.

Members of minority groups in particular hold the police and the criminal justice system in low esteem and the rest of the population has an increasingly diminished respect for the law. For example, most contacts with the police are through traffic enforcement. Also, people are aware that police exercise discretion and the decision to enforce a law is a subjective one. When a person is stopped for speeding and they realize that the police have allowed countless others to drive in excess of the speed limit without interference, their obvious question is, "Why me?" When there is a visible difference between the officer and the individual, then the perceived answer to that question is found in that distinction. If there is a racial dissimilarity, then the person is likely to assume that the reason for the stop is an underlying racial prejudice on the part of the officer.

Of course the greatest abuser of selective enforcement is the Federal Government because many federal criminal laws duplicate existing state laws and federal investigators and prosecutors have the authority to exercise discretion in selecting certain cases while leaving others for state prosecutors. The selection process can be based on such subjective criteria as public notoriety or for politically motivated reasons. Federal prosecutors likewise can accept or reject cases referred to them by local authorities, again, based on subjective criteria. The so-called "Brady Bill" that prohibited felons and certain others from possessing firearms was only enforced and prosecuted less than fifty times during the first few years after its ratification in the mid-1990s, despite thousands of referrals from local law enforcement. The remaining thousands of cases were processed locally. The Brady Bill expired in September 2004; however, a bill enacted in 1998 requires background checks when buying guns in a gun shop, and that bill is still in effect.

It should be noted here that this commentary is not intended to be an indictment of either the police or the criminal justice system. They are forced to operate with insufficient resources to accomplish their legally proscribed mission. It is a question of simple economics; when there are insufficient resources to meet demands then priorities must be established. Some needs are met at the expense of others and some are not met at all. Rather, the criticism and responsibility lies with legislators who, for their own political purposes, enact laws with little regard for how or even if they will be enforced. As mentioned previously, for many politicians the enactment of the law is an end unto itself, or rather, a means to enhance political careers by claiming that they are tough on crime or on some particular behavior. This leads to the final principle for this chapter: *Part of the legislative process should include input from members of the criminal justice system most affected by that legislation.*

Discussion Questions

1. What are some possible explanations for why scholars cannot come to a consensus about what law is?
2. Describe the difference between civil law and criminal law.

3. The Rockefeller Drug Laws are another series of laws that are considered unpopular. Describe why these laws are unpopular, focusing the conversation on unintended consequences and other discrepancies caused by these laws.

4. Identify ways to make the criminal justice system more effective that don't involve building more prisons.

5. Law creates crime, so we can decrease crime if we legislate fewer things as illegal. Do you agree/disagree with this statement? Why?

6. Come up with a list of laws that have outlived their relevance and give a brief explanation as to why they have outlived their relevance.

7. In this chapter, it was argued that to increase citizen support of regulatory law that such laws should be enacted at the lowest level of government practical. Explain the pros and cons of this approach.

8. Discuss the possible consequences of sending people to prison for the full length of their term, i.e., not allowing them to plead down their offense.

9. In this chapter the argument was made that the police do not pay enough attention to street prostitutes who act as conduits to transfer diseases to the general population. Can this problem be addressed by police action? Why? If you say that it can't, than how might this problem be addressed?

10. Discuss steps that the police and the criminal justice system could take to increase the support that minorities have for the law.

Notes

1. Bastiat, F. (1850) The Law (first published as a pamphlet) Retrieved from: http://bastiat.org/en/the_law.html#SECTION_G004.

2. Duhaime, L. (2007). Hammurabi's code of laws (circa 1780 B.C.). Retrieved from http://www.duhaime.org/LawMuseum/LawArticle-105/1760-BC—Hammurabis-Code-of-Laws.aspx.

3. State v. Horton, 139 N.C. 588, 51 S.E. 945, 946 (1905).

4. (Bash, (1996) 130 Wash.2d at 607, 925 P.2d 978).

5. Atwater et al. v. City of Lago Vista et al, 532 U.S. 318 (2001.

6. Beccaria, C. (1977). *On crimes and punishment* (6th ed.). Indianapolis, IA: Bobbs-Merrill Co.

7. Ibid.

8. Bureau of Justice Statistics. (2011). *Number of persons under correctional supervision.* Washington, DC. Retrieved from Bureau of Justice Statistics Website: http://bjs.ojp.usdoj.gov/content/glance/tables/corr2tab.cfm.

9. Ibid.

10. Seper, J. (2004, January 26). Illegal criminal aliens abound in U.S. *The Washington Times.* P.1.

11. Ibid.

12. Ibid.

13. Ibid.

14. Ibid.

15. Ibid.

16. Ibid.

17. Task Force on Federalization of Criminal Law. (1998). *The federalization of criminal law.* Washington, DC. American Bar Association.

18. Ibid.

Bibliography

Atwater et al. v. City of Lago Vista et al, 532 U.S. 318 (2001).

Bash, (1996) 130 Wash.2d at 607, 925 P.2d 978.

Bastiat, F. (1850) The Law (first published as a pamphlet) Retrieved from: http://bastiat.org/en/the_law.html#SECTION_G004.

Beccaria, C. (1977). *On crimes and punishment* (6th ed.). Indianapolis, IA: Bobbs-Merrill Co.

Bureau of Justice Statistics. (2011). *Number of persons under correctional supervision.* Washington, DC. Retrieved from Bureau of Justice Statistics Website: http://bjs.ojp.usdoj.gov/content/glance/tables/corr2tab.cfm.

Duhaime, L. (2007). Hammurabi's code of laws (circa 1780 B.C.). Retrieved from http://www.duhaime.org/LawMuseum/LawArticle-105/1760-BC—Hammurabis-Code-of-Laws.aspx.

Seper, J. (2004, January 26). Illegal criminal aliens abound in U.S. *The Washington Times.* P.1.

State v. Horton, 139 N.C. 588, 51 S.E. 945, 946 (1905).

Task Force on Federalization of Criminal Law. (1998). *The federalization of criminal law.* Washington, DC. American Bar Association.

CHAPTER TWO

Prohibition

Introduction

The effects of regulatory law during the period in American history commonly known as Prohibition will be examined as a case study in an effort to better understand the motivations and unintended consequences of nation-wide efforts to control human behavior. Prohibition began with the passage of the 18th Amendment to the U.S. Constitution in 1919 and lasted until it was repealed in 1933. This experience provides the opportunity to review the conditions prior to and after the thirteen-year period during which the manufacture, distribution and sale of alcoholic beverages was outlawed. Prohibition was intended to reduce the consumption of alcohol, seen by prohibition advocates as a major cause of crime, poverty, high death rates, a weakening economy and declining quality of life.

This period in history provides us with valuable insight into the pitfalls of omnibus efforts to control social behavior. We can readily appreciate the logical arguments of the movement to protect people from behavior that has the potential of not only self-destruction but also the calamitous consequences for family and the community at large. Absent effective social pressures, it also seems logical to enact legislation to achieve well-intentioned results. So, why did the effort fail, particularly when statewide prohibitions appeared to have some measure of success? Where did the federal government go wrong? And, why was there so much resistance to measures that had the potential to improve the quality of life in general and avoid the obvious consequences of alcoholism, public intoxication and the unsavory behavior that usually accompanies it. This chapter will attempt to answer those questions and will review the events leading up to enactment of the 18th Amendment, as well as the conditions that hastened its repeal.

Background

Although the term "Prohibition" brings to mind the Roaring Twenties, moonshiners, speak easy establishments, bootleggers, rumrunners, etc., the seeds of the prohibition movement began centuries earlier during the time of the early settlers in America. Facing extreme challenges in securing sufficient food and shelter, there was legitimate concern that drunkenness could hamper the social cohesiveness necessary for their survival. When the first breweries were established in Massachusetts and New York in the early to mid-1600s, the colonies levied taxes not only on alcohol production but also on consumption. In fact, fines were levied on persons who drank too much and even for those who remained in any inn or similar establishment for an extended period of time.[1] In 1733, the Georgia colony had the dubious distinction of being the first colony to establish a prohibition edict. General James Ogelthorpe's efforts to enforce a dry (i.e., alcohol free) colony were thwarted by bootleggers from the Carolinas and the edict was rescinded in 1742.[2]

The movement to control alcohol consumption became more organized in the 1800s with the founding of the Women's Christian Temperance Union (WCTU) and the Anti-Saloon League. Both of these organizations sprung up in response to the social deterioration seen throughout the country, particularly in rural areas. Laborers would routinely go to saloons after work on Saturdays and go home drunk, having spent all their wages. Women and children were mistreated and often neglected. Drunks were often seen passed out on the streets outside saloons and the signs of social decay were widespread.

The WCTU, formed by Susan B. Anthony, had similar goals to the Anti-Saloon League; however the Anti-Saloon League appeared to be better organized as it was operating like a business. There was a small paid staff augmented by an army of volunteers. Massive printing capabilities ensured a steady flow of propaganda materials that were widely circulated by volunteers. And, the operation was funded by Protestant churches as well as by private donors. These groups aggressively lobbied politicians of all parties and because they constituted a widely supported, single-purpose movement, they were able to exert extraordinary pressure on politicians regardless of ideology. Those politicians soon discovered that their careers could be enhanced or destroyed depending on their support for prohibition. The temperance activists also garnered the support of business leaders who long realized that drunkenness took its toll on productivity. Industrialists such as John D. Rockefeller Sr., Henry Ford and Pierre DuPont were among those who supported the movement.[3]

The first state laws prohibiting the manufacture and sale of alcoholic beverages were enacted in Tennessee in 1838 and in Maine in 1846. The movement gained momentum until the 1860s, when the attention of the country shifted to the Civil War. During this time, large-scale immigration from Ireland and Germany brought the tradition of beer consumption. German beer makers such as Anheuser, Blatz, Busch, Miller, Pabst and Schlitz began to set up breweries throughout the United States. Federal taxes from this industry accounted for about one third of the federal budget, particularly important in funding the Civil War.

By 1900, the prohibition movement had again risen to prominence and the political pressure of the Anti-Saloon League and the crusade of WCTU, now led by Carrie Nation, led to the enactment of prohibition laws in eighteen states.[4] Concern about recent immigrants' cultural attachment to alcohol and the ever-expanding beer industry brought renewed energy to the effort to control alcohol. However, the beer industry was now providing about 70% of the nation's budget, an obstacle that the prohibitionists had to overcome. Two events turned the tide in favor of the prohibitionists. The first was a national income tax that reduced the country's reliance on taxes from the beer makers. The second occurred in 1917 when America entered World War One. With Germany now as an enemy, Congress began investigations into links between the

brewers and German-American organization. Anti-German senti-
ment fueled by propaganda was commonplace and helped pave the
way for passage of the 18th Amendment.

The Prohibition Era: Passage of the Volstead Act

In 1919, shortly after the ratification of the Eighteenth Amendment, Congress, overriding a veto by President Woodrow Wilson,
passed the National Prohibition Act (commonly known as the Volstead Act, named after its author, Congressman Andrew J. Volstead). This act prohibited the importing, exporting, transporting, selling, and manufacturing of intoxicating liquor. Intoxicating
liquor was defined as anything having an alcoholic content of more
than 0.5%. Exceptions were made for alcohol used for religious
purposes as well as for liquor that had been purchased for home
use prior to July 1919 and alcohol prescribed for medicinal use.
However, in 1921, because of abuses by many physicians, Congress
enacted a law that established limits to how much liquor a doctor
could prescribe for a patient: no more than one pint per patient
during a ten-day period.

The first year of prohibition witnessed a substantial decline in
the consumption of alcoholic beverages. This was not necessarily
the result of a reduction in demand but rather because legitimate
sources of alcohol were terminated. During the prohibition era,
the demand for alcohol actually increased.[5] Consequently, numerous of illegal supply channels were created to satisfy that demand.

Prohibition Enforcement

The Volstead Act also set up guidelines for enforcement.[6] Congress, in 1920, appropriated two million dollars for enforcement
of the Volstead Act and another 6.5 million dollars in 1921. Federal responsibility for enforcement of the Volstead Act was assigned
to the Prohibition Unit of the Treasury Department. This existing
unit had been created to enforce the Harrison Act of 1914 that prohibited the sale and use of narcotics. A Narcotics Division was cre-

ated within the Prohibition Unit to separate the enforcement of narcotic and liquor laws.[7] In 1927, the office of Commissioner of Prohibition, consisting of 27 administrative districts, was created. Each district was headed by a chief administrator and contained an enforcement office that was divided into three sections: General Enforcement, Major Investigations, and Case Reports.[8]

Almost 18,000 agents were appointed during the Prohibition Era.[9] Of that number, over 13,000 were either terminated for cause or resigned, leaving an annual staffing of between 1,500 to 2,300 agents.[10] These agents were authorized to enforce all violations of the Volstead Act. They focused primarily on illicit distilleries (stills), smuggling and bootlegging, however, because of limited resources, they relied on local law enforcement for support. Many agents were ill-prepared to do their jobs because there were no standard qualifications, training was optional, and a large number of agents were political patronage appointments.[11]

Illegal distilleries had always operated in wooded, rural areas of the country. They were relatively inexpensive to construct and the main ingredients, primarily corn and other grains, were readily available, thus providing the farmers with additional revenue. After the Volstead Act, the increasing demand for illegal alcohol resulted in a proliferation of stills throughout the country. With an initial investment of about five hundred dollars, a still could pay for itself within a few weeks. The smoke and odor emanating from those stills made them relatively easy to find. Federal agents routinely located and destroyed illegal stills. Yet, because of relatively light fines, short jail sentences and the appeal of an enormous potential for profits, the stills soon reappeared.

Although illegal stills provided most of the liquor for American consumption, substantial amounts of superior quality liquor were smuggled over land and sea. Large-scale smuggling, primarily from Canada, supplied the major markets in New York, Illinois and other Northern states. Entrepreneurial criminals also smuggled alcohol into Canada for processing into liquor that was eventually smuggled back into the United States. U.S. Customs agents, state police and the newly established U.S. Immigration Border Patrol patrolled these borders.

One of the more famous smugglers was Roy Olmstead. Olmstead was dismissed from the Seattle police department after being caught smuggling liquor. He then began one of the largest smuggling operations in the country. Employing over fifty people, he supplied liquor from England via Canada to Seattle's best hotels and restaurants. In order to operate, Olmstead paid off police and city officials and even influenced the mayor. In sharp contrast to the low-grade and sometimes poisonous domestic liquor, Olmstead endeavored to provide quality whisky to his clients. Using speedboats and an elaborate storage and distribution operation, and under the protection of local law enforcement, Olmstead was able to operate without interference for about four years. Ultimately, federal agents were able to gather evidence using electronic equipment to tap Olmstead's phone and arrested him.[12] This was the first use of wiretaps in the United States. The U.S. Supreme Court (Olmstead v. U.S., 1928) ruled that wiretaps on telephones did not violate either the Fourth or Fifth Amendments to the U.S. Constitution regarding search and seizure.[13]

Smuggling had been successful on a large scale for a number of reasons. To begin with, the U.S. borders with Canada and Mexico are each thousands of miles long. The U.S. also has thousands of miles of ocean coastline. Canada and Mexico did not have laws banning the manufacture or export of alcoholic beverages. The liquor brought across the border at the North or at the South borders found its way hundreds of miles into the interior of the United States. Bootleggers maintained large fleets of trucks and automobiles running on regular schedules between Mexican and Canadian points and cities such as St. Louis, Kansas City and Denver.

In addition to the Canadian and Mexican borders, federal enforcement had to deal with smugglers bringing liquor into the country by ship. Under the Volstead Act, the U.S. Coast Guard and U.S. Customs Marine Patrol had primary responsibility for patrolling the coastline for smugglers. Although the U.S. Navy was also considered for use in this effort, the Attorney General of the United States ruled that such enforcement would be unconstitutional.[14]

The island of Nassau in the Bahamas became a major source of supply for the Eastern Coast of the United States. During Prohibition, imports to Nassau from Europe increased from 50,000 quarts to ten million quarts annually.[15] Fleets consisting of ships with liquor from Bermuda, Nassau and even from Europe remained anchored outside the 12 mile limit (the limit of United States jurisdiction) off the New York and New Jersey coast awaiting their contacts from the mainland. Smugglers using high-speed motorboats would make their runs to the liquor ships after nightfall to ferry the illegal cargo to waiting outlets throughout the Northeastern states. Although many were caught by either the Coast Guard or by other enforcement officers, sufficient numbers were able to get through, thereby providing a constant supply of liquor.

William McCoy, one of the more famous rumrunners, transported quality English and Scotch liquor from the Bahamas up the Eastern coast of America. His ship operated like an enormous liquor store with shelves loaded with a variety of fine quality merchandise. He even offered tastings to his customers. Each trip earned him about $300,000 profit. Because he only traded in genuine imported liquor as opposed to moonshine, his products earned the label, "The Real McCoy."[16]

Urban production of alcohol was also used to supplement the major suppliers. Small, portable stills could be purchased for about seven dollars. Their use as well as the operation of larger stills was quite common in cities and residential areas. According to Potter (1998), thousands of inner city residents were organized into microbreweries.[17] Outlets for most of the supplies of illegal liquor were referred to as speakeasies. These businesses, which were hidden in basements, behind legitimate storefronts or anywhere that could accommodate them, admitted only those who were known to the proprietors. They had modern alarm systems to avoid being shut down. By 1925, there were over 100,000 speakeasies operating in New York City alone.[18]

When such establishments were located, the Volstead Act provided procedures for locking-up any building or part thereof where alcoholic beverages were manufactured, stored or sold. This procedure, commonly referred to as "padlocking," required a court order from a federal judge declaring the premises a "common nuisance" under the National Prohibition Act. According to Greenberg (1999), from 1921 through 1925, more than 11,000 padlock injunctions were issued nationwide.[19]

In addition to whiskey smuggled during prohibition, there were also stores of legal whiskey that had been produced prior to the Volstead Act in warehouses in various parts of the country. Some was stolen by bootleggers but there were large quantities kept in distilleries under government control. George Remus, an enterprising attorney, found a way to take legal possession of that liquor. Remus was an intelligent, successful criminal defense lawyer who by 1920 was earning $50,000 a year. He noticed that his clients were quickly becoming very wealthy dealing in bootlegged alcohol. Remus studied the Volstead Act and found loopholes that allowed him to legally buy distilleries and pharmacies so that he could sell liquor to himself under government licenses for medicinal purposes. He would arrange for most of the liquor to be hijacked and diverted to speakeasies and other illegal outlets. Remus moved his operation to Cincinnati as it was within driving distance to most of America's bonded whiskey manufacturers. He made over 40 million dollars within a few years by bribing hundreds of police, judges and government officials, including the U.S. Attorney General. Remus was ultimately arrested and sentenced to two years in a federal prison.[20]

Enforcement, Politics and Corruption

To simply say that Prohibition was a controversial issue would be an understatement. Because law enforcement relies to a great degree upon voluntary compliance and because prohibition was so unpopular with a significant proportion of Americans, federal enforcement efforts were constantly being frustrated. Federal agents complained that local law enforcement was reluctant to identify and stop illegal liquor operations because of collusion between local officials and criminals.[21] Opposition came from the state level as well; the New York State Legislature, for example, passed a law in 1920 authorizing the sale of beer with 2.75% alcohol (substantially higher than the Volstead Act allowed) and in 1923, the Legislature repealed the state's only prohibition law.[22]

Fiorella H. LaGuardia, a prominent New York politician who served several terms in the House of Representatives and later became mayor of New York, testified before the National Prohibition Law Hearings before the Committee on the Judiciary, U.S. Senate, 69th Congress, 1st Session (1926), he stated ...

> It is impossible to tell whether prohibition is a good thing or a bad thing. It has never been enforced in this country ... At least 1,000,000 quarts of liquor are consumed each day in the United States. In my opinion such an enormous traffic in liquor could not be carried on without the knowledge, if not the connivance of the officials entrusted with the enforcement of the law.... (p. 649-652).[23]

Instances of corruption by federal agents, state and local law enforcement and political figures were numerous. Also, because of the enormous profits involved in the illegal liquor trade, bootleggers and smugglers were able to offer substantial bribes to federal and local law enforcement for their cooperation. The relatively low salaries of those officers together with the public's general indifference to alcohol consumption made those bribes even more attractive. For example, William Dwyer, one of the most successful smugglers in the New York City area, had bribed a large number of police and Coast Guard personnel in order to conduct his smuggling enterprise.[24] Also, in Chicago, a sheriff was prosecuted for coordinating the activities of a large number of bootleggers and prisoners and allowing them to conduct business from jail.[25] Corruption even reached the highest offices of the Federal Government, with a conspiracy to sell liquor permits from the Treasury Department in exchange for political contributions.[26]

In addition to the effects of corruption on the overall enforcement effort, there were regularly occurring conflicts between federal and local law enforcement officers. Local enforcement, particularly during the 1920s, relied on cooperation between local, small-town law enforcement officers and their community. Sheriffs often recruited volunteers and deputized them as needed for short-term enforcement objectives. These relationships were complicated and compromised when federal agents called upon local authorities for their cooperation in raids on illegal stills in their jurisdiction. Because of the unpopularity of prohibition in many of these communities, the illegal stills usually operated with the tacit approval of local law enforcement. This problem was further exacerbated when federal agents used unnecessary violence while enforcing the law, leaving local officers with the resulting community outrage.[27]

Although a substantial number of federal agents could not resist the temptation of substantial bribes, there were some, under the leadership of Eliot Ness, who were able to operate within the law. Special Agent Eliot Ness was only 26 years old when he was hired to run the Justice Department's Chicago Prohibition Bureau in 1929. Because bribes and corruption were commonplace in the Department, Ness had strict standards for selecting his subordinate agents. They had to be single, under 30 years old, be able to work long hours, intelligent, able to fight with or without weapons, and have keen investigative abilities. He also wanted newly-hired or assigned agents that were not known to the Chicago gangsters. Because of their honesty and devotion to duty they became known as *The Untouchables*. Although Ness and his agents conducted multiple raids on Al Capone's liquor operations, they were never able to gather enough evidence to convict him of those crimes. However, Capone was eventually convicted on tax evasion charges and eventually died in federal prison.[28]

Organized Crime

The prohibition era opened opportunities for illegal profits for those who could meet the public's demands for alcoholic beverages. Local gangs found that enormous profits could be made from the bootlegging and sale of beer and liquor. These gangs, particularly in the larger cities, used violent methods including bombings, arson and murder to intimidate speakeasy owners into purchasing alcohol from them. Gang violence also included the waging of turf wars against rival gangs who attempted to do business in disputed territories. These armed conflicts often resulted in the loss of innocent life and the terrorizing of neighborhoods. According to Bowen (1966), in Chicago alone over 400 murders a year were reported.[29]

Although gangs operated in many of the larger urban areas, Chicago gangs under the leadership of Johnny Torrio, and other notorious criminals, such as Al Capone, "Bugsy" Moran, the O'Banions and others established a model for organizing their criminal enterprises. Torrio in particular, utilizing his administrative skills, transformed street racketeering into a corporate structure founded on legitimate organizational principles. While gangs in other cities were competing violently for territory, the Chicago gangs coordinated their efforts by dividing the city along agreed upon boundaries.[30] Thus, they were free to operate with little or no interference from rival gangs.

After thirteen long, agonizing years of lawlessness, corrupted officials at every level of government and countless deaths not only from gang violence but also from adulterated liquor, the country finally made its opposition to prohibition known by electing Franklin D. Roosevelt president; the repeal of the 18th Amendment followed shortly thereafter. The legacy of organized crime continues to this day to provide a model structure that influenced criminal activity even after the repeal of the 18th Amendment. Modern organized crime operations still provide legally prohibited goods and services to meet public demands.

Many states maintained laws banning the manufacture and sale of liquor even after the repeal of the Eighteenth Amendment, until 1959 when Oklahoma, the last dry state, repealed its prohibition laws. The terms "wet" and "dry" were commonly used to identify states and groups that were in favor of or against prohibition. Although there are currently no statewide prohibitions against the sale of alcoholic beverages, many local jurisdictions throughout the country chose to remain dry. There are also various restrictions on the sale of alcohol. In addition to age restrictions, many jurisdictions prohibit the sale of alcoholic beverages on certain days of the week and hours of the day.

Summary

Prior to national prohibition, many states and locales enacted laws prohibiting alcohol production and sale and some later rescinded those laws. Once the 18th Amendment was ratified and the Volstead Act enacted, the states no longer had those options. Resistance to the law, although not universal, was nevertheless effective. The demand for alcoholic beverages increased and there were more than ample entrepreneurs ready to meet those demands. The ease of manufacturing together with the ready availability of ingredients attracted many everyday people to produce alcoholic beverages not only for themselves but also to sell to friends and neighbors. Despite efforts of federal agents to shut down large-scale stills, there were sufficiently large numbers operating to provide a steady supply of liquor to illegal markets.

Considering the enormous borders and coastlines of America, the prospect of any semblance of control was daunting and unattainable even under the best of circumstances. But, circumstances were not at their best. Governmental resources were inadequate and enforcement agencies routinely hired people who were not properly vetted, ill-trained and unmotivated. Because of the enormous profits involved, many key government officials were easily corrupted and often operated as pawns of the criminals.

The lack of local community support not only made the job of federal enforcement more burdensome, but often functioned to undermine those efforts. Eventually, faced with the futility of trying to control the country's desire for alcohol and with the change of administration, the 18th Amendment was finally repealed.

Commentary

We began this chapter with three questions: Why did nationwide prohibition effort fail, where did government go wrong and why was there so much resistance? As indicated previously, the United States is not a homogeneous society. We have been and still are divided politically, racially, ethnically, religiously, economically and ideologically. We see these differences in such issues as abortion, gay marriage, immigration and a host of other political and social issues. Moreover, because we tend to associate with people and locate ourselves in communities or regions where we have much in common, those differences can be found clustered in cities, towns, counties and even states. We are not *a one size fits all* nation.

The third principle of this book is apropos to this reasoning: *In order to gain maximum support and be most reflective of community standards, regulatory laws should be enacted at the lowest level of government that is practical.* Prior to Prohibition many states enacted laws prohibiting manufacture and sale of alcohol and later some states repealed those laws while other states maintained those restrictions. Additionally, after the repeal of Prohibition, several states retained their prohibition laws. Even today, while there are no statewide prohibitions, there are numerous jurisdictions within states that prohibit the sale of alcoholic beverages.

When decisions are made on a local or state level, citizens who are dissatisfied with those decisions can become politically active and lobby legislators to reverse those decisions or, if not responsive to those efforts, elect new legislators who reflect their values. The lower in the political hierarchy these decisions are made, the more impact community pressure can have. If, on the other hand, those who object are in the minority and the efforts at reversal are not successful, there is always the option of relocating to a community that more closely reflects their standards.

However, this is not the case when decisions are made on a national level. It is conceivable that a constitutional amendment can pass over the objections of the representatives of an entire state or even more than one state. In such a case, the residents of those states have little recourse. Electing new representatives would not likely make any difference and moving to another country, although possible, would not be a viable decision for most.

In a free society, a high percentage of voluntary compliance with law is essential. Law enforcement can deal effectively with a small percentage of dissidents. However, if the proportion of violators increases beyond the capacity of the criminal justice system to effectively process, then system adjustments in the form of priorities and alternatives must be made. Which violators will be arrested and which will not, who will be tried and who will not, and finally who will be imprisoned and who will not must be determined. As more laws meet with substantial resistance the more dysfunctional the criminal justice system will become. This issue will be developed more fully in Part Two of this book.

Discussion Questions

1. Why were Americans historically split on the question of alcohol consumption?

2. Why did alcohol consumption actually increase during prohibition?

3. What were the major contributing factors to the failure of prohibition?

4. In the end, prohibition was a failure; however, it did seek at the onset to achieve "well intentioned results." List and discuss those well intentioned results.

5. Given that national prohibition failed, in your opinion, do you think that prohibition bans against other popular drugs such as nicotine (cigarettes), marijuana, or caffeine could be successful? Why?

6. Given what you have read about why prohibition failed, come up with a strategy that would allow the government to enact prohibition again while avoiding the pitfalls of the first attempt. If you don't think that such a strategy can be devised, please explain why not.

7. In your opinion, are there any similarities between the Woman's Christian Temperance Union, Anti-Saloon League, and groups like Alcoholics Anonymous? If so, please discuss those similarities. If you don't think there are any similarities, please explain why/how the groups are different.

8. If the government had imposed harsher fines and longer jail sentences for violations of prohibition statutes, would prohibition efforts have been more successful? Why?

9. Part of the reason why prohibition failed was because the laws did nothing to decrease the demand for the product that had been outlawed (alcohol). What changes could have been made to prohibition statutes that could have addressed this issue?

10. If prohibition had been enacted today instead of in the 1920s, would problems such as long borders and the like have still had the same consequences on enforcement efforts? Why?

Notes

1. Cherrington, E. H. (1920). *The evolution of prohibition in the United States of America.* Montclair, NJ: Patterson Smith Publishing.

2. Ibid.

3. Peterson, G.L. (1937). *History of the brewing industry and brewing science in America.* (city, state, publisher).

4. Haskin, F. J. (1923). *The American government* (2nd. Ed.). Washington D.C.: Frederick J. Haskin, Publisher.

5. Warburton, C. (1932). *The economic results of prohibition.* New York: Columbia University Press.

6. Bowen, C. D. (1966). *Miracle at Philadelphia: The story of the Constitutional Convention May to September 1787.* Boston: Little, Brown & Co.

7. Greenberg, M. A. (n.d.) *Prohibition enforcement: Charting a new mission.* Springfield: Charles C. Thomas Publisher.

8. Schmeckebier, L. F. (1929). *The Bureau of Prohibition: Its history, activities and organization.* Washington, D.C.: The Brookings Institution, pp. 154-62.

9. Greenberg, M. A. (n.d.) *Prohibition enforcement: Charting a new mission.* Springfield: Charles C. Thomas Publisher.

10 Ibid.

11. Potter, C. B. (1998). *War on crime: Bandits g-men and the politics of mass culture.* New Brunswick: Rutgers University Press.

12. McClary, D. C. (2002). *Olmstead Roy (1886-1966) king of king county bootleggers.* Retrieved from http://www.historylink.org/index.cfm?DisplayPage=output.cfm&File_Id=4015.

13. Greenberg, M. A. (n.d.) *Prohibition enforcement: Charting a new mission.* Springfield: Charles C. Thomas Publisher.

14. Ibid.

15. Bloomfield, H. V. L. (1966). *The compact history of the U.S. Coast Guard.* New York: Hawthorn Books, Inc.

16. Behr, E. (1996). *Prohibition: Thirteen years that changed America.* New York: Arcade Publishing.

17. Potter, C. B. (1998). *War on crime: Bandits g-men and the politics of mass culture*. New Brunswick: Rutgers University Press.

18. Bowen, C. D. (1966). *Miracle at Philadelphia: The story of the Constitutional Convention May to September 1787*. Boston: Little, Brown & Co.

19. Greenberg, M. A. (n.d.) *Prohibition enforcement: Charting a new mission*. Springfield: Charles C. Thomas Publisher.

20. Coffey, T. M. (1975).*The long thirst-prohibition in America: 1920-1933*. New York, NY: WW Norton & Co.

21. Potter, C. B. (1998). *War on crime: Bandits g-men and the politics of mass culture*. New Brunswick: Rutgers University Press.

22. Greenberg, M. A. (n.d.) *Prohibition enforcement: Charting a new mission*. Springfield: Charles C. Thomas Publisher.

23. *The National Prohibition Law*, Hearings before the Committee on the Judiciary, U.S. Senate, 69th Congress, 1st Session (1926): 649-52.

24. Kobler, J. (1973). *Ardent spirits: The rise and fall of prohibition*. New York: G.P. Putnam's Sons.

25. Potter, C. B. (1998). *War on crime: Bandits g-men and the politics of mass culture*. New Brunswick: Rutgers University Press.

26. Ibid.

27. Ibid.

28. Heimel, P. W., & Ness, E. (2000). *The real story*. (2nd Ed.). Nashville, TN: Cumberland House Publishing, Inc.

29. Bowen, C. D. (1966). *Miracle at Philadelphia: The story of the Constitutional Convention May to September 1787*. Boston: Little, Brown & Co.

30. Behr, E. (1996). *Prohibition: Thirteen years that changed America*. New York: Arcade Publishing.

Bibliography

Behr, E. (1996). *Prohibition: Thirteen years that changed America*. New York: Arcade Publishing.

Bloomfield, H. V. L. (1966). *The compact history of the U.S. Coast Guard*. New York: Hawthorn Books, Inc.

Bowen, C. D. (1966). *Miracle at Philadelphia: The story of the Constitutional Convention May to September 1787*. Boston: Little, Brown & Co.

Cherrington, E. H. (1920). *The evolution of prohibition in the United States of America*. Montclair, NJ: Patterson Smith Publishing.

Coffey, T. M. (1975).*The long thirst-prohibition in America: 1920-1933*. New York, NY: WW Norton & Co.

Greenberg, M. A. (n.d.) *Prohibition enforcement: Charting a new mission.* Springfield: Charles C. Thomas Publisher.

Haskin, F. J. (1923). *The American government* (2nd. Ed.). Washington D.C.: Frederick J. Haskin, Publisher.

Heimel, P. W., & Ness, E. (2000). *The real story.* (2nd Ed.). Nashville, TN: Cumberland House Publishing, Inc.

Kobler, J. (1973). *Ardent spirits: The rise and fall of prohibition.* New York: G.P. Putnam's Sons.

McClary, D. C. (2002). *Olmstead Roy (1886-1966) king of king county bootleggers.* Retrieved from http://www.historylink.org/index.cfm?Display Page=output .cfm&File_Id=4015.

Peterson, G.L. (1937). *History of the brewing industry and brewing science in America.* (city, state, publisher).

Potter, C. B. (1998). *War on crime: Bandits g-men and the politics of mass culture.* New Brunswick: Rutgers University Press.

Schmeckebier, L. F. (1929). *The Bureau of Prohibition: Its history, activities and organization.* Washington, D.C.: The Brookings Institution, pp. 154-62.

The National Prohibition Law, Hearings before the Committee on the Judiciary, U.S. Senate, 69th Congress, 1st Session (1926): 649-52.

Warburton, C. (1932). *The economic results of prohibition.* New York: Columbia University Press.

CHAPTER THREE

Illegal Drugs

Introduction

It is by no coincidence that a parallel exists between the prohibition of alcohol and narcotics. Both movements were focused on the evils of the substances, arguing that they resulted in crime, poverty and social disorganization. Both movements began on the state and local levels and eventually resulted in congressional action, and both ultimately achieved much the same results. However, there are significant differences between the anti-alcohol and anti-narcotics movements. The anti-alcohol, or temperance, movement began in the states after much debate, while the anti-narcotics movement did not. Alcohol legislation was the product of an organized nation-wide lobby while narcotics legislation was enacted in the absence of grass roots public support. The major difference of course is that national laws against narcotics still exist. This chapter will trace the various legal efforts to control the use of narcotics, the several wars on drugs and the unanticipated consequences of those efforts, specifically on the criminal justice system.

The term, "illegal drugs" encompasses a broad range of substances. They can be grouped into a few categories, however: *Natural Sources* such as Opiates (heroin, morphine and opium) Cocaine and Marijuana; *synthesized substances,* including Lysergic Acid Diethylamide (L.S.D.), Methamphetamine, PCP (Angel Dust), etc. as well as *illegally used prescription drugs.*

For example, opiates were popular in America, especially among women. Several surveys found that women were much more likely to use opiates than men. Even accounting for the widespread use of opiates by prostitutes, female use of opiates was twice the rate of male use. Doctors often prescribed opiates for menstrual and menopausal conditions as well as various other female ailments. They were also available in pharmacies in the form of tonics and elixirs.[1]

Cocaine comes from the coca plant grown in South America. It became popular in the late 1800s in Europe after it had earned the praise of renowned psychologist Sigmund Freud. In 1883, Coca-Cola, made in part with syrup extracted from the coca leaves, was first introduced in the U.S..

Marijuana from the hemp plant was cultivated in the early colonies and was an important revenue-producing crop for the early settlers. The hemp plant provided a strong fiber suitable for a variety of uses including canvas, clothing and rope. Marijuana was also used as a medicinal plant in the latter half of the 19th century.

There are a number of synthesized substances that produce a variety of effects on mood and perception such as amphetamines, which can distort or heighten sensation and induce hyperactivity, Lysergic acid diethylamide (LSD), which is a psychedelic drug that can produce colorful visual and geometric patterns as well as a sense of time distortion, Barbiturates, which are depressant drugs that effect the central nervous system, Methamphetamine (Crystal Meth), which enters the brain and triggers a cascading release of dopamine, inducing intense euphoria, and Crack Cocaine, which affects the brain chemistry of the user, causing euphoria, supreme confidence, loss of appetite, insomnia, alertness and increased energy.

Background

As with alcohol, drugs have been used for social as well as religious purposes by various cultures for thousands of years. Their use in America during most of the 1700s and 1800s met with little organized resistance. In the early 1900s, the drug market was virtually unregulated. Doctors or pharmacists distributed medicines, which frequently contained cocaine or heroin derivatives, without prescription. It was not until the enactment of the Harrison Act of 1914 that the federal government attempted to control non-medical drug use. The Act was entitled: "An Act to provide for the registration of, with collectors of internal revenue, and to impose a special tax upon all persons who produce, import, manufacture, compound, deal in, dispense, sell, distribute, or give away opium or coca leaves, their salts, derivatives, or preparations, and for other purposes."[2]

The bill's major supporter was Secretary of State William Jennings Bryan, a man of strong prohibitionist beliefs. Ostensibly, the bill was not initially intended to address the abuse of drugs in the United States but to instead fulfill the obligations of the Hague Convention treaty of 1912, an international treaty aimed at dealing with opium problems in Asia.[3] On the surface, the law did not appear to prohibit drug use, but rather to ensure the orderly marketing of those drugs by requiring the licensing of manufacturers, pharmacists and physicians prescribing narcotics. However, language in the law, specifically, that doctors may prescribe these drugs in the course of professional practice only, was interpreted by law enforcement to prohibit doctors from prescribing opiates to an addicted patient. Because addiction was not considered a disease, many doctors were arrested and some imprisoned for violating the Harrison Act.[4]

In the early 1900s, Mexican immigrants introduced the recreational use of marijuana and by the 1920s it became increasingly popular as an alternative to alcohol during prohibition. By the 1920s doubts about the efficacy of the drug control laws began to surface. A 1926 editorial in the Illinois Medical Journal, commenting on the Harrison Act, opined:

> As is the case with most prohibitive laws, however, this one fell far short of the mark. So far, in fact, that instead of stopping the traffic, those who deal in dope now make double their money from the poor unfortunates upon whom they prey ... It is costing the United States more to support bootleggers of both narcotics and alcoholics than there is good coming from the farcical laws now on the statute books (p. 447).[5]

Opposition to drug laws also began to emerge from law enforcement as well. During the 1930s August Vollmer, former chief of the Berkeley California Police Department, professor and author of several books on police administration, former president of the International Association of Chiefs of Police and one of the pioneers in the movement to professionalize police, concluded:

> Stringent laws, spectacular police drives, vigorous prosecution, and imprisonment of addicts and peddlers have proved not only useless and enormously expensive as means of correcting this evil, but they are also unjustifiably and unbelievably cruel in their application to the unfortunate drug victims. Repression has driven this vice underground and produced the narcotic smugglers and supply agents, who have grown wealthy out of this evil practice and who, by devious methods, have stimulated traffic in drugs. Finally, and not the least of the evils associated with repression, the helpless addict has been forced to resort to crime in order to get money for the drug which is absolutely indispensable for his comfortable existence.... Drug addiction, like prostitution and like liquor, is not a police problem; it never has been and never can be solved by policemen. It is first and last a medical problem, and if there is a solution it will be discovered not by policemen, but by scientific and competently trained medical experts whose sole objective will be the reduction and possible eradication of this devastating appetite. There should be intelligent treatment of the incurables in outpatient clinics, hospitalization of those not too far gone to respond to therapeutic measures, and application of the prophylactic principles which medicine applies to all scourges of mankind (p.117-18)[6]

The Federal Bureau of Narcotics (FBN) was created to enforce the Harrison Act. Although the Harrison Act was targeted at opiates and cocaine, the FBN included a provision within the Uniform Narcotic Drug Act to allow marijuana to be included in the Harrison Act. In 1937, the Marijuana Tax Act was passed which, in essence, extended the power of the Harrison Act to tax and regulate marijuana. The Harrison Act, as well as the Marijuana Tax

Act, although not overtly prohibition laws, ultimately had the same effect. Compliance with the law was virtually impossible and many physicians were arrested for violating misleading and somewhat ambiguous sections of the law. After the repeal of the 18th Amendment, the FBI, which had achieved national recognition for its dealings with prohibition gangsters, was included in the efforts to control illegal drugs.

With the passing of the Boggs Act and the Narcotics Control Act in the 1950s the penalties for marijuana and narcotics violations dramatically increased. The Boggs Act (1951) established mandatory minimum sentences for drug violations while the Narcotic Control Act of 1956 lengthened minimum sentences and allowed the courts to impose the death penalty on anyone over the age of 18 who sold heroin to a minor.[7]

While drug enforcement agencies were focused primarily on narcotics and marijuana, amphetamines and other mind-altering and hallucinogenic drugs gained popularity. Because many of these drugs were legal, Congress passed the Drug Abuse and Control Amendments of 1965, which placed the manufacture and distribution of amphetamines, barbiturates, and LSD under the control of the federal government. These amendments prohibited the manufacture and sale of such drugs.

In 1968, the FBN was merged with the Bureau of Drug Abuse and Control (BDAC) to create the Bureau of Narcotics and Dangerous Drugs (BNDD). The U.S. Department of Justice was given authority over these merged agencies and was further authorized to enforce federal drug laws. The Office for Drug Abuse and Law Enforcement (ODALE) was established in 1972 in order to provide assistance to local drug enforcement agencies. During that same year, the Office of National Narcotic Intelligence (ONNI) was established to gather and propagate any information that might assist state and local law enforcement. In 1973, the Drug Enforcement Administration (DEA) was created and absorbed the functions of the BNDD, ODALE, and ONNI. The DEA was created for the purpose of investigating and enforcing all drug laws. The DEA was also charged with the responsibility of coordinating federal, state and local efforts to control the drug trade.

The Federal Bureau of Investigation (FBI), although not solely responsible for drug enforcement, shares jurisdiction with the DEA particularly with regard to the role of organized crime in the drug trade. Both agencies are under the Department of Justice. A number of other federal agencies assist in drug-related enforcement, including the Customs Service, the U.S. Coast Guard and the U.S. Border Patrol (drug interdiction). The United States Coast Guard's primary responsibility in this effort is to intercept maritime vessels at sea.

War on Drugs

Within a few years of the passage of the Harrison Act it was obvious that a war was in the making. Opium was being used by hundreds of thousands of people and the illegal traffic of narcotic substances was almost equal to the legitimate medical use of drugs. Most notable was the establishment of national crime organizations smuggling drugs into the United States primarily from Canada and Mexico. It was also estimated that, similar to the experience with alcohol prohibition, national use of illegal drugs had increased since the passage of the Harrison Act. Particularly hard hit with increases were the cities of New York and San Francisco; the result of which was a series of sterner law enforcement efforts.

During the World War II era, American drug use was seen as a marginal social problem not important enough to compete with the war effort that dominated the nation's attention. By the 1950s the prevailing concept of drug abuse and addiction was that of heroin addiction on the streets and alleys of urban ghettos.[8] However, the war on drugs began again in earnest in the 1950s. In 1954, President Eisenhower established the U.S. Interdepartmental Committee on Narcotics. It was at this venue where he became the first president to literally declare a war on drugs. The Anti-Vietnam war era of the mid-1960s witnessed the widespread use of drugs particularly among the so-called *Baby Boomers,* primarily college students and others in their late teens and early twenties. Marijuana was used openly and its use celebrated in films and song.

Hippy communes, where drugs, especially marijuana, were prevalent began to spring up throughout the country. LSD was promoted by academics as beneficial and it appeared that an entire generation was open to the experimentation of drugs of various kinds. Because these drugs could only be acquired illegally, large-scale import and distribution networks began to emerge to serve the ever-increasing demand. Before the 1970s, drug abuse was considered primarily a social disease that should be subject to treatment. However, it was soon viewed as a law enforcement problem that should be addressed with aggressive criminal justice policies.

In his 1971 "War on Drugs" speech, President Richard Nixon declared that drug abuse in America was public enemy number one. This speech led to the creation of the Drug Enforcement Agency and the National Institute for Drug Abuse. Funds were also allocated for drug research and treatment within the United States.[9]

One of the most notable events of the War on Drugs was the enactment of the Rockefeller drug laws. Noting that drug treatment programs were a failure, New York's Governor Nelson Rockefeller urged the passage of the harshest drug laws in the nation. These laws provided for mandatory minimum sentences. The Rockefeller drug laws are significant because they led to a nationwide trend of similar anti-drug laws with mandatory minimum sentences. Even though they were not effective, politicians still passed "zero tolerance" laws in order to appear to be tough on crime.[10] Drug arrests began to increase significantly, resulting in an overburdening of the criminal court systems across the country.

Cocaine emerged as the drug of choice for upper middle class whites; heroin was associated with African Americans, and marijuana tended to be popular with Latinos. Crack cocaine arrived on the scene in the late 1970s and its modest price appealed primarily to low income inner-city residents.

During the Reagan administration the Antidrug Act of 1986 was enacted, which established a 100:1 ratio for mandatory minimums associated with cocaine. 5,000 grams of powdered cocaine or 50 grams of crack cocaine could result in a 10-year minimum sentence. The government's war on drugs reached its ultimate stage when in 1994 the Omnibus Crime Bill sponsored by Senator Joe

Biden included provisions allowing for the execution of drug king-pins.[11] Other significant legislative actions included the Omnibus Anti Drug Abuse Act of 1988, and the Civil Asset Forfeiture Reform Act of 2000.

Over the past several decades, there has been a substantial and steady increase in the number of drug violation arrests. According to the BJS, in 1970, there were 322,300 arrests, in 1980, 471,200 arrests, in 1990, 1,008,300 arrests, by 2000, 1,375,600 arrests, and in 2007, 1,645,500 arrests—over four times as many as in 1980.

The budgetary implications of marijuana enforcement alone on the criminal justice system are staggering. For example, in 2000, the estimated law enforcement cost at the state and local level was $5.1 billion, the judicial and legal budget due to marijuana prosecutions amounted to $2.94 billion and the corrections budget devoted to marijuana prisoners was $484 million. This amounted to approximately $8.5 billion for one year only. Again, these figures are only at the state and local level. Consider that the cost to the federal government for all drug enforcement for the year 2002 was $13.6 billion and one can see that a significant portion of the cost of government is devoted to drug enforcement.[12]

There are serious social as well as legal implications associated with drug use. The toll on the medical industry is striking. According to the 2011 American College of Emergency Physicians fact sheet:

> In 2005, an estimated 3.4 million people used marijuana on a daily or near-daily basis.[13] That statistic is about the same as it was in 2004.[14] There were 215,656 emergency department mentions of marijuana/hashish in 2004, almost double the number from 2001.[15]
>
> From 2004 to 2005, the number of cocaine users nationally held steady at approximately 2.4 million.[16] There were 872,000 first-time cocaine users in 2005.[17] The number of cocaine-related emergency department visits has spiked in recent years, from 193,034 emergency department mentions of cocaine in 2001, to 383,350 in 2004.[18]
>
> An estimated 108,000 new heroin users were reported in 2005, down from 149,000 in 1999, although the number

of heroin users has increased by nearly 50% since 1994.[19]
There were 162,137 emergency department mentions of
heroin in 2004, up from 93,064 mentions of heroin/mor-
phine in 2001.[20]
More than half a million (638,484) drug-related emergencies were reported in 2001 — nearly a 75% increase over
1990 (371,208).[21] Nearly 20,000 people in the year 2000
died of drug-related causes.[22] It should be noted, however,
that these figures would also include overdoses of legally-
prescribed drugs as well as those obtained illegally.[23]
After a long climb, the first significant downturn in youth
drug use in nearly a decade was reported among 8th,
10th, and 12th graders, according to the 2002 Monitoring the Future study.[24]
Illegal drugs exact an enormous toll on society, taking
52,000 lives annually and draining the economy of $160
billion a year.[25] Everyone pays the toll in the form of
higher healthcare costs, dangerous neighborhoods, and
an overcrowded criminal justice system.[26]

Narcoterrorism and Transnational Organized Crime

The illegal drug trade has proved to be a reliable source of income in the world. The growing demand for drugs, particularly in
the United States, ensures a constant source of drug money. International drug cartels are well known for their innovative efforts
to smuggle drugs into the U.S. through our borders, particularly
with Mexico, as well as by ships and planes, both private and commercial. The Drug Enforcement Administration routinely inter-
cepts huge amounts of drug shipments with street values in the
millions of dollars. For decades, terrorists from around the world
have also used drugs to fund their operations. Narcoterrorism is
defined as the use of illicit drugs to advance political purposes and
to fund terrorist activities (Enrenfeld, 2002). Although their motivations are somewhat different, the activities of both groups are
quite similar. Both use ruthless violence and intimidation, partic-

ularly on civilian victims. Both resort to kidnappings, assassinations and extortion to intimidate and control public officials. And the use of legitimate businesses or charities as fronts for their operations are common to both groups. The major difference is that terrorist organizations are motivated by ideology while organized crime cartels are profit oriented.[27]

Narcoterrorism is a worldwide problem and is not limited to Al-Qaeda only; it also includes such organizations as Hamas, Islamic Jihad, Hizballah, the IRA in Ireland, the FARC in Colombia, the Sendero Luminoso in Peru, Laskar Jihad in Indonesia and the Chechens in Russia (Enrenfeld, 2002). Although each of these organizations has its own particular ideological agenda, they all fund their activities in large part with money from the international drug trade.

Summary

National efforts to curtail the use of drugs in America have failed to achieve a satisfactory level of success. Originating during the same period in history, the ideas of controlling the use of drugs and alcohol met with similar resistance and although national prohibition against alcohol was repealed, the nation continued in its efforts to control drug use through legislation and enforcement.

For nearly a century, there has been a steady increase in the use of drugs, along with escalating enforcement efforts, increases of organized drug cartels, several wars on drugs, increased drug smuggling, drug wars resulting in thousands of murders and kidnappings and the corruption of government officials (particularly police), followed by more laws, more enforcement resources, more people imprisoned, and enormous strains on the criminal justice system. Police make ever-increasing numbers of arrests and courts are burdened with caseloads that overwhelm judicial capacities, resulting in continuing pressure on the correctional system to ease overcrowding by the early release of prisoners. Even alternatives to incarceration are unable to adequately handle the flow of citizens arrested on drug-related charges.

Added to this in the enormous infusion of drug money in the coffers of international terrorists and the destruction and mayhem that money supports. Part Two of this book will provide a further review and analysis of the impact of drug laws on the criminal justice system.

Commentary

There were many reasonable and compelling arguments for the passage of the laws prohibiting drugs and alcohol. Non-medical drug use and abuse obviously presents serious risks to the individual, families and to society at large. It impairs judgment, leads to unnecessary health risks and can increase the potential for accidents to the individual as well as innocent others. It can also result in diminished capacity to function normally in society. With the passage of the Harrison Act of 1914 and the subsequent Volstead Act of 1919, it seemed that the country would take control of the social vices of drugs and alcohol. However, after the devastating failure of the Prohibition movement and the resulting rise of organized crime syndicates, it should have become apparent that unless there is more universal support for social control laws, similar fates await comparable legislation. Ironically, only a few years after the repeal of the 18th Amendment, the federal government chose to enact the Marijuana Tax Act.

Even early experiences revealed that these laws not only fail to achieve their objectives but quite likely have had the opposite affect by encouraging an increase in the use of drugs. Just as with Prohibition, crime syndicates were quick to seize the opportunity to provide legally-prohibited goods. Criminal entrepreneurs adopt many of the practices of legitimate businesses, primarily, expansion and diversification. Consider a company that begins with a single product offered to a local market. If successful, that company will seek to expand its market to include additional territories. Eventually, the company will offer additional lines of merchandise through its expanded market. Criminal enterprises are similarly established to meet the demands for illegal merchandise.

The criminal enterprise eventually seeks to increase its profits through expansion. These efforts are accompanied with or followed by offering additional illegal products or services. The term, "pusher" is an apt description. Their objective is to cultivate new customers, particularly the young, who could help pay for their use by further encouraging their peers to use those substances. According to the American College of Emergency Physicians fact sheet: 21% of 8th graders, 38% of 10th graders, and 50% of 12th graders have tried illicit drugs in their lifetimes.[28] This suggests that half of students today will have tried an illicit drug by the time that they finish high school.[29]

There is also the loss of human potential to be considered. Millions of people with criminal records who are not likely to reach their potential because of lost opportunities for careers and otherwise mainstream lives are relegated to a continued life of crime. Prisons are well-known training grounds where inmates can join a prison gang and learn new criminal skills, or simply fine-tune their trades. Regardless of the initial arrest charges, the majority of convicted criminals are more likely than not to recidivate. Experience has shown that nearly half of all prisoners (44%) are re-arrested within one year of release and within three years over 65% of all prisoners are rearrested. Those arrested for drugs share the same recidivism experience.[30]

More tragic is the loss of human life. There are those who die immediately from drug overdoses while many more shorten their lives from the long-term effects of these substances. Additional deaths can be attributed to drug-related causes, such as HIV/AIDS contracted from contaminated needles. Finally, we could add to the list of fatalities the countless numbers of criminals who are murdered in drug-related incidents, including territorial disputes, as well as innocent victims frequently caught in cross-fires. These deaths are not limited to the United States, but also occur in other countries in which drug cartels produce and transport illicit drugs to the United States. Mexico, for example, has experienced tens of thousands of murders; many of the victims were innocent citizens, government officials and law enforcement officers. According to the Mexican government, over 40,000 people have been killed since 2006, with more than 15,000 murdered in 2010 alone.[31] Add to this the death and destruction at the hands of international terrorists whose activities are funded in large part by drug money.

Similar to other problems of Prohibition, the issue of corruption and related misconduct of governmental officials, particularly police, must also be addressed. Although the issue of police corruption will be dealt with in greater detail in Part II of this book, any discussion of illegal drugs would not be complete without some reference to this problem. Two conditions have probably had the greatest impact on the corruption problem. They are: the enormous amount of money that is taken in by drug dealers and the apparent lack of seriousness with which the criminal justice system actually deals with those arrested on illegal drug charges. It is not unusual to find hundreds of thousands of dollars in small bills and large quantities of drugs in apartments housing urban drug "factories." When police come upon these places they cannot help but be tempted by the bribes that the dealers are willing to offer. In some cases, those bribes can easily surpass an officer's annual salary. The other issue is the frustration experienced by officers who, after making a felony arrest, enter a judicial system where the offenders are offered a plea deal to a lower sentence with the possibility of serving either a short sentence or even probation. Neither of these conditions excuses the corruption but provides an understandable context for this type of misconduct.

Finally, this topic must also include the issue of the legalization of certain narcotics. It should be emphasized that nothing in this chapter is intended to argue for legalization of drugs. This is a complex subject that could take volumes to adequately explore. Proponents of legalization point to many of the issues previously raised, including the enormous drain of government resources and the large numbers of people with criminal records.

However, if drugs are legalized there are still illegal markets to be cultivated. Teens and preteens, for example, are not likely to be able to buy drugs legally. There is also the likelihood of abuse of newly legalized drugs that can only be obtained with a physician's prescription. Street dealers often supply prescription drugs along with other controlled substances. There is also the question of increased drug use. If drugs became legal would the numbers of people using drugs increase substantially? Remember the toll drugs have taken in terms of health-related problems; 20,000 deaths in 2001 alone. Would that number rise? Is there enough public support for legalization? Despite motivated advocates for legalization, efforts to legalize marijuana have not been able to garner sufficient public support (California being the latest effort).

So, where do we go from here? One trend is the decriminalization of drugs, particularly marijuana. As of July 1, 2011, fourteen states have decriminalized possession of small amounts of marijuana. Decriminalization does not mean that the possession of a small amount of cannabis would be legal but that it would not subject a person to an arrest on a criminal charge. The offender would instead be given a modest fine with no criminal record to follow the offender. One of the motivations for this movement is economic. States would not have to spend scarce criminal justice resources arresting, prosecuting and incarcerating those offenders. Instead, fines for possession of marijuana would more likely aid financially strapped states. Additionally, there is some logic to decriminalization, at least at first blush. Law enforcement can now focus more of its resources on the drug lords. Ignoring the little guy and going after Mr. Big seems to make more sense.

There are major flaws in that argument, as well. The law of supply and demand must be considered. Will the demand for marijuana increase as a result of relaxed enforcement efforts? Current trends show that use of marijuana as well as most other drugs is on the rise and there is no reason to believe that decriminalization will alter that trend (Substance Abuse and Mental Health Services Administration, 2010). Even if decriminalization itself does not lead to a further increase in the use of marijuana, the demand is certainly likely to increase if current trends continue.

That leaves the drug cartels and their leaders to contend with. Past experience has shown that enforcement efforts have not had a significant effect on the flow of illegal drugs into this country. With the enormous amount of money involved and the growing demand for drugs by Americans, the War on Drugs has become a war of attrition. For every person arrested, whether dealer or drug lord, there are several others ready to take his or her place. Further, for every cartel that is put out of business, others are prepared to fill the void. We need only to look at Mexico to see the extent that these cartels are willing to go to profit in the drug trade. They are prepared to bribe, assassinate, kidnap and terrorize to achieve their ends.

Is the focus on the supply side of the equation the best way to proceed? Can we really hope to stem the tide of illegal drugs by virtually ignoring the demand side of the equation? Increases in use of illegal drugs will only fuel the violence of those cartels, not only in Latin America but in the United States as well. It should be obvious that unless the demand can be reduced, the problems associated with illegal drugs will only worsen.

Discussion Questions

1. In this chapter, the author hinted at the idea that plea bargaining may in some way be correlated with police corruption. Do you agree? Explain.

2. Discuss President Ronald Reagan's role in the war on drugs.

3. Discuss the arguments for and against the legalization of drugs.

4. What are some possible explanations for why the police target people who possess drugs far more frequently than people who sell drugs?

5. In your opinion, should non-violent drug offenders be incarcerated or given alternative sentences, such as community service or probation? Explain your answer.

6. Discuss the racial disparities that exist in incarceration for drug crimes.

7. Discuss the advantages and disadvantages of minimum sentences for drug possession.

8. Compare and contrast the efforts of law enforcement during prohibition to the efforts of law enforcement during the war on drugs.

9. Which criminological theory best explains the philosophy behind the war on drugs?

10. Discuss how one might go about reducing the recidivism rate of drug offenders.

Notes

1. Brecher, E. M. (1972). *Licit and Illicit Drugs: The Consumers Union Report on Narcotics, Stimulants, Depressants, Inhalants, Hallucinogens, and Marijuana—including Caffeine, Nicotine, and Alcohol.* Boston, MA: Little Brown.

2. Public Law No. 223, 63rd Cong., approved December 17, 1914.

3. Brecher, E. M. (1972). *The consumers union report on licit and illicit drugs chapter 8. The Harrison Narcotic Act (1914).* Retrieved from: http://www.druglibrary.org/schaffer/Library/studies/cu/cu8.html.

4. Ibid.

5. (1926). Stripping the medical profession of its powers and giving them to a body of lawmakers. The proposed amendment to the Harrison Narcotic Act-—everybody seems to know all about doctoring except the doctors. *Illinois Medical Journal,* 49, p. 447.

6. Vollmer, A. (1936). *The Police and Modern Society.*

7. Musto, D. F. (2002). *Drugs in America: A documented history.* New York, New York: University Press.

8. Inciardi, J. A. (1990). Handbook of drug control in the United States. Greenwood Publishing Group.

9. President Nixon Declares "War" on Drugs. (2006). In K. L. Lerner & B. W. Lerner (Eds.)*Medicine, Health, and Bioethics: Essential Primary Sources,* (pp. 297-300) Detroit: Gale Retrieved February 17, 2011, from Gale Virtual Reference Library via Gale: http://go.galegroup.com/ps/start.do?p=GVRL&u=cuny_johnjay.

10. Kohler-Hausmann, J. (2010). The Attila the hun law: New York's Rockefeller Drug Laws and the making of a punitive state. *Journal of Social History,* 44(1), 71-95.

11. Head, T. (2011). History of the war on drugs. Retrieved from http://civil-liberty.about .com/od/drugpolicy/tp/War-on-Drugs-History-Timeline.htm.

12. Miron, J. A. (2005). *The budgetary implications of marijuana prohibition.* Retrieved from http://www.prohibitioncosts.org/mironreport.html.

13. American College of Emergency Physicians. (2011). Illegal drug use. Retrieved from http://www.acep.org/content.aspx?id=26004.

14. Ibid.

15. Ibid.

16. Ibid.

17. Ibid.

18. Ibid.

19. Ibid.

20. Ibid.
21. Ibid.
22. Ibid.
23. Ibid.
24. Ibid.
25. Ibid.
26. Ibid.
27. Schmid, A. P. (1996). The links between transnational organized crime and terrorist crimes. *Transnational Organized Crime, 2,* (4), 40-82.
28. American College of Emergency Physicians. (2011). Illegal drug use. Retrieved from http://www.acep.org/content.aspx?id=26004.
29. Ibid.
30. Langan, P. A., & Levin, D. J. (2002). *BJS special report, recidivism of prisoners released in 1994.* Retrieved from United States Department of Justice Website: http://www. justice.Gov /ndic/pubs38/38661/movement.htm.
31. (2011, October 25). Mexican drug trafficking. *New York Times.* Retrieved from http://topics.nytimes.com/top/news/international/countries andterritories/mexico/drug_trafficking/index.html.

Bibliography

American College of Emergency Physicians. (2011). Illegal drug use. Retrieved from http://www.acep.org/content.aspx?id=26004.

Bonnie, R. J., & Whitebread, II, C. H. (1970). The forbidden fruit and the tree of knowledge: An inquiry into the legal history of American marijuana prohibition. *Virginia Law Review, 56* (6), 971-1203.

Brecher, E. M. (1972). *Licit and Illicit Drugs: The Consumers Union Report on Narcotics, Stimulants, Depressants, Inhalants, Hallucinogens, and Marijuana—including Caffeine, Nicotine, and Alcohol.* Boston, MA: Little Brown.

Brecher, E. M. (1972). *The consumers union report on licit and illicit drugs chapter 8. The Harrison Narcotic Act (1914).* Retrieved from: http://www.druglibrary.org/schaffer/Library/studies/cu/cu8.html.

Head, T. (2011). History of the war on drugs. Retrieved from http://civilliberty.about.com/od/drugpolicy/tp/War-on-Drugs-History-Timeline.htm.

Human Rights Watch. (2009). *Decades of disparity.* Retrieved from http://www.hrw.org/en/node/81105 /section/4.

Inciardi, J. A. (1990). Handbook of drug control in the United States. Greenwood Publishing Group.

Kohler-Hausmann, J. (2010). The Attila the hun law: New York's Rockefeller Drug Laws and the making of a punitive state. *Journal of Social History, 44*(1), 71-95.

Langan, P. A., & Levin, D. J. (2002). *BJS special report, recidivism of prisoners released in 1994.* Retrieved from United States Department of Justice Website: http://www.justice.Gov/ndic/pubs38/38661/movement.htm.

(2011, October 25). Mexican drug trafficking. *New York Times.* Retrieved from http://topics.nytimes.com/top/news/international/countriesandterritories/mexico/drug_trafficking/index.html.

Miron, J. A. (2005). *The budgetary implications of marijuana prohibition.* Retrieved from http://www.prohibitioncosts.org/mironreport.html.

Musto, D. F. (2002). *Drugs in America: A documented history.* New York, New York: University Press.

President Nixon Declares "War" on Drugs. (2006). In K. L. Lerner & B. W. Lerner (Eds.)*Medicine, Health, and Bioethics: Essential Primary Sources,* (pp. 297-300) Detroit: Gale Retrieved February 17, 2011, from Gale Virtual Reference Library via Gale: http://go.galegroup.com/ps/start.do?p=GVRL&u=cuny_johnjay.

Public Law No. 223, 63rd Cong., approved December 17, 1914.

(1926). Stripping the medical profession of its powers and giving them to a body of lawmakers. The proposed amendment to the Harrison Narcotic Act- — everybody seems to know all about doctoring except the doctors. *Illinois Medical Journal,* 49, p. 447.

Rachel Ehrenfel Funding Terrorism: Sources and Methods: Workshop held at Los Alamos National Laboratory March 25-29, 2002 Confronting Terrorism—2002.

Schmid, A. P. (1996). The links between transnational organized crime and terrorist crimes. *Transnational Organized Crime, 2,* (4), 40-82.

Vollmer, A. (1936). *The Police and Modern Society.*

CHAPTER FOUR

Gun and Prostitution Laws

Introduction

Regulatory laws include controls on a variety of human behaviors. There are laws that control traffic both vehicular and pedestrian, games of chance, possession of certain weapons, picture taking, marriage, sexual relations, certain speech and so on, too many such laws to adequately cover in this book. This chapter will examine the laws involving guns and prostitution. Although not directly related, they each pose a different set of challenges to the criminal justice system and illustrate the impact on that system by other regulatory laws as well.

The right to bear arms guaranteed by the Bill of Rights would appear on the surface to be straightforward; however, it has unfortunately been subject to a variety of interpretations. The evolution of firearms from single shot flintlock muskets and pistols to automatic and semi-automatic weapons has further clouded the issue. Prostitution, the oldest profession, is illegal in every state in the country except Nevada, yet it is practiced openly in most places. Because these topics are for the most part separate and distinct issues and present a different set of challenges to the criminal justice system, each will be explored individually in this chapter.

Gun Laws

Gun control laws can be divided into two groups: federal laws and state laws. Federal laws control the manufacture and transportation of guns and prohibit the sale of guns to certain individuals, such as felons and those with a mental illness. State laws further define who may possess guns and the conditions under which guns may be purchased and the conditions under which they may be possessed.

History

The discussion of guns must begin with the Second Amendment of the U.S. Constitution, which simply states, "A well regulated Militia, being necessary to the security of a Free State, the right of the people to keep and bear Arms, shall not be infringed." The idea of the armed citizenry may have originated in 10th century Great Britain, when King Alfred needed protection against the Norman invasions. He required every adult male to possess weapons as a "ready-force to defend the crown and the kingdom."[1]

There are two motivating factors underlying the inclusion of the 2nd Amendment in the Constitution. After living under British control, citizens of the individual states were fearful of a despotic national government. There was also the very practical need for self-defense. As Alexander Hamilton wrote, " … the right to bear arms is one of the natural rights."[2] As straight-forward as the 2nd Amendment may appear, it has continued to be a source of controversy as to its original intent particularly as applied to a changing society. The words "militia" and "right to bear arms" are at the crux of the controversy.

Without a standing army, the new nation needed to rely on citizens in the event of an invasion or other emergency. Citizens had to be mobilized quickly without the need for arming and extensive training. As stated in Article I, Section 8 of the Constitution, the federal government can activate the militia for the following purposes: "To provide for calling forth the militia to execute the laws of the union, suppress insurrections, and repel invasions." This strategy proved to be crucial as the country was, within a short time, plunged into the War of 1812 and the United States was again invaded by the British army. However, over time and with the creation of a standing army as well as army reserves and state-controlled national guards, the original intent of a ready militia gradually became less relevant.

Along with this evolution from a young nation into a more structured society, professional law enforcement agencies substantially reduced the need for citizens to possess guns for self-protection. Consequently, segments of society became concerned with the proliferation of weapons, particularly handguns. Over the years, this concern led to the mobilization of advocacy forces both for and against firearm possession by citizens. Legislators, responding to these forces, enacted laws controlling the possession of certain types of guns. The following are some examples of those laws:

> In 1911, New York State passed the Sullivan Act. The act prohibited New York City residents from possessing a handgun without a city permit.
>
> In 1934, following the repeal of prohibition, the National Firearms Act was America's first attempt at federal gun control. Gang violence of the 1920s, in which criminals increasingly used machine guns as well as shotguns and rifles with shortened barrels, provided the impetus for this legislation.
>
> In 1938, the Federal Firearms Act required federal licensing of gun dealers.
>
> In 1968, the Gun Control Act was enacted, " ... to provide support to federal, state and local law enforcement officials in their fight against crime and violence." This act followed the assassinations of Martin Luther King, Jr. and Robert Kennedy and prohibited the sale of guns to drug addicts, mental patients and persons convicted of certain crimes. It also required serial numbers on all new firearms.[3]
>
> In 1986, the federal government reversed some provisions of previous gun control laws by permitting sales of firearms between private individuals as well as the interstate sales of rifles and shotguns, thus allowing the sale of firearms at gun shows.[4]
>
> In 1993, the Brady Handgun Violence Prevention Act required background checks of gun purchasers by local au-

thorities and imposed a waiting period of up to five days
to prevent handgun sales to those prohibited under the
1968 act.[5]

These laws did not come without judicial challenges, however, and
resulted in a number of rulings by lower courts and several appeals
to the U.S. Supreme Court. Over the ensuing years a number of important U.S. Supreme Court rulings were instrumental in applying
the 2nd Amendment to a changing society. Some of the early cases
merely addressed the jurisdictional issues of whether the second
amendment applied to the states or the federal government, such as
United States v. Cruikshank (1875) and Presser v. Illinois (1886).

However, in the more recent cases courts ruled on the right to
own guns. In *District of Columbia v. Heller* (2008), for example,
the court held for the first time, in a 5-4 decision, that the Second
Amendment guarantees a law-abiding, responsible citizen's right
to possess an operable handgun in the home for self-defense. Because the District of Columbia is a federal enclave, this ruling did
not specifically apply to the states.

In *McDonald v. City of Chicago* (2010), the Court extended this
right to state and local governments in addition to the federal government. The Supreme Court added that the Second Amendment
should not be interpreted as conferring a "right to keep and carry
any weapon whatsoever in any manner whatsoever and for whatever purpose." The Court identified a non-exhaustive list of "pre-
sumptively lawful regulatory measures," including "longstanding
prohibitions" on firearm possession by felons and the mentally ill,
as well as laws forbidding firearm possession in sensitive places
such as schools and government buildings and also imposing conditions on the commercial sale of firearms. The Court also noted
that the Second Amendment does not prohibit laws banning "dangerous and unusual weapons" not in common use at the time, such
as M-16 rifles, and other firearms that are most useful in military
service.

In addition to federal laws, each state legislature has enacted
laws controlling the possession of handguns. These laws vary by
state and are too numerous to review individually. However, the

states can be classified as to their level of restrictive laws. The following is a review of those classifications. (It should be noted that the makeup of these categories has changed over the past years and are not likely to remain static):

> Three states, Vermont, Arizona and Alaska, allow firearms owners to carry guns without a permit.
> Thirty-six states grant handgun permits to any adult after a one-day class and a background check.
> Nine states grant permits to those who are able to show a need to carry a handgun.
> Two states (Illinois and Wisconsin) refuse to allow citizens to carry handguns.[6]

The majority of states permit the possession of handguns with few restrictions. However, the controversy continues. Do handguns improve or diminish public safety? Attempts have been made to answer this question with mixed results. Analysis can be divided into two general categories: defensive gun use and comparison of violent crimes in states with restrictive vs. permissive laws.

Defensive Gun Use

Perhaps the most cited sources of data on defensive gun use were the National Self-Defense Survey of 1993 and a 1998 article by Kleck and Gertz that was based on the survey.[7] In the 1993 anonymous survey, researchers randomly dialed phone numbers, obtaining a sample of 4,977 people 18 years and older from the 48 contiguous states. Of that number, 1,832 subjects received full interviews. The remaining 3,145 did not report a defensive gun use. Those who reported using a gun in self defense were grouped into one or more of the following categories: brandished or showed a gun; verbally referred to a gun; pointed gun at offender; fired gun; and wounded or killed the offender. The results when projected nationally showed an estimate of over 2 million instances of defensive gun use involving all guns and over 1.5 million instances involving handguns.

Works by Kleck and Gertz (1995), as well as Lott and Mustard (1997), also show estimated annual defensive gun uses that range from between 1 to 2 million.[8,9] It should be noted that most of these figures are estimates based on limited surveys. These figures are in sharp contrast to estimates of about 68,000 to slightly over 80,000 defensive gun use incidents as reported in the National Crime Victimization Surveys during roughly the same time frame. Critics of these studies point to flawed methodologies in their research and findings based on unrealistic assumptions.[10]

State Comparisons of Violent Crime

Similar controversies revolve around the question of whether there is a relationship between a state's gun control laws and the incidents of violent crime in that state. A number of studies attempt to evaluate the effectiveness of restrictive vs. permissive gun control legislation based on crime statistics. Several studies show a correlation between permissive gun control laws and lower crime and conversely, between stricter gun control laws and increases in violent crime.[11] As with defensive gun use data there is much controversy over study methodologies and conclusions. Most notable is the question of causality. People often confuse *correlation* with *causation*. Correlation is the statistical relationship of two variables that occur together. Causation is a process in which a change in one variable results in a change in another variable. In this case, an easing of gun control restrictions is said to result in lower incidents of crime. Without getting too deeply into statistics, there is a world of difference in the two. There are many alternative explanations as to why a correlation exists between two events or variables. For example, it could be a coincidence or there could be a third variable which influences changes in the first two variables.

Summary

America's experience with guns has evolved over the years from a necessary tool used for national protection, as well as hunting for survival and self-protection, to a multi-purpose commodity. Although guns are still used for self-protection, people also collect guns as a hobby or for sports and of course, crime.

The development of more sophisticated and lethal weaponry has resulted in a societal rift pitting gun control groups against those who argue for less stringent laws against gun possession. U.S. Supreme Court rulings have functioned to adapt the Second Amendment to a changing nation and states have struggled to balance Constitutional rights with public safety.

During this transition several studies have attempted to associate gun possession with reduced crime. These studies have, for the most part, been conducted by pro-gun advocates while the sharpest critics of those studies have had anti-gun sentiments. The basic facts are not in dispute but the interpretation of the data appears to be at the heart of the controversy. Complicating the issue even further is the rhetoric and conjecture associated with some of those positions. Because this subject is highly charged with emotion on both sides of the debate it is difficult to find truly objective analysis of the data.

Commentary

History has witnessed a clash of forces both for and against national anti-gun legislation. Numerous states have passed permissive handgun laws that allow a person, not otherwise prohibited, to purchase handguns. The only condition is the completion of a gun safety course approved by their state. These courses range from a few hours to a few days. This is in sharp contrast with other states that have very restrictive laws regarding handgun possession. This dichotomy highlights the schism that exists in this country regarding gun possession and argues against extensive national anti-gun legislation. Despite many convincing arguments against permissive handgun possession, national prohibition would certainly lead down the same path as other similar prohibition legislation. We have learned painful lessons that unpopular prohibition of any product simply leads to the establishment of illegal distribution networks. The law of supply and demand will ultimately apply. New York City is an example of this process. With one of the nation's strictest gun control laws, New York City has become a booming marketplace for the smuggling and sale of illegal weapons. Although the bulk of these weapons are obtained for nefarious reasons, many otherwise honest people purchase these guns for self-defense. Arguments have been made that easy access to weapons in nearby states facilitates the transport of these weapons into New York City and stricter laws would diminish this problem. However, the prohibition of illegal drugs in every other state does not seem to affect the availability of those drugs in New York. It all comes down to the adequacy of governmental resources to control these activities.

The fact that individual states still have the authority to determine the ability of their citizens to possess firearms is consistent with the third principle: *In order to gain maximum support and be most reflective of community standards, regulatory laws should be enacted at the lowest level of government that is practical.*

Prostitution

Introduction

Often referred to as the oldest profession, prostitution is a common practice in most societies. Some see prostitution as a means of survival for otherwise hopeless lives. For others it is a form of slavery and oppression. Although morally frowned upon and illegal in all but one state, (Nevada) this practice has generally been recognized as a part of life in American society. Prostitutes can be seen plying their trade in urban tourist areas but can also be less visible in other venues. From the street *hooker* to the Internet's social networks, to high-end escort services, the prostitution trade operates with little interference from law enforcement. The crime of prostitution is not given high priority due to its image as a victimless crime. Although the "victimless" label may be accurate in some cases, there are in fact many victims in the prostitution business.

Background

Prostitution per se was not a crime in Colonial America. It was, however, treated as a form of vagrancy as well as a violation of laws against fornication or adultery or being a common streetwalker.[12] In the late 1700s, seaport cities such as New York attracted prostitutes in the streets as well as in taverns where sailors would gather between voyages.[13] Concerns over sexually transmitted diseases, particularly syphilis, resulted in legislation aimed at controlling the spread of those diseases. For example, in 1870, St. Louis, Missouri enacted a Social Evil Ordinance that required the Board of Health to register and administer medical examinations to all known prostitutes and to license brothels.[14] In 1875, the U.S. Congress passed the Page Act that outlawed the importation of women into the United States for the purpose of prostitution.

In the early 1900s, prostitution became a high-profile national issue, leading the U.S. Congress, in 1910, to pass the Mann Act, that made it a federal crime to transport a female across state lines for the purpose of prostitution. During the periods of the first and second world wars, prostitution was rampant in the towns adjacent to military training camps. There was increasing concern over the spread of syphilis among military personnel and the devastating effect it could have on the war effort. The Chamberlain-Kahn Act of 1918 authorized the government to quarantine any woman suspected of being infected with a sexually transmitted disease.

In 1971, the state of Nevada began to formally regulate prostitution giving rural counties the option to license brothels.[15] In 1981, the Centers for Disease Control and Prevention in its *Morbidity and Mortality Weekly Report* reported five cases of young males with a condition that would be later referred to as AIDS. Although initially HIV infection was thought to be limited to gay males, it soon spread to the general population via a variety of means, including prostitution.

Prostitution Today

Some argue that prostitution is a victimless crime. After all, it is a contract voluntarily entered into by two parties with an exchange of money for services, a transaction comparable to one with a barber, auto mechanic, housepainter, etc. Even in the pornography industry, which is protected by the First Amendment to the U.S. Constitution, people legally exchange sex for money. Several prostitutes' rights groups have been formed around the country, such as COYOTE (Call Off Your Old Tired Ethics), FLOP (Friends and Lovers of Prostitutes), HIRE (Hooking Is Real Employment), and PUMA (Prostitute Union of Massachusetts Association.[16] Prostitution is also somewhat glamorized in Hollywood movies, such as *Pretty Woman*, *Mighty Aphrodite*, *L.A. Confidential*, *Moulin Rouge*, etc.

Traditionally considered a women's trade, prostitutes also consist of males and transgender males who engage in sex for money with other males. Many male and female prostitutes are or appear to be underage, which makes them particularly attractive to certain segments of the population.

Those who argue for legalization of prostitution emphasize the *voluntary* and *victimless* nature of the transaction. As to the issue of voluntarism, many street prostitutes are under the control and virtual ownership of a pimp. In a technical sense, a pimp is the agent for a prostitute who takes a portion of the prostitute's earnings. The relationship between the pimp and prostitute is often abusive and possessive. Many prostitutes are underage and incapable of legal consent and still others must perform in order to receive drugs for which they have no other means of payment. Also, illegal immigrants are routinely forced into prostitution to pay for their transport to America. According to a 1998 study by Farley and Barkan, of 135 prostitutes in San Francisco:

Eighty-eight percent of these respondents stated that they wanted to leave prostitution. They also voiced a need for: a home or safe place (78%); job training (73%); treatment for drug or alcohol abuse (67%); health care (58%); peer support (50%); and self-defense training (49%). Forty-eight percent stated that they needed individual counseling; 44% wanted legalized prostitution; 43% needed legal assistance; 34% needed childcare; and 28% wanted physical protection from pimps.[17]

Although the term, "victimless" may apply to certain segments of the trade, closer analysis reveals a number of categories of victims. Prostitutes are routinely exposed to dangerous situations by their pimps and clients. Because of the intimate nature of the sexual act and the isolation in which the act takes place, prostitutes are often physically assaulted, raped and even murdered by their clients. Even pimps, who are supposedly their protectors, are known to rape, beat, confine and disfigure their workers in order to keep them in line and to set an example for their other workers.

Victims also consist of those infected by sexually transmitted diseases (STD's). The prostitute functions as a locus for not only the commonly known STD's such as gonorrhea, herpes, syphilis and Chlamydia but also for a host of other diseases including pelvic inflammatory disease, hepatitis B, human papilloma virus and HIV. Many of these diseases have become drug resistant due to incomplete medical treatments. The transmission of these diseases from the prostitute does not end with the clients. Secondary infections continue on to other sexual contacts of the clients, including spouses and other partners, thus adding another class of victim.

The federal government still has the authority to quarantine individuals under 42 USC § 264 (Regulations to Control Communicable Diseases) which provides, in part " … to prevent the introduction, transmission, or spread of communicable diseases from foreign countries into the States or possessions, or from one State or possession into any other State or possession …." Although the states and local governments also have responsibility of enforcing quarantines, the Centers for Disease Control (CDC) may declare quarantines with regard to specific diseases, including cholera, diphtheria, infectious tuberculosis, plague, smallpox, yellow fever, viral hemorrhagic fevers and SARS (Executive Order of President George W. Bush, 2003). However, STD's are not included in governmental policies for quarantine. Instead, according to the CDC's Division of STD Prevention Mission Statement, what is needed is " ... national leadership, research, policy development, and scientific information to help people live safer, healthier lives by the prevention of STDs and their complications." This is accomplished by providing various government and non-government organization with timely science-based information and interpreting that information to the public and policy makers.

Prostitution Enforcement

The crime of prostitution is listed as a misdemeanor in all but one state (Nevada) with penalties ranging from 30 days to up to one year in jail and/or a fine that can range from a minimum of $50 to a maximum of $10,000, depending on the state. Nevada permits counties to approve the operations of brothels as long as they observe the prostitution laws of Nevada and the brothel owners and prostitutes are licensed and registered.

Because there are usually no complaining victims, arrests for prostitution are, for the most part, discretionary on the part of the local police department and political leaders. Federal enforcement is limited to upper class prostitution rings such as the so-called Hollywood Madam, Heidi Fleiss, and the Emperor's Club VIP in which former New York Governor Eliot Spitzer was a client. Because these cases tend to achieve extensive media attention they usually result in substantial prison sentences. The manner in which high-profile cases are handled in the judiciary will be examined in more detail in Chapter Seven of this book.

Police departments with detective units responsible for vice enforcement usually require some level of enforcement or quota. Enforcement may take the form of individual arrests or sweeps in which multiple arrests are made. Additionally, sweeps are also conducted in advance of significant functions such as political conventions and major sporting events. For example, in preparation for the 1984 Summer Olympics in Los Angeles, police officers conducted sweeps of Hollywood and other areas, resulting in the arrest of approximately 15,000 prostitutes.[18]

In a 1984 study, Pearl (1987) estimated the costs of prostitution arrests and found that more than $120 million a year was being spent by police on prostitution.[19] That amounted to an average of nearly $2,000 per arrest.[20] These figures do not include court costs.[21] The study also points out that reports of violent crime were up 32% in 1985 from a decade before.[22] However, arrests for violent crimes rose only 3.7%, and arrests for homicide and robbery dropped 15%.[23] During the same year, police officers arrested 74,550 people for prostitution in America's 16 largest cities.[24] That means that the average big-city police department spent 213 man-hours a day enforcing prostitution laws.[25] Pearl (1987) concluded that, "arrests for prostitution, a misdemeanor, exact a disproportionately high toll on law enforcement resources" to the point that agencies can no longer "afford" to keep the act "illegal."[26]

The city of San Francisco's Task Force on Prostitution investigated the effectiveness of prostitution enforcement and concluded:

> The total costs accounted for in this report amounts to $7,634,750.00. Given the many areas in which we found that information is not available, or there are hidden costs, the overall expense to the taxpayer exceeds $7.6 million annually.
> Despite the heavy emphasis on enforcement as a solution, the incidence of prostitution does not decrease over time. In 1991, there were 2, 518 prostitution-related arrests; in 1992, 4,785; in 1993, 3,218; in, 1994, 5,269. Moreover, these policies are not eliminating problems articulated by the neighborhood residents.[27]

From 1994 to 2004, national arrest estimates for prostitution have ranged from about 73,000 to slightly over 100,000, with about

86,000 occurring in 2004.[28] Because of overtaxed correctional resources (which will be explored more fully in Chapter Eight) judges are reluctant to sentence prostitutes to jail time but instead impose an affordable fine.

It should be noted that because crimes against persons or property, such as robbery and burglary, are usually reported to police, the number of arrests for these crimes may indicate police effectiveness in addressing such crimes. However, because crimes of prostitution are rarely reported it is difficult to place the number of arrests into any meaningful context. For example, if the number of prostitution arrests increases or decreases is that an indication of the number of crimes being committed or is it the result of police discretionary decisions?

The discretionary nature of enforcement as well as the lack of complaining victims creates a fertile environment for police corruption. The light sentences or fines imposed by the courts are not sufficient enough to deter the prostitute from further violations but are seen merely as part of the cost of doing business. Knowing the amount of the potential fine ahead of time provides the police officer and the prostitute a point of negotiation for a bribe in order to avoid the arrest. It is not the amount of the fine but rather the interruption of business and potential loss of income that motivates the bribe offer. However, police must still make some arrests in order to show that they are not ignoring the problem. In order to meet arrest quotas for vice crimes, particularly gambling and prostitution, some vice detectives have resorted to the practice of arrests by appointment. A date is selected when the corrupt officer will arrest a willing offender, after which the gambler or prostitute can go about their business without police interference until the next appointment date. Other corruption methods involve payoffs and/or sexual favors to police to simply ignore an entire illicit operation. Also, because of the numerous arrests, vice officers and prostitutes eventually get to know each other. The level of familiarity or social link provides an environment that may also contribute to the corruption process.

Alternatives to Enforcement

The arrest process typically results in the prostitute returning to the street with only a temporary interruption of business. The arrest, however, can provide an opportunity for intervention and a break in the cycle. One such effort began in San Francisco in 1993. The program, Standing Against Global Exploitation (SAGE), includes a rehabilitation center that offers prostitutes mental health counseling and drug rehabilitation services to help them leave prostitution, and begin new careers. At SAGE, peer counselors and former prostitutes offer interventions to prostitutes and those exiting prostitution such as assessments, referrals, peer support, vocational training, counseling, mentoring and rehabilitation. Similar programs exist in such places as New York, Kansas City, Atlanta, Denver, Seattle and St. Paul, Minn.[29]

Summary

Prostitution in America can be traced to at least the 1600s and continues to today. Although currently illegal and, for the most part, morally unacceptable, prostitution is apparently tolerated and accepted as part of American society. Early measures to control the spread of STD's through the quarantine process have all but disappeared as the growth of these infections expands throughout society. The criminal justice process has also failed to control street prostitution. Criminal sanctions in the form of fines are viewed as business overhead, similar to paying taxes, and have not had a significant deterrent effect. Prison sentences are usually limited to high-profile and highly publicized prostitution operations. Police corruption is often associated with vice crimes such as prostitution due to the "victimless" character of the crime and the discretionary enforcement powers of the police.

Commentary

If the purpose of law is to discourage crime through enforcement and criminal sanctions, then the current prostitution laws have failed to achieve that purpose. Apprehension should be inevitable and punishment should be sufficiently stern so as to deter further criminal behavior. By simply imposing a fine on street prostitutes, the criminal justice system has entered into a de facto partnership with the offenders, taking a share of the profits similar to a business tax, thus leaving prostitutes free to return to the streets to continue practicing their trade. These fines hardly pay the costs of enforcement and court time. Even more troubling is the fact that those criminal justice resources are detracted from more serious crimes. There is an argument for concentrating on quality of life offenses as long as those enforcement practices have a deterrent effect on the commission of those offenses. There is apparently little or no such deterrence to street prostitution. The cost of enforcement greatly outweighs the benefits to society. The second principle would be appropriately applied to prostitution laws: *If a law fails to achieve its intended purpose or if there are legitimate reasons why it should not be enforced as written then it should be revised or repealed.*

So why have laws against prostitution in the first place? As previously discussed, many street prostitutes are virtually trapped in their condition, not only by their pimps, but also by their addiction to drugs and lack of access to viable alternative life styles. They are often victimized by their pimps as well as by their clients. The widespread transmission of a host of dangerous and sometimes deadly diseases can be directly attributed to prostitution. Prostitution locations also attract other criminal activities, particularly drug dealers and robbers who prey on potential clients.

Perhaps a better approach would be a combination of enforcement and mandatory treatment in such programs as SAGE. The arrest process would then be aimed at ultimately reducing street prostitution.

Discussion Questions

1. Given the amount of gun violence that occurs on city streets, should handguns continue to be sold legally in the United States and carried by U.S. citizens? Why or why not?

2. Are there certain types of firearms that should not be sold legally in the United States or owned by U.S. citizens? Explain.

3. If you were charged with establishing a series of rules and regulations to control gun ownership, what rules and regulations would you be likely to include?

4. Discuss the arguments for and against increased control over gun ownership?

5. In your mind, should gun ownership be a right or a privilege? Why?

6. If citizens were not allowed to possess guns, do you think that violent crime would increase or decrease? Explain your answer.

7. Discuss how the prostitute may be the victim of prostitution.

8. Should prostitution be legalized? Explain your answer.

9. Describe some of the possible benefits to prostitutes if prostitution were legalized (in addition to not being arrested)?

10. Discuss some possible steps that could be taken to decrease the amount of police corruption that stems from prostitution.

11. How do you think the police should respond to the victimization of prostitutes?

12. Laws against prostitution have done little to curb the supply and demand for prostitution. What else might be done that could decrease the problem?

Notes

1. Esposito, G. (2011, January 16). Their rights as Englishmen: A brief history of the Second Amendment-Part I. Retrieved from http://jonathanturley.org/.

2. Edel, W. (1995). *Gun Control*. West Port, CT: Greenwood Publishing Group, Inc.

3. Krajicek, D. J. (n.d.). Guns and gun control in covering crime and justice, criminal justice journalists. Retrieved from http://www.justice journalism.org/crimeguide/toc.html.

4. Prontonne, S. (1997). *Gun control issues.* Commack, NY: Nova Science Publisher, INC.

5. Volokh, E. (2009). *Implementing the right to keep and bear arms for self-defense: An analytical framework and a research agenda.* 56 UCLA Law Review 1443. Retrieved from http://www2.law.ucla.edu/volokh/2am.polf.

6. Lott, Jr. J. R. (2000). *More guns, less crime: Understanding crime and gun control laws* (3rd. ed.). Chicago, IL: University of Chicago Press.

7. Kleck, G., & Gertz, M. (1995). Armed resistance to crime: The prevalence and nature of self- defense with a gun. *Journal of Criminal Law and Criminology, 86,* 150–187.

8. Kleck, G., & Gertz, M. (1995). Armed resistance to crime: The prevalence and nature of self-defense with a gun. *Journal of Criminal Law and Criminology, 86,* 150–187.

9. Lott Jr., & Mustard, D. (1997). Crime, deterrence and right-to-carry concealed handguns. *Journal of Legal Studies, 26,* 1–68.

10. Webster, D. & Ludwig, J. (2000). *Myths about defensive gun use and permissive gun carry laws.* Washington, DC. Berkeley Media Studies Group.

11. Lott, Jr. J. R. (2000). *More guns, less crime: Understanding crime and gun control laws* (3rd. ed.). Chicago, IL: University of Chicago Press.

12. Miller, E. M., Romenesko, K., & Wondolkowski, L. (1993). Prostitution: An International Handbook on Trends, Problems, and Policies. Retrieved from http://prostitution.procon.org/view.resource.php?resourceID=000117.

13. Gilfoyle, T. J. (1996). The urban geography of commercial sex: Prostitution in New York City, 1790-1860, *the other Americans: Sexual variance in the national past.* Retrieved from http://prostitution.procon.org/view.resource.php?resourceID=000117.

14. Sneddeker, D. R. (1990). *Regulating vice: Prostitution and the St. Louis social evil ordinance, 1870–1874.* Gateway Heritage.

15. Symanski, R. (1974). Prostitution in Nevada. *Annals of the Association of American Geographers, 64* (2).

16. Jenness, V. (1990). From sex as sin to sex as work: COYOTE and the reorganization of prostitution as a social problem. *Social Problems, 37* (3).

17. Farley, M., & Barkan, H. (1998). Prostitution, violence against women, and posttraumatic stress disorder.*Women & Health, 27*(3): 37-49.

18. Becklund, L. (1987, July 10). Prostitution arrests cost $2,000 each, study finds. *Los Angeles Times.*

19. Pearl, J. (n.d.). Cost-benefit analysis of prostitution laws. *University of California's Hastings Law Journal.*

20. Ibid.

21. Ibid.

22. Ibid.

23. Ibid.

24. Ibid.

25. Ibid.

26. Ibid.

27. (1996). San Francisco Task Force on prostitution final report. Retrieved from http://www.bayswan.org/5cost.html.

28. Puzzanchera, C. M. (2006). *Easy access to FBI arrest statistics 1994-2004.* Washington, DC: National Center for Juvenile Justice (NCJJ).

29. Dittmann, M. (2004). Getting prostitutes off the streets. *Journal of the American Psychological Association, 35* (9).

Bibliography

Becklund, L. (1987, July 10). Prostitution arrests cost $2,000 each, study finds. *Los Angeles Times.*

Centers for Disease Control, Division of STD Prevention Mission Statement. Retrieved from http://www.cdc.gov/std/dstdp/.

Dittmann, M. (2004). Getting prostitutes off the streets. *Journal of the American Psychological Association, 35* (9).

Doherty, B. (2008). *Gun Control on Trial.* Washington, D.C: Cato Institute.

Edel, W. (1995). *Gun Control.* West Port, CT: Greenwood Publishing Group, Inc.

Eno, W. P. (1903). Rules of the Road.

Esposito, G. (2011, January 16). Their rights as Englishmen: A brief history of the Second Amendment-Part I. Retrieved from http://jonathanturley.org/.

Farley, M., & Barkan, H. (1998). Prostitution, violence against women, and posttraumatic stress disorder.*Women & Health, 27*(3): 37-49.

Gilfoyle, T. J. (1996). The urban geography of commercial sex: Prostitution in New York City, 1790-1860, *the other Americans: Sexual variance in the national past.* Retrieved from http://prostitution.procon.org/view.resource.php?resourceID=000117.

Jenness, V. (1990). From sex as sin to sex as work: COYOTE and the reorganization of prostitution as a social problem. *Social Problems, 37* (3).

Kleck, G. (1995). Armed resistance to crime: The prevalence and nature of self-defense with a gun. *Journal of Criminal Law and Criminology, 86* (1).

Kleck, G., & Gertz, M. (1995). Armed resistance to crime: The prevalence and nature of self- defense with a gun. *Journal of Criminal Law and Criminology, 86,*150–187.

Krajicek, D. J. (n.d.). Guns and gun control in covering crime and justice, criminal justice journalists. Retrieved from http://www. justicejournalism.org/crimeguide/toc.html.

Legal Community Against Violence. (2011). *Summary of Second Amendment case law-federal cases.* Retrieved from Legal Community Against Violence Website: http://www.lcav.org/content/SecondAmendFedCases.asp.

Long, A. P. (2004). *The great southern Babylon: Sex, race, and respectability in New Orleans, 1865-1920.* Baton Rouge, LA: Louisiana State University Press.

Lott, Jr. J. R. (2000). *More guns, less crime: Understanding crime and gun control laws* (3rd. ed.). Chicago, IL: University of Chicago Press.

Lott Jr., & Mustard, D. (1997). Crime, deterrence and right-to-carry concealed handguns. *Journal of Legal Studies, 26,* 1–68.

Miller, E. M., Romenesko, K., & Wondolkowski, L. (1993). Prostitution: An International Handbook on Trends, Problems, and Policies. Retrieved from http://prostitution.procon.org/view.resource.php?resourceID=000117.

Pearl, J. (n.d.). Cost-benefit analysis of prostitution laws. *University of California's Hastings Law Journal.*

(1981, June 5). Pneumocystis Pneumonia—Los Angeles. *Morbidity and Mortality Weekly Report.*

Prontonne, S. (1997). *Gun control issues.* Commack, NY: Nova Science Publisher, INC.

Puzzanchera, C. M. (2006). *Easy access to FBI arrest statistics 1994-2004.* Washington, DC: National Center for Juvenile Justice (NCJJ).

(2007). *Right to carry states map.* Retrieved from http://johnrlott. tripod .com/2007/05/right-to-carry-states-map.html.

(1996). San Francisco Task Force on prostitution final report. Retrieved from http://www.bayswan.org/5cost.html.

Sneddeker, D. R. (1990). *Regulating vice: Prostitution and the St. Louis social evil ordinance, 1870–1874.* Gateway Heritage.

Symanski, R. (1974). Prostitution in Nevada. *Annals of the Association of American Geographers, 64* (2).

Volokh, E. (2009). *Implementing the right to keep and bear arms for self-defense: An analytical framework and a research agenda.* 56 UCLA Law Review 1443. Retrieved from http://www2.law.ucla.edu/volokh/2am.polf.

Webster, D. & Ludwig, J. (2000). *Myths about defensive gun use and permissive gun carry laws.* Washington, DC. Berkeley Media Studies Group.

CHAPTER FIVE

Vehicle and Traffic Laws

Introduction

Traffic enforcement is one of the major functions of most police departments and accounts for the most official contacts between the public and the public. This is especially true in large urban areas where the need for traffic safety and the maintenance of a smooth flow of both vehicular and pedestrian traffic requires a significant proportion of police patrol time. Vehicle and traffic laws have grown in number and complexity as the availability of motor vehicles has expanded dramatically over the past century. Frequent enactment of additional traffic laws places even more demands on already strained resources. With traffic enforcement, as well as with other police responsibilities, the issue of sufficient resources is of serious concern. This chapter will review the history and evolution of traffic laws and some of the problems facing police and the public in the enforcement of those laws.

History

Although self-propelled vehicles can be traced back to the late 1700s, most agree that the age of the American automobile began around the turn of the 20th century. Auto companies such as Oldsmobile, Ford and Cadillac began mass production around 1900. Perhaps the first traffic law came into effect in 1901 when New York required owners to register their automobiles. However, it wasn't until 1920 that license plates were required in all states and driver's licenses were not required until the 1930s.

As the use of automobiles began to increase, the need for such laws as speed limits, traffic lights, stop signs, one-way streets and a variety of other regulations became apparent. Ironically, many of these rules were first introduced in the book, "Rules of the Road" by William P. Eno in 1903. Eno proposed such regulations as slow traffic staying to the right, passing on the left, pedestrian crosswalks and stop signs, as well as other innovations.[1]

Most of the early safety laws focused on external interactions aimed at providing a smooth flow of traffic and preventing collisions between cars and injuries to pedestrians. It was not until fairly recently that laws addressed activities within the vehicle. Seat belt laws, for example, were first introduced in New York State in 1984. New Jersey, Illinois, Missouri, Michigan and New Mexico followed shortly after.[2] More recently, the increased use of cell phones, particularly those with texting capabilities, led to a variety of state and local ordinances against distracted driving. Unlike criminal laws that require intent, traffic violations are considered "strict liability laws," which means that a person can be guilty without having any criminal intent. For example, if a person unknowingly exceeds the speed limit they can still be held legally responsible for their actions.

Traffic Laws and Violations

With the proliferation of new traffic laws there has also been an increase in public disregard for those laws. Drivers routinely exceed speed limits, pass on the right, use cell phones, text while driving and so on. A survey of teenagers conducted by the American Automobile Association (AAA) found that 51% of teenagers talk on their cell phones while driving, 46% text while driving, 40% admit to exceeding the speed limit by 10 miles per hour or more, and 11% say that they have driven under the influence of alcohol or drugs.[3]

Another driver survey of the AAA found that nearly 80% rated aggressive drivers as a " ... serious or extremely serious traffic safety problem."[4] In the same survey, nearly half of drivers reported exceeding the speed limit by 15 mph on major highways in the past

30 days, and 15% even admitted exceeding the speed limit by 15 mph on neighborhood streets.[5] In another survey by the AAA conducted in 2010, about 52% of drivers reported feeling less safe than they did five years prior, also, over 65% of drivers reported talking on cell phones while driving within the past month, nearly 35% admitted to doing so on a regular basis, and 24% reported that they text or email while driving.[6] In the same 2010 survey, 45% of drivers said that they have driven more than 15 mph over the speed limit in the month prior and about one in three drivers considered it acceptable to do so.[7] Most drivers (over 65%) often feel pressured from other drivers to drive faster than they would prefer.[8] As to red light running, about one third of drivers admitted to doing so during the past month.[9] Finally, about 10% reported that they drive without wearing their seatbelts on a regular basis.[10]

It is quite apparent that there is a general and growing disregard for traffic laws. It is not uncommon to see police cars riding along with the rest of the traffic that is exceeding the speed limit. Traffic does slow down, however, when a police officer is apparently issuing a summons on the side of the road. Unfortunately, the slower traffic is only temporary as drivers resume speeding after they pass the police car.

Police readily admit that there are not enough police to enforce all the laws, therefore they must focus on drivers who commit the most flagrant violations. For example, if a speeder is weaving in and out of traffic that person might be stopped even though everyone else is exceeding the speed limit at a similar pace. Thus, police use their discretion to the exceptional violator, the one that stands out of the pack. This discretionary practice functions as tacit approval of those other drivers who are exceeding the speed limit and establishes, de facto, a new, unofficial, higher speed limit. A problem occurs when the new higher speed limit becomes the norm and drivers gradually exceed that unofficial limit. This incremental process can easily get out of hand and result in a wholesale disregard for traffic laws.

Unfortunately, the perception that they are somehow immune from the law lulls many speeding drivers into a false sense of security. Drivers can and do get stopped for speeding and to their dismay, receive summonses for doing so. The excuse, "everyone else is doing it" rarely dissuades the officer. Because police have wide discretion in traffic enforcement and one officer is not bound by the standards of another, an offense ignored by one officer can legitimately be enforced by another.

Traffic Enforcement

The federal government has had a significant impact on the enforcement of traffic laws. By providing incentives in the form of grants administered by the State Highway Safety Offices (SHSO), the federal government helped to shape the enforcement strategies of nearly all the states. For example, Section 405, of the Occupant Protection Incentive Grants, provided grant money to states that meet four of the following six criteria:

> A law requiring seat belt use by all front seat passengers (FY 1999 and FY 2000) and beginning in FY 2001, by all passengers.
> A primary enforcement seat belt law.
> Minimum fines or points for violations of seat belt and child restraint laws.
> A statewide special enforcement program for occupant protection.
> A statewide child passenger protection education program.
> A child passenger protection law.

In order to qualify for these funds, states must submit annual reports showing compliance with the criteria and meet performance goals and objectives. Congress has revised its grant program several times, adding new incentive grants, penalties and sanctions. Other grant programs involve offences related to Alcohol-Impaired Driving Countermeasure Incentive Grants and Child Safety and Child Booster Seat Incentive Grants. Grants can be substantial, amounting to as much as over $12 million to New York, $15 million to Texas and over $21 million to California during fiscal year 2010.

One of the notable criteria for receiving grant money is the state's enforcement statistics. Municipalities share in these grants as well as the income from summons fines, resulting in a strong economic incentive to issue summonses. The higher the rate of enforcement, the greater the financial rewards to local government, resulting in pressure on local police to actively participate in the enforcement objectives. This is accomplished in two ways. First, teams of officers establish checkpoints where violators may be spotted and stopped with minimum traffic disruption. Checkpoints located at parkway entrance and exit ramps are used to check for seatbelt compliance while checkpoints for driving under the influence are most likely to be operated during early morning hours and on weekends.

The second and perhaps the most controversial method is the use of activity quotas. Because the word "quota" is objectionable to the public and police officers alike, police departments avoid the use of the phrase and substitute more acceptable terms such as "activity expectations," "performance goals" and "benchmarks." Nevertheless, the intent is the same; police officers must make a minimum number of arrests and issue a minimum number of traffic summonses or face consequences. In a *New York Times* article, a police commander was secretly recorded telling his subordinate supervisors that officers in his command must write more summonses or face consequences. A specific number was given for officers on a particular shift. They were expected to write, " ... as a group — 20 summonses a week, five each for double-parking, parking at a bus stop, driving without a seat belt and driving while using a cell phone."[11] In Los Angeles, two police officers were awarded a $2 million judgment against the city for requiring them to meet summons quotas and for actions against the officers by the department affecting their careers after they reported the misconduct and refused to meet the quotas.[12] Numerous similar media reports of quotas and reaction thereto are readily available online.

Quotas raise a number of questions. For example, what is the purpose of traffic law enforcement and do quotas serve to accomplish that purpose? This question can be answered in terms of means and ends. Theoretically, the desired end result, as most would agree, is the smooth, safe flow of traffic. The means would be strategies aimed at controlling street, road and highway traffic. Controlling tactics would focus on targeted enforcement efforts employed to modify or change driving habits and behaviors so that they will comply with existing laws. These tactics would include but not be limited to summons issuance. Success, that is, achievement of the desired end result, would be measured in terms of the degree in which traffic is safe and flows smoothly. However, if the intended end result is increased revenue, then it makes little difference where and when traffic summonses are issued.

The use of quotas also has a detrimental effect on police relations with the public. It reduces the amount of discretion police officers have to determine if a summons is the best way to deal with a particular violation. There are times when extenuating circumstances may suggest that a warning to the driver might be the preferable course of action. The fact that police must meet quotas reduces legitimate enforcement of law to a perceived numbers game, a game in which the citizen is the loser. The citizen is left with the belief that the reason for the summons was not necessarily his behavior but for a fine to contribute to the government's coffers.

There is also the claim that quotas lead to racial profiling by police. Even if individual officers are completely unbiased in fulfilling their quotas, there is the possibility that a combination of quotas and police deployment practices may actually result in a disproportionate number of citations against minorities, particularly in larger cities. For example, police departments normally deploy higher numbers of officers to high-crime neighborhoods. People of color have traditionally inhabited these neighborhoods. The increased number of officers raises the probability that more offenses will be observed by officers in that neighborhood than in other places throughout the city that have fewer assigned officers. These opportunistic observations are likely to result in more summonses and arrests of minorities, thereby raising the specter of racial profiling.

Automated Enforcement

New technologies are available to augment traffic enforcement by police personnel, specifically the use of red light and speed cameras. These cameras have the benefit of not only freeing officers for other duties but they also function as totally impartial enforcers of the law. There is no question of quota, preferential or discriminatory treatment or any of the subjectivity questions usually associated with police officer enforcement. They operate around the clock, 365 day a year and instill a level of certainty of enforcement not attributable to police. Many states already use speed and red light cameras, albeit under limited circumstances. According to the Governors Highway Safety Association (GHSA) as of the end of 2011, 21 states, as well as the District of Columbia, permit some form of red light camera use.[13] Nine states prohibit their use, and 20 states have no state law concerning red light camera enforcement.[14] Twenty-five states and the District of Columbia have red light cameras currently operating in at least one location.[15]

Scofflaws

Despite efforts to increase summons issuance through quotas, the courts, particularly in large cities, lack sufficient resources to process those cases and collect fines. For example, a recent audit in Los Angeles revealed that there was an estimated $15 million in unpaid parking tickets.[16] Seattle had over $54 million in unpaid tickets, with one person alone accounting for $72,000.[17]

Summary

Street and highway safety is one of the primary functions of police. One method used to accomplish this mission is the enforcement of laws that prohibit behavior that tends to create unsafe conditions. In addition to that primary purpose, additional incentives to enforce those laws have taken the form of government grants and political pressures to increase revenue to municipalities in the form of fines for traffic violations.

Police enforcement is one of the activities necessary to qualify for federal grant monies by targeting certain behaviors identified in those grants. In addition, police activity quotas designed to meet grant requirements have been imposed on police officers. These practices result in a backlash from police officers and from the public alike and question the efficacy of traffic law enforcement efforts. Public displeasure with these tactics, including claims of racial profiling, is primarily directed at police officers. Despite current enforcement efforts, public disregard for traffic laws has been growing to a level that police seem unable to control with existing resources.

Commentary

It is obvious that public compliance with traffic ordinances is gradually eroding. There are two likely explanations: first, available police resources are inadequate to effectively enforce the volume of traffic laws currently in effect, and second, current strategies for the use of police resources are misdirected. Also possible is a combination of the two.

There is an underlying philosophy of balance scales in law enforcement. That is to say, violations of law are somehow offset by apprehensions (summonses and arrests). If there is an increase in violations of a particular law, an increase in apprehensions with regard to that law is evidence of police effectiveness. The use of activity quotas, not only in traffic enforcement but also in general practice, is an outgrowth of this philosophy. Although there is some logic to this approach, it tends to be an inefficient and often ineffective use of police resources. This is particularly true in regulatory law enforcement as compared to the enforcement of laws that are usually reported to police, such as assaults and robberies.

Take the example of the New York Transit Police efforts to control graffiti in the subways. During the period of the 1960s and 1970s, when spray paint and magic markers became widely used to graffiti public and private property, subway trains became an attractive target by youths and young adults. The result was that virtually every visible part of every one of the more than 6,000 train cars was full of graffiti. There were graffiti markings all over the inside windows, doors, seats and ceilings. The outsides of the trains were also covered with graffiti, sometimes in the form of massive murals. The New York Transit Authority had all but given up trying to keep the train cars clean, resulting in new graffiti being placed or spray-painted over existing graffiti. So extensive was the graffiti that is was impossible to tell the rate at which it was being applied.

The Transit Police response to this problem was to make arrests and issue summonses for graffiti in the amount of over 150,000 apprehensions per year. Because most of those apprehended were juveniles, the already strained juvenile justice system failed to impose any significant penalties, which simply encouraged them to continue their behavior. If public and private officials complained about the problem the police responded by increasing the volume of apprehensions; again, the philosophy of balancing the scales. Nevertheless, the volume of apprehensions appeared to have little effect on the problem and everyone, including the police, was resolved to the futility of the graffiti problem. This situation continued unchanged until the early 1980s when David Gunn, a newly appointed President of the Transit Authority, challenged the police to take a comprehensive approach to eliminating the graffiti problem and committed the operating personnel of the Transit Authority to coordinate their efforts with the police. It should be noted that the following is an overview of a rather extensive and complex program. For the sake of brevity, many elements of the program will not be discussed.

The first step was to understand the nature of the graffiti problem. There were three general categories of offenders. One group consisted of gang members and others who wanted to write their "tags," which are street names and street numbers. Gang members traditionally use tags to mark territorial boundaries. Self-proclaimed "graffiti artists" made up the second group. They were responsible for large colorful murals on the side of train cars. They preferred train lines that had outdoor stations so that their art can be easily photographed for their portfolios. The third group was made up of typical vandals bent on defacing property.

The strategy was to take a large, seemingly unsolvable problem and break it down to manageable parts. Each part consisted of one subway line. The first was the Flushing line that ran from Times Square to Main Street in Queens. There were a number of principles that were adopted in this effort. The first step involved a security inventory at train storage areas were trains were kept during periods of low demand. Broken fences and other means of unauthorized entry were secured to keep vandals from defacing the trains. Second, all the train cars on the targeted line were thoroughly cleaned of graffiti prior to going into service and would not stay in service unless they remained graffiti free.

About twenty-five officers, in addition to the normal complement, were assigned in uniform and plain clothes to patrol this line. Those in plain clothes would often wear reflective orange vests, similar to those worn by transit authority workers. After several arrests, the vandals were conditioned into thinking that anyone similarly dressed could be a police officer. This strategy had the additional benefit of providing a residual police presence after the main contingent of officers was redeployed.

Graffiti incidences on the targeted line were eventually reduced to a manageable level mainly because the incentives for graffiti murals and tags were removed. The vandals eventually moved to other areas where they could operate without interference and where their "artwork" would not be disturbed. After several weeks, the incidents of graffiti reached a manageable level and because new graffiti could be easily spotted, officers could concentrate on the times and areas were graffiti was likely to occur, making prevention and enforcement efforts more efficient.

When it became apparent that the Flushing line was under control, the original contingent of officers was gradually moved to the next line in the program. This pattern of deployment allowed the police and other Transit Authority personnel to gradually take control of one train line at a time until after about five years the entire system was clean of graffiti.

As far as enforcement was concerned, the level of apprehensions was reduced from over 150,000 per year to about 5,000. Consider the issue of qualitative vs. quantitative measures. When measured on the basis of quality the program should be considered a success, however, judging by the quantity of apprehensions alone, the program might not represent aggressive police enforcement.

Controlling highway speeding could be dealt with using an approach similar to the subway graffiti problem. In fact, the "Safe Corridor" program sponsored by the National Highway Traffic Safety Administration (NHTSA) provides an excellent place to begin. A "Safe Corridor" is an area or segment of highway identified as such due to increased accident rates, fatalities, traffic volume and/or other highway traffic criteria. Although the Safe Corridor program is not specifically designed to deal with a speeding problem only, the concept of declaring a segment of road as a full enforcement zone could achieve the desired results. Because the current problem of excessive speeding did not emerge overnight, corrective efforts will not provide immediate results but will require patience and a methodical course of action.

A segment should be of a distance that police resources can adequately control. It is more important to control a shorter distance of road than to be overly ambitious and select a segment that would require more resources than are available. Signage together with public announcements would alert drivers with sufficient notice of the total enforcement program. The public has been accustomed to hearing empty threats of full enforcement programs so it is important to back up those announcements with a full commitment to the program.

Monitoring the designated segment of road is vital to measuring results. After a period of full enforcement there should be a residual enforcement effect as drivers become conditioned to the new expectations. Once compliance with speed limits reaches a satisfactory level, police resources can be gradually reassigned to a new segment of road. Patience is critical and a reputation of full enforcement must be maintained. Early results may tempt administrators to take on larger areas than their resources can adequately control. If drivers realize that they can speed without a high risk of being stopped, the program will lose credibility.

Using a combination of automated speed enforcement cameras augmented by marked and unmarked police vehicles, police could take control of highways and roads in their jurisdiction one segment at a time. The duration of such a program depends on several factors, including the length of highway or road in the jurisdiction and the amount of police resources and speed cameras available.

Discussion Questions

1. Discuss the pros and cons of activity quotas.

2. Should police have more or less discretion in law enforcement? Why?

3. In some countries, there are no speed limits on freeways and people just drive at the speed that they are comfortable driving. Could such a policy ever work here in the United States? Why or why not?

4. If the government passes a law and doesn't encourage police to enforce that law, is that law really necessary? Can it be eliminated?

5. Do you agree or disagree with the use of automated technologies such as speed detection cameras?

6. What are some possible unintended consequences of the usage of automated technologies by the police?

7. Do you think that more people would follow the traffic laws if the police themselves also followed traffic laws and "led by example"? Why?

8. Do you think that the presence of more technology in vehicles, specifically hands-free calling devices, is contributing to more people breaking the law regarding cell phone use while driving? Why?

9. When trying to eliminate the presence of graffiti in a place such as the subway, what are some possible problems that one might face when trying to accomplish this goal?

10. What are some possible unintended consequences of the use of technological devices such as red light cameras by the police?

Notes

1. Cohen, S. L. (n.d.). The history of traffic laws. Retrieved from http://www.ehow.com/about_5436948_history-traffic-laws.html.

2. Morelock, S., Hingson, R. W., Smith, R. A., & Lederman, R. I. (1985). Mandatory seatbelt law support and opposition in New England—a survey. *Public Health Reports, 100* (4), 357–63.

3. Van Tassel, W. (2007, August). 17 EXPERTS: manager of the American Automobile Association driver improvement programs. *Seventeen Magazine.*

4. AAA. (2010). Traffic Safety Culture Index. Retrieved from: http://www.aaafoundation.org/resources/index.cfm?button=research.

5. Ibid.

6. Ibid.

7. Ibid.

8. Ibid.

9. Ibid.

10. Ibid.

11. Baker, A., & Rivera, R. (2010, September 9). Secret tape has police pressing ticket quotas. *New York Times.* Retrieved from http://www.ghsa.org/html/stateinfo/laws/auto_enforce.html.

12. Blankstein, A. (2011, April 11). Officers who alleged LAPD traffic ticket quota system win $2-million judgment. *Los Angeles Times.*

13. Governors Highway Safety Association (GHSA). (N.d.). Retrieved from http://www.ghsa.org/html/stateinfo/laws/seatbelt_laws.html.

14. Ibid.

15. Ibid.

16. Beltzer, Y. (2011, April 26). Controller issues audit on unpaid parking tickets. Retrieved from http://www.q13fox.com/news/kcpq-parking-ticket-scofflaws-cost-city-of-seattle-millions-20110206,0,5922128.story.

17. (2011, February 7). Seattle's biggest parking ticket offenders: Meet the man with $72,000 in tickets. *KCPQ.*

Bibliography

AAA. (2010). Traffic Safety Culture Index. Retrieved from: http://www.aaafoundation.org/resources/index.cfm?button=research

Baker, A., & Rivera, R. (2010, September 9). Secret tape has police pressing ticket quotas. *New York Times.* Retrieved from http://www.ghsa.org/html/stateinfo/laws/auto_enforce.html.

Beltzer, Y. (2011, April 26). Controller issues audit on unpaid parking tickets. Retrieved from http://www.q13fox.com/news/kcpq-parking-ticket-scofflaws-cost-city-of-seattle-millions-20110206,0,5922128.story.

Blankstein, A. (2011, April 11). Officers who alleged LAPD traffic ticket quota system win $2-million judgment. Los Angeles Times.

Cohen, S. L. (n.d.). The history of traffic laws. Retrieved from http://www.ehow.com/about_5436948_history-traffic-laws.html.

Governors Highway Safety Association (GHSA). (N.d.). Retrieved from http://www.ghsa.org/html/stateinfo/laws/seatbelt_laws.html.

Morelock, S., Hingson, R. W., Smith, R. A., & Lederman, R. I. (1985). Mandatory seatbelt law support and opposition in New England—a survey. Public Health Reports, 100 (4), 357–63.

(2011, February 7). Seattle's biggest parking ticket offenders: Meet the man with $72,000 in tickets. KCPQ.

Van Tassel, W. (2007, August). 17 EXPERTS: manager of the American Automobile Association driver improvement programs. Seventeen Magazine.

PART TWO

Impact on the Criminal Justice System

Over the next three chapters, it will become apparent that the criminal justice system is currently inadequate to deal effectively with the level of crime and disorder, particularly with regard to regulatory law violations. This level of lawlessness is somewhat hidden from official crime statistics, which only show reported crimes. Because these offenses are, for the most part, victimless, they are not reported to police in the traditional manner. Nevertheless, it is obvious that drug use is rampant, and anyone who drives on the streets and highways is reminded daily of the violation of traffic laws of all kinds, particularly speeding, failing to keep to the right lane, running stop signs and red lights, using cell phones and texting, etc. Similarly, prostitutes, many of whom are underage, openly parade city streets and many otherwise law-abiding citizens carry concealed, unlicensed weapons for protection.

It should be emphasized again that it is not the intent of this book to argue in favor of or against any of the behaviors prohibited by the regulatory laws covered in Part I but to examine the effects that those laws have on the criminal justice system. Society would certainly be better off without alcohol and drug abuse and their related problems of intoxicated driving, broken homes, domestic violence, health problems and premature deaths. We would also be better off if no one possessed hand guns or engaged in prostitution and if everyone drove safely. However, we do not live in a perfect world and the question is not whether these activities should be legal or not but rather whether the criminal justice system can realistically enforce all the laws that are currently in effect, particularly regulatory laws. That is the challenge we face.

The Criminal Justice System

As we proceed with an examination of the system from police through the courts and corrections we see progressive diminishment of capacity. That is, even though police admit that they cannot fully enforce all laws, they can still effect many more arrests than the courts can adequately manage, and the courts can sentence more convicted criminals than correctional facilities can house. At each stage therefore, alternatives to the preferred process must be utilized. Police, for example, using their discretion, can give warnings or simply ignore certain violations of law. The courts can decline to prosecute certain offenders, sentence offenders to periods of probation, give suspended sentences, adjourn cases contemplating dismissal of the charges (A.C.D.) which means that the charges will be dismissed after a specified period during which the defendant does not commit another offense or simply dismiss a case "in the interest of justice." Correctional departments can automatically reduce sentences for good behavior, give liberal paroles, or, when overcrowded, provide wholesale releases of non-violent inmates. It should be noted that the non-violent status applies to the final charge of the conviction and not necessarily to the original charge, so if a person committed a violent crime but during a plea bargain pled guilty to a reduced non-violent crime, that inmate would be considered non-violent.

It is impossible to completely separate each section of this book, as there is much overlap, particularly between the regulatory laws in section one with the impact of those laws on the criminal justice system that will be reviewed in the following three chapters. The criminal justice system, as presented in the flow chart above, consists of three main elements: the police, the courts and corrections. A basic overview of the system's operation begins with the arrest of a defendant by the police. The courts include, among others, the judge, prosecuting attorney, defense attorney, and where applicable, a jury to adjudicate the charges against the defendant. If found guilty, the defendant may be sentenced to a period of time under correctional supervision in either a jail or prison, or placed under the supervision of a probation officer or if imprisoned, may at some point be placed under the supervision of a parole officer after which the offender is returned to society. Each of the following three chapters will review this process in greater detail and will examine the effect of regulatory laws on each of the system's elements.

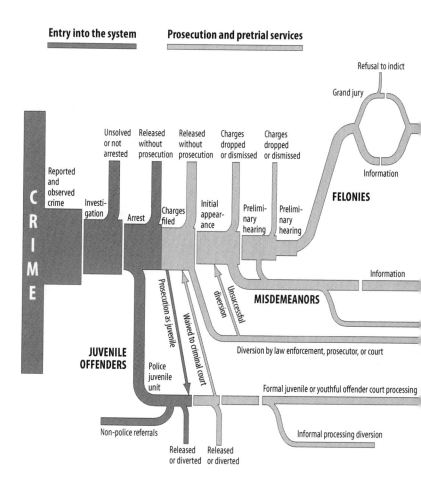

Entry into the system

Prosecution and pretrial services

Note: This chart gives a simplified view of caseflow through the criminal justice system. Procedures vary among jurisdictions. The weights of the lines are not intended to show actual size of caseloads.

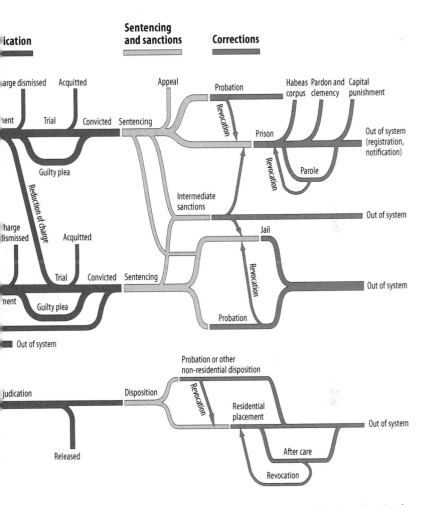

http://bjs.ojp.usdoj.gov/content/largechart.cfm

CHAPTER SIX

The Police

Introduction

Policing as we know it today is a relatively new phenomenon in society. Considering that societies have had laws for thousands of years, it is interesting that police departments have only been in existence for a relatively short period of time. Prior to the creation of police departments, people were responsible for protecting themselves. It was not until the emergence of densely populated urban centers and the need for order maintenance that cities began to establish police departments. This chapter will review the role and purpose of police in a free society with emphasis on the effects of regulatory law.

The Police Role in Society

Police fulfill several societal needs, namely: law enforcement, protection of life and property, fighting crime, order maintenance, and the provision of a variety of services to the public:

Law Enforcement

Perhaps the earliest need of societal groups has been the creation and enforcement of laws as a means of social control. Throughout the ages various civilizations employed their own unique methods of fulfilling that need. For example, in Egypt at about 1000 B.C. public officers appointed by the Pharaoh performed law enforcement duties. Their symbol of authority was a staff engraved with the name of the Pharaoh. A body of five elected officials called the *ephori* performed the Greek's form of law enforcement. They were given extensive power to investigate, arrest, judge and execute law violators. Rome, under the emperor Augustus formed the Praetorian Guard to protect the palace and the Urban Cohort to patrol the streets. These were staffed with men selected from the military. During the middle ages, societies began to employ citizens for the purpose of enforcement of law. The appointment of constables and shire reeves (the antecedent of sheriff) in England were examples of non-military government officials appointed for law enforcement.

Protection of Life and Property

Leaders of nations traditionally appointed people to provide a variety of services, including protection for themselves, their families, and their possessions. For the most part, the people themselves were left with the responsibility of their own safety and security. In ninth century England, for example, people were assigned to ten family groups, known as tithings, which were self governing and responsible for their own security. They were also held responsible as a group for offenses committed against the king by any member of the tithing. Family members were often assigned to keep watch at night for robbers as well as other emergencies, such as house fires. This tithing system also included the authority to exact punishment against those who committed crimes against the group.

Order Maintenance

The need to maintain order did not manifest itself until the industrial revolution and the accompanying increase in densely populated urban communities. Societies were ill equipped to control large crowds of disorderly persons except by the use of military force. One of the underlying motivations for England to create a professional police force was the Peterloo Massacre, the tragic manner in which the English army handled a demonstration attended by about 60,000 protestors. The setting was at St. Peters Square in Manchester, in 1819, at which a contingent of about 1,000 cavalry and infantrymen attempted to disperse the crowd, resulting in 18 protesters killed and about 700 injured as a result of saber wounds and trampling.

Crime Fighting

Law enforcement is considered a reactive process, taking action after a crime has been observed or reported; crime fighting is a proactive process of investigating suspected criminal enterprises to uncover evidence of criminal behavior. Undercover officers may infiltrate organized crime operations or other gangs for the purpose of gathering enough evidence to potentially bring charges against key individuals and thereby disband the criminal operation.

Providing Services

Governments typically provide a range of services to the public. For a number of reasons, such as the fact that police operate 24 hours a day, 7 days a week, they have traditionally been assigned to perform many of these services. Such non-enforcement activities as licensing, searching for lost children, providing emergency medical aid, traffic and crowd control have historically been performed by police. Police also work with juveniles through sporting activities as well as programs designed to deter them from criminal or other potentially harmful activities.

Law Enforcement: A Brief History

The London Metropolitan Police Department, created in 1829, is generally recognized as the first modern police department and served as a model for many police departments in the United States. For example, the New York Police Department, which was established in 1844, adopted many of the basic principles of the

London police, including a numbered badge, a uniform, probationary hiring, record keeping, assignments based on crime and
so on. One major difference between the political organization in
England and in the United States is that England's police come
under national jurisdiction while in the United States police are
controlled by state and local governments. This distinction resulted
in a lack of consistent standards for hiring and training in the
United States but more importantly, police came under the influence of local politicians. It is generally accepted that policing in
the United States evolved through three eras: the political era, the
reform era and the community era.[1]

The Political Era (1850s to 1900)

The first police departments were created during a time in history in which the spoils system controlled virtually all of political
life in America. This system derived its name from the adage, "to
the victor go the spoils." The victors in this case were those who
won elections to public office. The spoils were patronage jobs,
power and political influence. This system was marked by the
wholesale firing of government workers during changes in administrations and the hiring of friends, relatives, political supporters
and those who were willing to pay for their jobs. Police departments were not exempt from this system. Corruption was rampant
and politicians often relied on police to further their corrupt enterprises by collecting payoffs from illegal operations, including
gambling and prostitution. Police were also called upon to fix arrests of friends of the politicians, intimidate political rivals and
perform various other tasks for the political leaders. Police officers
typically worked 12-hour shifts; patrol work took up part of each
shift and the remainder was devoted to various duties as directed
by political leaders.

Police chiefs during this period functioned mainly as figure-
heads, powerless to hire or fire officers except at the direction of
those in political power. On the positive side, however, police were
also engaged in a broad range of social services, from running
soup lines to finding jobs for immigrant workers. Also, because

police patrolled predominately on foot, there was a high degree of interaction and familiarity between the police and the public.

The Reform Era

The reform movement began at about the turn of the 20th century. Frustrated with the level of political corruption, highly motivated social groups began coordinated activities to reform politics as well as law enforcement and other parts of the criminal justice system. The practice of granting positions through political patronage was the main target of the anti-patronage movement. Their goal was to separate policing from political influence. Some of their efforts included the election of police chiefs and granting them autonomy with broad discretionary powers. Following the Pendleton Act of 1883, which established the Federal Civil Service Commission, reform groups sought to also introduce the civil service merit system for hiring and promotions at the state and local levels. The civil service system would also provide tenure in office so that government workers could not be fired except for cause; thereby reducing dependency for employment on one's political benefactor.

Police chiefs, led by progressive administrators such as August Vollmer of Berkeley California and O.W. Wilson of Wichita Kansas, pioneered efforts to professionalize law enforcement. Seeking to raise policing to a level on par with other professions, the effort relied on college education in law enforcement subjects and a shift from community service to crime fighting, utilizing scientific methods such as crime analysis and finger printing.

The creation of the Uniform Crime Reports (UCR) by the Federal Bureau of Investigation (FBI) in the 1930s provided police with a means of keeping track of local crime trends as compared with crime in other jurisdictions around the country. The numbers of crimes and arrests began to take on a new dimension of importance. Because the Part I offenses of the UCR measured serious crime, such as murder, rape and robbery, they tended to serve as a report card for police department effectiveness. Other quantitative measures of police activity included response time to calls for service and the numbers of crime complaints cleared by arrest. To become more responsive to crime, police departments were restructured into centralized organizations and relied more heavily on the use of patrol cars.

Ironically, those elements of "professionalism" also functioned to separate police from the communities that they served. This gradual separation can be traced to such police practices as crime fighting priorities, deployment strategies and police discretion. There existed a significant division between police priorities and the priorities of the community. While police concentrated on UCR felony crimes, citizens tended to be more concerned with quality of life issues. Rowdy teenagers harassing people, abandoned cars, graffiti, drunks and other disorderly conditions that were driving people out of their communities received less police attention than major felonies.

Police also began to rely more heavily on automobile patrol. Cars were efficient and more practical than foot patrol. A police officer on foot can only patrol a relatively small area while an officer in a car could patrol larger sections of a city, respond more quickly to crimes and other emergencies and carry more equipment than an officer on foot. Automobile patrol also tended to remove police from routine interaction with the public. Interaction occurred primarily during law enforcement activities that were often marked by heightened emotions. This separation was most notable in inner city neighborhoods populated predominantly by minorities. The fact that most police who patrolled those neighborhoods were white tended to exacerbate the problem even further.

Civil rights and anti-Vietnam War demonstrations and riots of the 1960s highlighted the schism between the police and inner city communities that had been growing for decades. Some of those demonstrations were planned but others occurred spontaneously, often over an action of a white police officer that resulted in the death or serious injury of a minority citizen. Most police who were working during this era had never witnessed large-scale demonstrations and in some cases, this level of unpreparedness was actually credited with transforming a demonstration into a riot. Because of a lack of training in hostile crowd control, some demonstrators' attempts to goad police into overreaction succeeded, resulting in riots that lasted for days.

During the late 1960s and early 1970s, several national commissions were established to review these civil disorders. They included The President's Commission on Law Enforcement and Administration of Justice, The National Advisory Commission on Civil Disorders, The National Advisory Commission on Criminal Justice Standards and Goals, The President's Commission on Campus Unrest and The National Commission on the Causes and Prevention of Violence. A number of recommendations for better training, college education for police officers and the need for improved relations between police and the public resulted from these reviews. Ironically, recommendations for higher educated police echoed the concerns of Chief Vollmer from about half a century prior. In fact, The National Advisory Commission on Criminal Justice Standards and Goals (1973) recommended that by 1982 every police agency in the United States should require a four-year degree as a prerequisite for employment.[2] Currently, there are fewer than forty police departments that meet that standard.[3]

The Community Era

The Community Era began to emerge during the early 1980s when police professionals from organizations such as the International Association of Chiefs of Police, (IACP) the National Sheriffs Association, (NSA) the National Organization of Black Law Executives (NOBLE) and the Police Executive Research Foundation (PERF) coordinated their efforts to develop a strategy for a new direction for police. This strategy that became known as Community Policing had at its core several principles such as: customer-oriented policing, authority derived from the community, decentralized police organizations, proactive rather than reactive policing and a partnership between the police and the community committed to addressing community concerns. A major thrust of this concept is the idea of problem solving policing, an effort to uncover and respond to the underlying causes of crime and disorder. Community policing is considered a department-wide commitment to these principles rather than a program within a police agency.

Police executives are still struggling to adopt the concept of community-oriented and problem solving policing into traditional police agencies. For example, a decentralized organization requires the loosening of controls from the chief executive as well as from local commanders, a rather threatening concept since police executives are still accountable for the actions of their officers. It also requires a shift in success measurements from the traditional UCR standard of arrest and summons performance to the more ambiguous problem solving outcomes. Community policing also places a high priority on police/community interaction of which foot patrol is critical. Yet, as indicated earlier, foot patrol is a far less efficient method than motor vehicle patrol and requires more officers to provide the same level of patrol coverage. In short, community policing relies on quality of police service whereas traditional policing results are more quantitative.

A major challenge of community policing is how police executives will show results. The news media and the public have been conditioned to rate police departments in quantitative terms, such as how much crime was reported, how many arrests were made, how many summonses were issued and the response time to calls for police service. As police interaction with the public improves and walls of distrust are removed, people are more willing to report crime. How will this increase in reported crime be received? With greater emphasis on foot patrol, how will police maintain low response times without increasing department strength? These problems motivate many police chiefs to claim a commitment to community policing while maintaining the status quo.

Attitudes Towards Regulatory Laws

As stated earlier, regulatory laws differ from other laws in that the behaviors are not necessarily evil in nature nor do they inflict harm on others, as do *mala en se* laws such as murder, robbery, rape and larceny. Therefore, decisions to obey these laws do not necessarily rely on people's intent to do good or evil. Response to regulatory laws can be presented in a five-category continuum ranging from most likely to comply with those laws to those who are least likely. Those categories are: Civic Responsibility, Moral Agreement, Followers, Risk Takers and finally, Dissidents.

Civic Responsibility: People in this category believe that they have an obligation, as citizens, to comply with all laws whether or not they agree with those laws. For these people "legal and illegal" are the same as "right and wrong" and "good and evil."

Moral Agreement: These are people who will comply with the law when they have strong convictions about the efficacy of the law. However, they are likely to pick and choose which laws to obey based on their own moral and ethical convictions about the prohibited behavior. For example, they might use cocaine or marijuana but not patronize a prostitute.

Followers: Compliance with the law depends on what everyone else is doing. If highway traffic is moving at a speed above the limit these people will keep up with traffic but not necessarily exceed the prevailing rate so as not to stand out of the crowd.

Risk Takers: These are people who will take calculated risks to see how much they can get away with. They make rational choices based on potential gains versus possible losses. They will exceed speed limits and weave in and out of traffic if they are in a hurry or they will park illegally if they see that a traffic agent has just left the area.

Dissidents: People who simply do not care can be placed in this category. They are likely to have accumulated thousands of dollars in unpaid fines, drive without a license, have long criminal records for relatively minor offenses and simply do as they please with little concern for the consequences.

Enforcing Regulatory Laws

An arrest is defined as the taking of a person into custody to answer to a judge for a violation of law. In some cases, the officer may be authorized to issue a summons, which is in lieu of an arrest but still requires that person to appear before a judge to answer for a law violation.

One of the more significant differences between regulatory law violations and *mala en se* crime is the absence of a complaining victim. Additionally, police have broad discretion in the enforcement of many of these laws. Although they are authorized to enforce the laws they are not usually mandated to take any specific action. They may choose to simply order the person to desist from the prohibited activity, they may give a verbal or written warning, they can make an arrest, issue a summons, or take no action at all. Police discretion or the authority of a police officer to choose what action to take has proved to be problematic and has led to such problems as police corruption, claims of racial profiling, and complaints of police inattentiveness to certain crimes as well as selective enforcement.

Police Discretion

Discretion is not limited to police officers. Police chiefs, prosecutors, judges, juries, probation and parole officers, etc. all have the authority to make subjective decisions affecting people's lives and liberties. It is generally conceded that police cannot enforce all laws. Although police are required by law to take action when certain felonies or specific misdemeanors are committed, there is wide discretion in how police handle other laws. But, how much discretion should officers have? Should police officers be required to issue a summons in every instance of speeding, for example? Most would concede that this would require an army of police officers tying up traffic for miles and would simply be unrealistic. This question will be explored further in the Commentary Section. Police departments generally have a formal requirement that police must respond to all violations of the law. At a minimum, they should take some corrective action; however, that action is often left to the discretion of the officer. Of course, there are exceptions, as police executives also have the discretion to order officers to fully enforce certain laws and make arrests or serve summonses in every instance in which those particular laws are violated. Absent these department mandates, individual officers are free to decide.

Members of the public are keenly aware of police power to choose whether to take action or not. The result is a perception of unfair treatment if the police decide to issue a summons or make an arrest. A person cannot help but wonder why he or she was singled out. If everyone else is speeding why did this officer pick me? If I were another police officer or if I had a P.B.A. card, I would certainly be released. There is a natural search for some explanation for being selected. If there were a racial or obvious religious difference it would be natural for someone to grasp at that reason for the officer's attention. In any event, the officer's action would be perceived as being subjective or even personal.

One of the major objections to police discretion is the uneven application of the law. There are differences in the use of discretion among officers. One officer could decide not to take any action, while another officer under the same circumstances might choose to issue a summons. This is particularly evident when a department fails to provide clear guidelines for the use of discretion. Activity quotas can also have a bearing on the outcome, depending on whether the officer reached the quota or not.

Enforcement Activity Quotas

Can police departments realistically operate without some expectation of officer performance? This raises the question of how much is enough, thus the quota. If it is generally acknowledged that police cannot fully enforce all laws, then how can a police supervisor accept an officer's claim that he did not witness any law violations during his tours of duty? As pointed out previously, people openly violate laws on a regular basis. One tactic used by supervisors against officers with little or no enforcement activity is to spend time on patrol with that officer and point out instances in which a summons can be issued. Because those instances may involve circumstances in which the officer might have chosen not to issue a summons, the officer quickly learns that it is better to make those decisions personally. Supervisors may also give offending officers undesirable assignments or other forms of harassment.

In a perfect world, police officers would be evaluated on their contribution toward achieving the police purpose, quality of service to the public, contribution to public order, etc. However, given the nature of police work, where officersusuallyperform their duties outside the direct observation of a supervisor, it would be difficult to rate an officer's performance based on the quality of their work. Additionally, qualitative assessments of officer performance tend to be subjective and may lead to claims of unfair treatment. With the ready availability of records documenting the actions of the officers, supervisors can prepare performance evaluations in an objective and non-controversial manner. If one officer made more arrests and issued moresummonses than another, then it would be reasonable for that officer to receive a higher rating. Also, if an officer met his or her quota, that officer would be considered a cooperative and productive worker.Although more practical and easier to manage, the quota system subordinates legitimate police outcomes to bureaucratic expediency.

The issue of quotas again begs the question, what are the desired outcomes? Is it simply to ensure that officers are performing those police duties that qualify for government subsidies or grants, or is the purpose to modify and control unlawful behavior? What happens when the rest of the criminal justice system fails to play their role in the enforcement effort? When summonses are not paid are follow-up measures sufficient or are offenders allowed to rack up thousands of dollars in fines? As indicated previously, dissentients will routinely fail to pay traffic fines, resulting in a loss of millions of dollars nationally. For example, as indicated in the previous chapter, New York reported that in 2009 there was $454 million in unpaid parking tickets[4] and the Los Angeles Controller reported in 2011 an estimated $15 million in unpaid parking tickets.[5]

Racial Profiling

One of the more troubling aspects to the issues of discretion and activity quotas is the allegation of racial profiling, which is the use of race or ethnicity as a basis for police decisions to stop people for traffic as well as for other violations. The disproportionate numbers of minorities who receive citations as compared with white citizens tends to support these claims and leads people of all races to lose respect for the police. In particular, it tends to alienate minority communities, reducing the ability of law enforcement agencies to work with them. While members of those communities are fearful of victimization and seek police protection from predatory criminals, there is a level of resentment when police focus on the regulatory offenses committed by community residents. The perception that police are enemies of low-income minority neighborhoods, whether true or not, hinders attempts to build trust or rapport between police and those community residents.

Police departments as well as the governmental entities in which they serve have promulgated guidelines designed to curtail the practice of using race as a deciding factor in applying the law. The Florida Police Chiefs Association (FPCA), for example, recommended policies to its members to deal with the problem of racial profiling without undermining legitimate traffic enforcement. In a policy statement, the FPCA urged members to clearly prohibit racial profiling and subject violators to disciplinary actions. They further recommended that members of internal affairs units investigate allegations of racial profiling.[6] Many states, including Missouri, have enacted laws that require all peace officers in the state to report specific information including a driver's race for each vehicle stop. Law enforcement agencies are required to report the data to their state and states may withhold funds from agencies that do not comply with the law.[7]

The issue of racial profiling can be somewhat clouded by the realities of police deployment policies. For example, most street crime occurs in inner city minority neighborhoods and because police deployment is based to a large extent on reported crime there will of necessity be more police in those neighborhoods than in other parts of the city. Because more police are there, more violations of regulatory laws, including traffic laws, will be observed. Add to this the quotas that are imposed on police and these opportunistic observations will necessarily result in more stops of minorities. Finally, because whites comprise a higher percentage of police personnel the likelihood of more minorities being the subject of police actions by white police officers is highly probable.

Police Corruption

As indicated earlier, police corruption has existed since the beginning of policing in America. Police departments came under local governmental jurisdiction and police quickly became instruments of local politicians. Working twelve-hour shifts with only about four hours on patrol, police spent the remaining time attending to the political leaders' business. This business involved activities that were designed to either further politicians' ambition and/or to increase the wealth of the politician. Other activities of the police were varied of course by jurisdiction but usually involved such legitimate activities as sweeping streets and safety inspections, as well as collections from illegitimate businesses for the privilege to operate within the jurisdiction of the political leader.

Decades prior to the enactment of civil service legislation police functioned under a political patronage system. In addition to having the correct political affiliation, a person had to pay political bosses for a police job. In examining the problem of police corruption it becomes apparent that corruption is related to power and authority over people. Paraphrasing the old adage, "power corrupts" is appropriate here when one considers that the problem of corruption is fundamentally linked to those so-called victimless crimes, behavior that is regulated by law.

Corruption continues to be a major problem plaguing law enforcement. Many police executives cite the *Rotten Apple Theory* in an attempt to explain incidents of corruption uncovered in their departments. According to that theory, corruption is the result of a few, dishonest police officers who fell through the cracks of the hiring investigation process. Although this may explain some incidents of corruption there is ample evidence that other forces are also at work, primarily the enforcement of regulatory criminal law. History has shown that these laws are at the heart of most incidents of police corruption. The lure of substantial financial rewards for police to ignore or even facilitate those criminal enterprises provides a strong incentive that is difficult for police officers to resist. The absence of complaining witnesses together with apathy on the part of the public and the judicial system's unwillingness to seriously prosecute many of those who violate regulatory laws also contributes to police corruption.

Fair or not, the New York Police Department (NYPD) has been the subject of most high-profile corruption investigations. Beginning with the Lexow Commission in 1895, there have been a total of six commissions created to investigate corruption in the NYPD. The Knapp Commission in 1972 and the Mollen Commission in 1992 conducted two of the more recent and highly publicized investigations. The Knapp Commission looked into corruption activities of police officers, detectives and supervisors. Police were routinely collecting "protection" bribes from criminals involved in such activities as prostitution and gambling as well as illicit narcotics. "Good will" gratuities to police officers from legitimate sources such as restaurants and retail businesses were also a generally accepted practice. The Knapp Commission identified two types of corrupt police officers: "grass eaters" and "meat eaters." Grass eaters would passively accept bribes that were offered to them while the meat eaters aggressively solicited bribes and would seek assignments dedicated to enforcing laws against gambling, prostitution and narcotics. The commission concluded that corruption was systemic in the New York Police Department and their recommendation included the appointment of a special prosecutor to investigate police corruption as well as the reorganization of the NYPD's Internal Affairs Division.[8]

Although large-scale, organized forms of corruption, particularly among high-level supervisors were virtually eliminated after the Knapp Commission, pockets of corrupt officers were still active. Large-scale arrests of corrupt officers by internal affairs and local prosecutors occurred periodically. Incidents of this type usually began with a sting operation in which a small group of officers would be caught either extorting money and drugs or simply accepting a bribe from an undercover officer posing as a drug dealer. In exchange for their cooperation in uncovering evidence of similar activities from other officers in their command, those officers would receive favorable consideration from prosecutors. Operations of this type often led to the arrest of dozens of corrupt officers.

Despite the NYPD's effectiveness in uprooting corruption, arrests of large numbers of officers often resulted in bringing negative public reaction to what might appear to be an unmanageable police organization. Ironically, if the department simply arrested the few officers who were caught in the initial sting without further inquiry, the public reaction would have probably been more positive. After all, the department was uprooting those few rotten apples. It takes courage for a police commander to delve deeper and uncover a larger problem that is likely to reflect poorly on that commander and possible adversely affect his or her career.

The Mollen Commission was established in 1992 by then Mayor David Dinkins in response to the arrest of NYPD officers by police in another jurisdiction for possession and sale of drugs. Although the ring leader, Officer Michael Dowd, had been the target of several internal affairs investigations during his nearly ten-year career, charges were never brought against him and the mayor sought a review of the effectiveness of the NYPD to police itself. Officer Dowd agreed to cooperate with the investigation and his testimony helped shed some light on the underlying contributing factors to police corruption. His testimony included admissions to a variety of crimes including the use and sale of illegal drugs as well as the extortion of money and drugs from dealers. Unlike the systemic corruption uncovered by the Knapp Commission, the Mollen Commission investigation found that small groups of officers known as "crews" coordinated their efforts to identify drug sites and plan raids for the purpose of extorting money and drugs from the dealers, after which they would let the suspects go free. The amount of money extorted was not particularly high but with the volume of shakedowns executed by Officer Dowd, he and his crew took in from $300 to $400 per day, with even larger amounts, in the thousands, during the holiday season. Drugs that were appropriated would either be retained for personal use or sold to other dealers. Handguns that were confiscated from dealers were also sold for hundreds of dollars, sometimes to other criminals. Perhaps the largest bribes were for protecting drug operations. Officer Dowd and his partner received about $4,000 per week each for protecting drug operations in their precincts.

According to the Commission's findings, the most serious police corruption today comes from the drug trade. "Some corrupt police officers went so far as to conspire with drug dealers to protect, assist, and strengthen their drug operations. They worked hand-in-hand with drug traffickers and other criminals to thwart law enforcement efforts" (p. 31).[9] The Commission also acknowledged that vast amounts of money generated by the drug trade can easily be stolen by police or offered to them as bribes. "Drug money is everywhere. Officers stop cars with trunk loads of cash, search apartments with closets stacked with money, and meet drug dealers who will gladly pay them thousands of dollars just to be left alone" (p. 60).[10]

Contrary to the rotten apple model, when asked if he planned to engage in criminal activities when he joined the police force Officer Dowd adamantly stated that he did not. In fact his stated reasons for becoming a police officer were similar to those of the vast majority of officers: to serve people and because it looked like an interesting job. Other corrupt officers revealed that their illegal activities evolved from well-intended motivations. Initially, they would conduct unlawful raids of apartments in order to make drug arrests and later falsify police reports to show probable cause. As they realized the potential profits, they decided to keep the money, weapons and drugs and let the dealers go free. The Commission also found that the "notion that most corrupt cops 'slipped through the cracks' during recruitment ... is not always true." Additionally, " ... many—although not all—of these corrupt cops looked similarly 'ideal' while in the Department ..." (p.20).[11]

The Mollen Commission also uncovered evidence of false arrests, falsified documents and perjury related to drug-enforcement activities. Furthermore, these activities were often tolerated and even encouraged by police commanders. Not all false arrests were drug-related however, some were timed to generate overtime for officers who took hours after their normal tours to process arrests. Arrest quotas have also been associated with false arrests. In some instances, officers make illegal arrests to meet quotas imposed by commanders and also to receive preferential treatment or assignments. For example, a New York Transit Police commander made assignments based on officer arrest and summons activity. Those with lower than average activity would be given less desirable assignments while officers with higher activities received highly sought after preferential assignments. Two officers from that command were subsequently arrested for a series of false arrests that were made in order to maintain their plain-clothes assignment.[12]

Summary

Police departments are a relatively new concept given the thousands of years of various efforts to enforce laws. The industrial revolution together with emerging urbanization and dense populations created a need for methods to control crime and disorder. Unlike the British model of nationalized policing, American police evolved at the local level. Local politics together with the spoils system and its accompanying corruption quickly involved the police. Several efforts to reform governments and separate politics from police had only partial success. Progressive police chiefs made important strides toward professionalizing policing and established means of measuring police success. The advent of motorizing policing together with the need to show success in statistical terms through numbers of arrests, summonses, speedy response to calls for service and crime reports helped define policing in quantitative rather than qualitative measures. Attempts to achieve favorable numbers tended to separate police priorities from those of the public they served. Individual police officers also perceived their function as achieving acceptable numbers of apprehensions that together with deployment strategies based on crime rates led to complaints of racial profiling.

Policing has historically been plagued with corruption, initially at the direction of political leaders and later with the enforcement of unpopular regulatory laws. The prohibited behaviors often involve substantial profits that attract criminal syndicates eager to offer substantial bribes to police in order to operate without interference. Additionally, police often pursued opportunities to become personally involved in those criminal activities by either providing protection for criminal syndicates or by engaging in illegal operations on their own.

Several commissions, both federal and local, have been created to investigate policing effectiveness in dealing with disorders as well as corruption issues. These commissions found that police regularly engaged in such corruption activities as taking bribes and making false arrests and often did so with the active or tacit approval of supervisors and higher-ranking officials. Recommendations included raising hiring standards, particularly with regard to education, and improvements in training.

Commentary

Two areas of law enforcement deserve particular attention and commentary: they are activity quotas and police corruption. Both of these issues are strongly related to regulatory law enforcement and both have significant implications for policing.

It is generally acknowledged that most police departments use some form of quota system. This practice, although expedient, has several inherent flaws, primarily in its misdirection of purpose. It is a question of means and ends. Police enforcement is a means to achieve an end result of compliance with the law. Quotas, absent some strategic purpose, become an end unto itself, which is the antithesis of problem solving policing. When police executives and officers themselves perceive the police enforcement role as simply doing something a specific number of times then the objective of achieving compliance with the law becomes lost in the process.

One of the problems with regulatory law is that, unlike traditional crimes such as robbery and burglary, there are seldom any reports of regulatory law violation. Without reported crime, there is nothing to measure enforcement efforts against. For example, if store robberies are being reported in a certain district of the city and police are deployed to apprehend the robbers then those arrests should lead to a reduction in the number of robberies and would indicate that the effort had been successful. Because regulatory law violations are seldom reported, without some objective measurement of the volume of violations, there is no feedback mechanism to gauge the success of enforcement efforts.

Random enforcement can only hope to achieve random results. It is a scattergun, hit or miss philosophy as compared with enforcement programs that are better focused on achieving measurable objectives. Problem solving policing, for example, begins with the identification of a problem followed by the design and implementation of enforcement efforts to resolve the problem. Feedback mechanisms are then employed to measure the impact of those enforcement efforts on the problem followed by modifications of enforcement strategies, as necessary. As illustrated in the example of the graffiti program in Chapter Five, it comes down to the way success is measured. This brings us to the fifth principle: *Because police service is qualitative in nature, measures of that service should be expressed in qualitative rather than quantitative terms.*

Why do police become corrupt? As indicated earlier, the rotten apple theory may provide some insight into the problem but experience has shown that the reasons are not that simple. Let's begin with the concept of power. The ability to exercise control over people's activities or to provide them with favorable or profitable circumstances presents temptations on the part of both the powerful and those subject to that power. Add to that circumstances that provide an element of privacy, reducing the likelihood that a bribe might be uncovered, and you have the basic ingredients for corruption.

Take building inspectors and their relationship with contractors for example. The inspector has the power to cause extensive delays at a construction site, subjecting the contractor to cost overruns, late completion penalties and lost revenues from delayed future projects. Contractors are more than willing to bribe inspectors to overlook minor violations of construction codes and many of those inspectors either succumb to the temptation or even initiate an offer to cooperate with the contractor, for a price. The fact that only the inspector and contractor are aware of the transaction further facilitates and encourages the corrupt activity.

Police interaction with regulatory law offenders presents a similar environment for corruption. Unlike *mala en se* violations of law, there are usually no complaining witnesses to regulatory law violations so that only the officer's power to arrest and the secrecy of the transaction are present.

But, to return to the original question, why do police become corrupt? A substantial number of police officers and other students who intend to become police officers attend my classes at John Jay College of Criminal Justice. I often ask them to discuss their reasons for wanting to join the police force. Although their reasons are many, most can be placed in four categories: they want to provide a public service, they believe they can make a difference in society, they believe that it will be an interesting job and finally, a member of their family is or has been a police officer. The Mollen Commission also found that the vast majority of police officers, including Officer Dowd, had honorable motives for becoming police officers. As noted in the Mollen investigation, while in the department officers experience a gradual erosion of values. Police seldom achieve a sense of satisfaction from their job. Nor do they usually feel appreciated by the public. For example, at funerals of officers killed in the line of duty, hundreds of police officers from numerous regional departments line up in formation to honor the fallen officer. Rarely seen are residents from the slain officer's precinct.

Although people appreciate it when police save lives and arrest murderers, rapists and robbers, they tend to resent enforcement of laws that limit their freedom. When the government enacts regulatory laws, they pit police officers against the otherwise honest citizenry they are there to protect and serve. Police witness people getting away with crime, particularly violations of regulatory laws, and making large amounts of money doing so. They see young criminals driving BMW's and flaunting oversized gold jewelry. They often witness firsthand what has become known as the revolving door of justice. They can arrest a drug dealer on one day and find that same dealer out on the streets a few days later, leaving them with the sense that no one cares. There is a disillusionment and disappointment with a system that fails to live up to its own standards of due process and the rule of law. This is particularly true of people who enter policing with high expectations of the justice system and who later witness a cavalier, assembly-line process that has been substituted for a system that is purported to represent justice.

These feelings of disillusionment are further compounded by a perceived hostility from the public, the "us vs. them" mentality. Both the Knapp and Mollen Commissions found that police often feel resentment from the general public, especially when they enforce regulatory laws, traffic laws in particular. This perceived isolation from the public tends to foster strong bonds among officers and leads to the feeling that they must protect each other because no one else will. This bond of protection is most evident in the often cited "blue wall of silence." Even officers who are not corrupt are not likely to expose those who engage in corruption. This code of silence tends to facilitate corrupt activities because dishonest officers do not fear the honest ones.

As long as the basic elements of corruption are present in society as well as in policing, it is unlikely that corruption can ever be eliminated. Perhaps corruption should be viewed as a symptom of more insidious disease that we should be concerned with: a society that requires corruption to achieve desirable ends.[13]

Discussion Questions

1. Explain the terms "meat eater" and "grass eater" as used in the Knapp Commission Report.

2. According to the author, the use of discretion by police leads many citizens to ask "why me" when they are stopped by the police. How might this *why me* question be removed from the encounter without eliminating the use of discretion by police?

3. Discuss how an all-out prohibition of racial profiling might undermine the ability of the police to effectively discharge their duties and to combat crime?

4. Are differences in the amount of summonses issued according to race proof of racial profiling? Explain.

5. How might racial profiling by police happen by accident? Provide a detailed example.

6. Discuss what led to the Knapp Commission and what the Knapp Commission found.

7. Discuss what led to the Mollen Commission and what the Mollen Commission found.

8. Compare and contrast the corruption found by the Knapp Commission with the corruption found by the Mollen Commission.

9. What can be done to curb the monetary incentive for police officers to engage in acts of corruption?

10. What if anything could be done to eliminate or at least reduce the reach and power of the "blue wall of silence"?

Notes

1. Kelling, G. L., & Moore, M. H. (1988). The evolving strategy of policing. *Perspectives on Policing, 4.*

2. National Advisory Commission on Criminal Justice Standards and Goals. (1973). The police. Washington, D.C.: Government Printing Office.

3. Burns. (2010). Reflections from the one-percent of local police departments with mandatory four-year degree requirements for new hires: Are they diamonds in the Rough? *Southwest Journal of Criminal Justice, 7* (1), 87-108.

4. Einhorn, E. (2009, February 22). So easy for scofflaws to slip through cracks in New York City collection system. *Daily News.* Retrieved from http://www.nydailynews.com/news/2009/02/22/2009-02-22_so_easy_for_scofflaws_to_slip_through_cr.html.

5. Beltzer, Y. (2011, April 26). Parking ticket scofflaws cost LA millions. *NBC.* Retrieved from http://www.nbclosangeles.com/traffic/transit/Parking-Ticket-Scofflaws-Cost-LA-Millions-120730799.html.

6. The Florida Police Chiefs Association (2011). Racial profiling. http://www.fpca. com/profiling.htm.

7. Koster, C. (2010). Missouri Attorney General, vehicle stops report http://www.fpca.com/profiling.htm.

8. (1972). New York. (City): Commission to Investigate Allegations of Police Corruption and the City's Anti-Corruption Procedures.

9. The City of New York. (1994). *Commission to investigate allegations of police corruption and the anti-corruption procedures of the police department.*

10. Ibid.

11. Ibid.

12. Glaberson, W. (1989, March 15). 2 New York City Transit officers are guilty in false-arrest scheme. *New York Times.* Retrieved from http://www.nytimes.com/1989/03/15/nyregion/2-new-york-city-transit-officers-are-guilty-in-false-arrest-scheme.html.

13. Ashman, C. H. (1973).*The finest judges money can buy.* Los Angeles: Nash Publishing.

Bibliography

Ashman, C. H. (1973).*The finest judges money can buy.* Los Angeles: Nash Publishing.

Beltzer, Y. (2011, April 26). Parking ticket scofflaws cost LA millions. *NBC.* Retrieved from http://www.nbclosangeles.com/traffic/transit/Parking-Ticket-Scofflaws-Cost-LA-Millions-120730799.html.

Burns. (2010). Reflections from the one-percent of local police departments with mandatory four-year degree requirements for newhires: Are they diamonds in the Rough? *Southwest Journal of Criminal Justice, 7* (1), 87-108.

Einhorn, E. (2009, February 22). So easy for scofflaws to slip through cracks in New York City collection system. *Daily News.* Retrieved from http://www.nydailynews.com/news/2009/02/22/2009-02-22_so_easy_for_scofflaws_to_slip_through_cr.html.

Glaberson, W. (1989, March 15). 2 New York City Transit officers are guilty in false-arrest scheme. *New York Times.* Retrieved from http://www.nytimes.com/1989/03/15/nyregion/2-new-york-city-transit-officers-are-guilty-in-false-arrest-scheme.html.

Kelling, G. L., & Moore, M. H. (1988). The evolving strategy of policing. *Perspectives on Policing, 4.*

Koster, C. (2010). Missouri Attorney General, vehicle stops report http://www.fpca.com/profiling.htm.

National Advisory Commission on Criminal Justice Standards and Goals. (1973). The police. Washington, D.C.: Government Printing Office.

(1972). New York. (City): Commission to Investigate Allegations of Police Corruption and the City's Anti-Corruption Procedures.

The City of New York. (1994). *Commission to investigate allegations of police corruption and the anti-corruption procedures of the police department.*

The Florida Police Chiefs Association (2011). Racial profiling. http://www.fpca.com/profiling.htm.

(2011). *The Peterloo Massacre.* http://www.peterloomassacre.org.

(n.d.). Views of corruption control. http:// policeandlaw.org/ ... /Views%20of %20Corruption%20Control.pdf.

CHAPTER SEVEN

The Courts

Introduction

The courts or the judicial system is the second phase of the criminal justice process. After a person is arrested they are required by law to be presented in criminal court to answer for the crime with which they are charged. The entire criminal justice process from apprehension to incarceration is subordinate to the court process. Regardless of the professionalism of the police in effecting an arrest, conducting an investigation and uncovering evidence, and the competence of the prosecutor in presenting that evidence, the ultimate outcome depends entirely on the judicial process, particularly the judge, and where applicable, the jury.

Historical Perspective

Courts or similar forums for adjudicating disputes as well as criminal charges have existed for thousands of years. The tribunals of ancient Greece, the Sanhedrin of Israel and the courts of Rome are but a few examples. The European legal systems began to evolve during the Middle Ages and continued to make binding decisions regarding civil and criminal matters. The courts of England, in addition to ruling on existing law, created new law by making decisions that were in agreement with previous decisions (i.e., that adhered to precedent). This process, known as common law, or the doctrine of *stare decisis,* became a unique characteristic of the English judicial system. Lawyers who diligently studied precedent setting cases were better equipped and more successful in defending their clients, particularly those who were targeted for conviction by the monarchy. This conflict led to the concept of *due process*, the right to a fair and public trial conducted in a competent manner. United States courts systems were influenced to a great degree by the English judicial system. Inhabitants of the original thirteen colonies that were under British rule were familiar with the existing court system, particularly at the lower court level. By 1787, with independence from England and the adoption of the U.S. Constitution, federal as well as state courts were established and maintained the concept of Common Law and Due Process. Each court system was composed of different levels: trials, appeals and final appeals. Each state organized its own court system according to state constitution and applicable law. The federal court system was structured in accordance with the U.S. Constitution.

The Criminal Court

The criminal court system is essentially adversarial, a conflict between prosecution and defense with a judge as referee and a jury as deciders. In this system, the prosecutor must prove guilt beyond a reasonable doubt based on evidence presented and the defense's role is to refute the prosecution's evidence and to cast doubt on the credibility of the evidence presented. The judge is responsible for ensuring that the rights of the accused are protected and that evidence meets admissibility tests. Finally, the jury has the duty to render a verdict based solely on the evidence presented in court. In the event that a jury cannot reach a verdict, the judge may declare a mistrial, in which case the prosecutor has the option to bring the case to trial again with another jury. Below is a more detailed discussion of the duties/responsibilities of each.

Prosecuting Attorney

The prosecutor in most jurisdictions is the elected district attorney or an assistant to the district attorney. Prosecutors perform legal functions related to the investigation and prosecution of felony, misdemeanor, juvenile delinquency, conservation and other types of cases. To the extent that the prosecutors are the lawyers for the state, their client is not the individual victim of a crime or the police, but society itself. They secure expert witnesses, secure additional information from law enforcement, investigate case data, review police reports and determine criminal charges for arrest and non-arrest cases, and secure and interview witnesses to ascertain the facts of a case. They also research case law, formulate trial strategy, determine if child victims are able to provide testimony, prepare felony cases for Grand Jury indictment and prepare witnesses for trial. Prosecutors also attend pre-trial hearings, file or respond to pre-trial motions and prepare and respond to post-trial motions. Furthermore, prosecutors determine sentences sought, conduct plea negotiations and represent the municipality at sentencing hearings.

In addition to local district attorneys, there are state attorney generals who prosecute cases that have statewide significance and work with local district attorney's offices in the prosecution of cases. At the federal level, prosecutors work at the Department of Justice in Washington, DC, and at U.S. Attorney's Offices throughout the United States. The majority of people working as federal prosecutors are Assistant U.S. Attorneys (AUSAs), who carry out the bulk of prosecutions in the federal courts.

Prosecutorial Discretion

Prosecutors have vast discretionary authority, perhaps to a greater degree than any other position in the criminal justice system, including police officers and judges. They can choose whether or not to bring charges against a defendant, what charges to bring and what level of penalty to seek. This authority provides an opportunity for the harshest punishment allowable or for leniency. Prosecutors can also decide whether to negotiate a plea arrangement with the defense which could result in a defendant serving little or no jail time for a crime that would otherwise result in a penalty of several years in prison.

In felony cases, prosecutors can press charges even if the victim of the felony refuses to make a complaint against the defendant. An uncooperative victim or witness can also be subpoenaed to testify against the defendant and even be held in contempt and either be fined or jailed if they refuse to testify.

Defense Attorney

Following an arrest and before the commencement of the court proceedings, the defendant contacts a criminal defense attorney and asks for representation in the case. Upon agreement to represent, the criminal defense attorney must be present with the accused during interrogations made by law enforcement officers, the prosecutor or any other authority except for the Grand Jury. Criminal defense attorneys speak on behalf of their client. They defend the legal rights of the accused and try to decrease or dismiss the charges against their client. The criminal defense attorney collects all the necessary data and studies the case prior to taking the case forward. Case preparation may include obtaining information from the police, detectives, witnesses and other individuals related to the crime. The defense attorney is also entitled to disclosure from the prosecution of all reports, documents and written notes relating to the case, including those containing statements from witnesses and law enforcement personnel.

Prior to or during the trial the defense attorney may consult with the prosecutor to negotiate a plea arrangement in which the accused receives a lesser sentence and or lesser criminal charge in exchange for a plea of guilty. During the trial, the defense attorney's role is to protect the rights of the accused by challenging questionable evidence, testimony or rulings by the judge. Upon a finding of guilt in the case, these objections may form the basis for an appeal of either the guilty finding or sentence.

In addition to defense attorneys personally engaged by the defendant, state, federal and local jurisdictions may provide public defenders that serve as court-appointed attorneys for those who cannot afford attorneys. Because public defender offices must accept all cases referred to them, the number of cases a public defender handles at one time can be capacious.

Most jurisdictions also maintain a list of private attorneys who agree to take on cases assigned by the court where public defenders are not available. These attorneys are paid at a standardized rate by the state. Finally, during pretrial or trial proceedings, judges have the authority to randomly assign any attorney to represent the accused person.

Judges

Lower court judges' duties vary according to the extent of their jurisdictions and powers. In general, the judge serves as a referee in the pretrial and trial proceedings and oversees the legal process in courts. Judges ensure that trials and hearings are conducted equitably and that the court safeguards the legal rights of all parties involved. During pretrial hearings judges determine whether the evidence presented merits a trial. They also decide questions of admissibility of evidence and timetable for trial proceedings. Judges may decide whether people charged with crimes should be held in jail pending trial, or they may set bail or other conditions for release of the accused.

During trial, judges ensure that all parties adhere to applicable law, rules of evidence and court decorum. They also rule on objections from the defense or prosecuting attorneys and attempt to maintain a neutral, objective demeanor during the trial. If unusual circumstances arise for which standard procedures have not been established, judges interpret the law to determine how the trial will proceed. Judges instruct juries on applicable laws, direct them to deduce the facts from the evidence presented and hear their verdict. When a jury trial is not required or when the parties waive their right to a jury, judges may decide cases. In such instances, the judge determines guilt or innocence and imposes penalties as necessary. Judges duties include work in their chambers or private offices. There, judges read motion documents, research legal issues and write opinions.

Appellate court judges have the authority to overrule decisions if they determine that judicial errors were made in a case or if legal precedent does not support the judgment of the lower court. Appellate court judges rule on a small number of cases and rarely have direct contact with the people who are or were on trial. Instead, they usually base their decisions on the lower court's records and on lawyers' written and oral arguments.

The Jury

Federal as well as local jurisdictions have established policies for the process of selecting jurors. Those policies outline qualifications a person must meet to serve on a jury. There are two types of juries relating to criminal matters: trial juries and grand juries. A criminal trial jury is usually made up of 12 primary jurors and a number of alternate jurors. Alternate jurors may be assigned to take the place of any of the primary jurors who might be dismissed or released prior to completion of the trial. Juries decide whether the evidence proves beyond a reasonable doubt that the defendant committed the crime as charged. A jury's deliberations are conducted in private, out of sight and hearing of the judge, witnesses and others in the courtroom. Guilty verdicts must be unanimous. The judge usually sets sentences, however, in cases of capital offenses a jury may also make recommendations regarding a death penalties. A grand jury, which normally consists of 16 to 23 members, has a more specialized function. The prosecutor may present evidence to the grand jury for them to determine whether there is "probable cause" to believe that an individual has committed a crime and should be put on trial. Members of the grand jury may question the prosecution and witnesses as needed. If the grand jury decides there is enough evidence, it will issue an indictment against the defendant. Grand jury proceedings are not open for public observation.

Selection of Jurors

Potential jurors are selected from a pool generated by random selection of citizens' names from lists of registered voters, or combined lists of voters and people with driver's licenses, in the judicial district. Those selected complete questionnaires to help determine whether they are qualified to serve on a jury. After reviewing the questionnaires, the court randomly selects individuals to be summoned to appear for jury duty. These selection methods are intended to ensure that jurors represent a cross section of the community, without regard to race, gender, national origin, age or political affiliation.

When a jury is needed for a trial, the group of qualified jurors is taken to the courtroom where the trial will take place. The judge and the attorneys then ask questions of potential jurors to determine their suitability to serve on the jury. This process is called *voir dire*. The purpose of voir dire is to exclude from the jury anyone who may not be able to decide the case fairly. At the request of the attorneys, the judge typically will excuse those who know any person involved in the case, or who have first hand information about the case, or who may have strong prejudices about the people or issues involved in the case. The attorneys also may exclude a certain number of potential jurors without giving a reason.

The Criminal Trial

There are several stages leading up to a criminal trial. A preliminary hearing or a grand jury, the discovery process, arraignment and determination of venue are steps that may be taken prior to a trial. The trial consists of jury selection, opening statements, presentation of evidence, witness testimony, cross examination, various motions, closing arguments, jury deliberation, verdict and if guilty, a sentence by the judge.

In most jurisdictions, a preliminary hearing is required within a relatively short time after an arrest. The purpose of this hearing is to determine whether probable cause exists for believing that the defendant committed the offense as charged. There is no finding of guilt at these hearings. They simply serve as a safeguard for the defendant to ensure that the arrest and indictment are justified. If the prosecution fails to establish probable cause then the judge may dismiss the charges. A grand jury may also be impaneled to determine if probable cause exists and if so, to direct the prosecutor to prepare an indictment specifying the facts in the case.

The discovery process requires that the prosecution provide the defense with all documentation related to the case, including any hand written notes of the police or others involved in the investigation. The defense is also required to disclose certain information to the prosecution, but each state sets certain limitations on disclosure by the defense.

Before a trial can begin a determination must be made as to the location of the trial (venue). Normally, the trial is located in the jurisdiction in which the crime was committed, however, the defense may request a different venue if it is apparent that because of the notoriety of the crime an impartial jury from the local population is not possible.

Potential jurors are selected at random from such sources as motor vehicle records, voter registrations and telephone records. The prosecutor, defense attorney and the judge may question (voir dire) potential jurors to determine their suitability for the particular case. Both the defense attorney and the prosecutor have the option of challenging a juror, that is, requesting the judge to dismiss a potential juror. These challenges take two forms. A preemptory challenge is one in which no explanation is required, while challenges for cause must be approved by the judge. There are limits and restrictions on the number of preemptory challenges that may be approved, however, challenges for cause are unlimited.

After jury selection the prosecutor and defense attorney make their opening statements, in which they outline their cases to the jury. These statements prepare the jury for evidence and testimony which will be presented during trial and also draw the jury's attention to particular issues that each side will argue.

After opening statements, the prosecutor presents evidence in the form of witness testimony and physical evidence. The prosecutor questions witnesses in an effort to provide testimony and or physical evidence that supports the charges against the defendant. Defense attorneys may raise objections to any part of the procedure, including questions asked of the witness, the relevance of testimony to the case, the credentials of expert witnesses, the admissibility of certain witness statements or the admissibility of physical evidence. Defense attorneys also have the option of cross-examining witnesses. Their questions are limited to the statements already made by the witnesses as well as the witnesses' credibility or competence.

After the prosecution's case is completed the defense attorney may make motions to dismiss the charges. Those motions may be based on a claim that the prosecution failed to establish a *prima facie* case, or that evidence of guilt beyond a reasonable doubt has not been proved. If the motions are denied then the defense has the opportunity to present its case. However, the defense may choose not to present any evidence or testimony at which time closing arguments may be made.

In the closing arguments, the prosecution and defense review facts in evidence and draw conclusions from those facts that best support their individual positions. The prosecution seeks to convince the jury that the evidence proves guilt beyond a reasonable doubt and the defense attempts to convince the jury that reasonable doubt exists.

After closing arguments the judge charges the jury. In the charge the judge explains the relevant sections of law, what is needed for a finding of guilt as well as the concepts of presumption of innocence and reasonable doubt. The judge also gives the jury certain rules to follow during deliberation. Jury deliberations take place in private and may be concluded in as little as a few hours or it may take several days to reach a verdict. Jury deliberations may end with one of three findings: guilty, not guilty or no verdict. If no verdict can be reached then it is considered a hung jury. The jury decision is then presented to the judge in open court. If the defendant is found not guilty then the charges are dismissed and the defendant is released. In the event of a finding of guilt the judge sets a date for sentencing. If the jury cannot reach a finding then the prosecutor has the option of retrying the case with a different jury. In this situation double jeopardy does not apply. If the defendant is found guilty, the defense has the option of filing appeals based on denials by the judge in response to objections or motions by the defense.

Alternatives to Trial

There are several means of processing criminal defendants in addition to the trial. The prosecutor may decline to prosecute an otherwise legitimate case, the judge may adjourn a case with the possibility of a dismissal of the charges, a defendant might plead guilty at arraignment or the prosecution and the defense may enter into a plea agreement.

Declination to Prosecute: As indicated above, the prosecutor may decline to prosecute the offender. This decision can be made even if the arresting officer acted in accordance with the law and police department procedures, the arrest was based on probable cause and there was no legal reason why the person should not be charged. Prosecutors generally arrive at this decision in cases where the interests of justice might not be served by proceeding with the case. An example would be a person who is in the final stages of an incurable disease and is not likely to live long enough to stand trial.

Adjournment Contemplating Dismissal: After arraignment, the judge may adjourn the case for an extended period of time, usually one year, with the understanding that the case will be dismissed if during that time the defendant does not commit another crime.

Guilty Plea at Arraignment: If a defendant pleads guilty at arraignment there is no need for a trial and the judge may impose a sentence consistent with the crime charged.

Plea Negotiations: The prosecution and the defense enter into an agreement for a reduced sentence and/or charges in exchange for a guilty plea. Plea agreements are subject to acceptance by the judge.

Plea Bargaining

In 1839, only about 15% of all felony convictions in Manhattan and Brooklyn resulted from guilty pleas. However, the percentage increased steadily and by 1926 approximately 90% of all felony convictions in the New York area were the result of a guilty plea (Moley, 1928). Today, well over 90% of criminal convictions result from plea negotiations. The primary justification for the use of plea-bargaining is economic. Judicial economy seeks to conclude cases in an efficient and speedy manner. However, this process has been the subject of much criticism due to the appearance of being overly lenient to criminals. "Revolving door justice" and "a slap on the wrist" are but two of the terms commonly used to describe the results of this process. In a plea bargain, the defendant agrees to plead guilty (often to a lesser charge than the one for which the defendant could stand trial) in exchange for a more lenient sentence (and/or so that certain related charges are dismissed). The decision to bargain may be based on the strength of the evidence, the seriousness of the crime, media coverage of the case and/or the potential of a guilty verdict by the jury.

Plea-bargaining involves three areas of negotiation: First is *charges bargaining*, which involves not only the initial charge but also additional charges related to the same crime. For example, if a person is arrested for robbery and possession of a dangerous weapon the plea agreement might include dropping one of the charges. Another is *sentence bargaining*, where the plea of guilty is made in return for a lighter sentence. Finally, *fact bargaining*, which is used infrequently, involves the stipulation of certain fact(s) which the prosecution might have difficulty proving in court in return for an agreement not to introduce other facts into evidence.[1]

If a plea agreement is reached the defendant waives the right to a trial but is still required to enter that guilty plea in court and a judge must approve the arrangement.[2] The judge may or may not take the plea bargain depending on the offense charged.[3] Additionally, defendants are required to enter into the court record a confession (allocution) of the details of the crime. Once approved, this plea agreement is not subject to appeal by either side. A plea of guilty by a criminal defendant is a conclusive resolution of the case and removes the need for judicial inquiry into the facts. Plea bargains are generally encouraged by the court system, and have become a necessity safety valve to help alleviate overburdened criminal court calendars and overcrowded jails.[4] This procedure has been subject to extensive judicial review and has not been found to be unconstitutional nor does it violate the rights of the defendant.[5]

The plea bargaining option provides incentives for almost all parties involved. For judges, accepting a plea bargain serves to eliminate the need for a trial in a typically heavy court docket. Judges are also concerned about overcrowded correctional facilities and the ever-present pressure to reduce prison populations by means of early release. Although plea bargains provide prosecutors with the opportunity to reduce their workload, there is also the surety of a conviction. Both prosecutors and defense attorneys are fully aware of the unpredictability of a jury. A plea bargain ensures a favorable resolution to the case. For the defense attorney, getting the defendant off with a lower penalty then they might otherwise receive represents at least a partial win, particularly in cases were the evidence is sufficient enough for a finding of guilt. Also, where a fixed fee for services was entered into the defense attorney can collect the full fee without going through the trial process. Public defenders can quickly reduce their onerous caseloads. The defendant, of course, avoids some or all potential jail time. There is also the advantage of less serious convictions on the defendant's criminal record, particularly if the reduction is from a felony to a misdemeanor. In many states, multiple felony convictions can result in substantial prison time, including life sentences.

Of course there are losers in the process. Society suffers when criminals are on the streets searching for people to victimize instead of being incarcerated. Also, the victims of the initial crimes and witnesses thereto, are subject to harassment and further victimization by the criminal they were willing to testify against. Finally, there are those arrested for crimes they did not commit, especially crimes that carry a mandatory sentence. They face the dilemma of choosing between a lenient sentence that may involve no jail time and a mandatory sentence, that if convicted may involve several years in prison together with a felony conviction on their record. As shown earlier, a guilty plea waives the right to a trial and is not subject to appeal. The U.S. Supreme Court in *North Carolina v. Alford* held that plea bargains are valid even if the defendant later claims innocence as long as the plea was entered into voluntarily.[6]

Summary

The courts represent the second step in the criminal justice process, where arrested persons are brought to answer for the charges against them. During colonial times, courts were established under the jurisdiction of the individual colonies with oversight from England. After the American Revolution, the colonial courts served as the basis for the state court systems. These systems evolved with the expansion of the country together with increasing population and urbanization into more complex structures. The major participants in the judicial process are the judge, prosecutor, defense attorney and the jury. The judge ensures that applicable laws and procedures are followed and that the rights of the defendant are protected. Prosecutors have wide discretion in determining whether to bring charges or not, recommending penalties, and the authority to engage in plea negotiations with the defense. Defense attorneys represent the defendant in all phases of the process from arrest to appeals. They develop defense strategies aimed at refuting the prosecution's case. The jury is charged with rendering a verdict based on facts admitted into evidence during trial.

Because there are many more arrests than the courts can adequately adjudicate through the trial process, several alternative means of resolving cases have evolved, the most common of which is plea bargaining. All parties to the judicial process have come to rely heavily on negotiations to expedite cases in an overburdened court system. Although plea bargaining is a legitimate practice, there has been an overreliance on this alternative to trial for logistical purposes. The result has been much criticism from law enforcement as well as from the public.

Commentary

Inadequate resources to process the number of arrests, particularly those involving regulatory laws and minor offenses, have resulted in an overreliance on the plea bargaining process. Unless involved as a victim or witness, the general public is not aware of the extent that plea bargaining is used to avoid trials. The scarce resource of a criminal trial is reserved primarily for cases involving well-known persons and or for those cases that have attracted media attention.

Of course there are some instances in which plea bargaining can further the interests of justice but these would be in the minority and would not even approach the proportion of cases resolved by negotiated plea deals. As indicated earlier, "revolving door of justice" is a term often used to portray a system in which the criminal is out on the streets even before the arresting officer has completed his paper work. Excessive use of plea bargaining is perceived as being soft on crime. However, in some cases relying on this process can be particularly unjust to the innocent. In order to encourage plea deals prosecutors often threaten the use of excessive charges that carry mandatory sentences so that an innocent person is left with having to choose between being released with a criminal record and standing trial with the possibility of conviction and having to serve years in prison. Defense attorneys also pressure their clients to accept the deal—a deal that many reluctantly do accept for fear of also alienating their attorney.

Career criminals have learned to "play the system" by capitalizing on the system's most vulnerable area, its resources. It is not unusual to see individuals with criminal records, particularly those involving violations of regulatory laws, that show a long list of arrests resulting in suspended sentences, probation or sentences of only a few weeks in jail. These experiences by career criminals tend to dilute the deterrent affect of arrest and prosecution. That is not to say that they are not concerned about being apprehended but that committing the crime is apparently worth the risk. Criminals are confident that if apprehended, they will simply walk out of court with another warning from the judge that next time things will not go so easily.

When the crime involves a victim or witnesses the police officer is often left to explain how the criminal could be treated so leniently. Police must also deal with the anger and frustration of the victim or witness who has taken time off from work to pursue the case because of police encouragement, appealing to their sense of civic duty and responsibility. This is particularly troublesome if the case involved several adjournments prior to the negotiated plea resulting in the criminal walking out of court to freedom.

This situation has the effect of frustrating law enforcement and may very well contribute to the problem of police cynicism, brutality and corruption. As police officers begin to lose respect for and confidence in the integrity of the criminal justice system they also begin to question the importance of their own role in the process. While in this state of frustration police officers can become susceptible to the temptation of seeking out their own version of justice. That may include resorting to "street justice" or joining the lucrative narcotics trade by accepting bribes to release dealers or extorting money and drugs from dealers.

Sadly, the trend in society is to add to the already burdensome volume of regulatory laws without a corresponding increase in the resources to arrest, try and imprison offenders. Given the current state of the economy in America, it is more likely that the problem will be exacerbated by further reductions in criminal justice resources. The first principle would be appropriate at this point as well in the following chapter on corrections. That principle is: *The enactment of a law requires a commitment to provide the resources and the will to enforce that law.*

Discussion Questions

1. Discuss step-by-step the process that a defendant will go through from the time of arrest to the time of sentencing in the U.S. judicial system.

2. Compare and contrast the functions of a trial jury with the functions of the grand jury.

3. Briefly describe each step in trial process.

4. Discuss the role and function of the prosecutor during the judicial process.

5. Discuss the use of discretion by the defense attorney during the judicial process.

6. Discuss the role and function of the judge during a trial.

7. Discuss what plea bargains are and why they are used.

8. What are the advantages and disadvantages of using plea bargains?

9. Discuss the meaning of the phrase "revolving door of justice."

10. Discuss the process by which jury members are selected.

Notes

1. (2011). Plea bargaining: Areas of negotiation. Retrieved from http://criminal.findlaw.com/crimes/criminal_stages/stages-plea-bargains/plea-bargain-areas-of-negotiation.html.

2. O'Keefe, K. (2010). Two wrongs make a wrong: A challenge to plea bargaining and collateral consequences statutes through their integration. *The Journal of Criminal Law & Criminology*, 100 (1), 247-76.

3. O'Hear, M. (2008). *Plea bargain and procedural justice.* Pearson Press.

4. (2011). Plea bargains. Retrieved from http://criminal.findlaw.com/crimes/criminal_stages/stages-plea-bargains/criminal_plea_bargain.html.

5. Sandefur, T. (2003). *In defense of plea bargaining.* Pacific Legal Foundation.

6. Gaines L. G., & Miller R. L. (2009). *Criminal justice in action* (5th Edition). Belmont, California: Thomson Learning Inc.

Bibliography

Gaines L. G., & Miller R. L. (2009). *Criminal justice in action* (5th Edition). Belmont, California: Thomson Learning Inc.

O'Hear, M. (2008). *Plea bargain and procedural justice.* Pearson Press.

O'Keefe, K. (2010). Two wrongs make a wrong: A challenge to plea bargaining and collateral consequences statutes through their integration. *The Journal of Criminal Law & Criminology*, 100 (1), 247-76.

(2011). Plea bargaining: Areas of negotiation. Retrieved from http://criminal.find law.com/crimes/criminal_stages/stages-plea-bargains/plea-bargain-areas-of-negotiation.html.

(2011). Plea bargains. Retrieved from http://criminal.findlaw.com/crimes/criminal_stages/stages-plea-bargains/criminal_plea_bargain.html.

Sandefur, T. (2003). *In defense of plea bargaining.* Pacific Legal Foundation.

CHAPTER EIGHT

Corrections

Introduction

Corrections, the third stage in the criminal justice process, includes prisons, jails, probation, parole and community-based rehabilitation. The major function of corrections is to ensure the proper supervision of detained persons awaiting trial and to carry out sentences imposed by the courts. After being found guilty, a person may be sentenced to a period of time under the supervision of corrections personnel. They are responsible for that person for the duration of the sentence either in a detention facility, or under the supervision of a probation or parole officer or some combination of those operations. There are four major goals of punishment in the American criminal justice system: retribution, deterrence, incapacitation and rehabilitation, see *United States v. LaBonte*, 117 S.Ct. 1673, 1687(1997).[1] Nowhere in the criminal justice process do scarce resources impact the efficacy of the system more than with corrections. This chapter will review the correctional process and the effect of its limited resources.

History

As with much of criminal justice, our corrections roots can be found in Europe. Early punishments for crime were centered on the idea of revenge. It was not until the Middle Ages and the influence of the Roman Catholic Church that the theory of deterrence and reformation received social acceptance.[2] Nevertheless, harsh and cruel punishment of the offender was still relied upon to deter criminals from future deviant behavior. Corrections in America progressed through several periods of development: Colonial, Penitentiary, Reformatory, Progressive, Medical, Community and Crime Control.

Colonial Period (1600s to 1790s)

During the 1600s, in the early colonies, the workhouse gained popularity as a means of dealing with debtors, beggars and persons awaiting trial. After conviction, punishment took the form of whipping, periods of time in the stocks or hanging. In 1682, the Quakers introduced a criminal code, The Great Law, emphasizing punishment of hard labor for serious crimes. Death penalties were only imposed for premeditated murder.[3] The development of a penal system did not actually begin until after independence from England.

Penitentiary Period (1790s to 1860s)

The first prison in America is considered to be the cellblock in the Walnut Street Jail in Philadelphia, built in the late 1700s. However, the two most influential penitentiary systems were developed in Pennsylvania and New York. The Pennsylvania System, which was established in 1790, stressed solitary confinement rather than hard labor. Inmates were confined to their cells for their entire sentence. Their only contact was a prison guard who they were able to see only once a day. Although they were occasionally allowed to read, most of their time they were encouraged to reflect on their crimes. The Quakers did not consider solitary confinement a punishment but rather an opportunity for reflection and remorse and its use was based on four principles:

1. Penance & labor—Prisoners should not be treated vengefully but rather be convinced that through hard work and selective forms of punishment they could change their lives.

2. Isolation & silence—Solitary confinement would prevent further corruption inside prison.
3. Contemplation—In isolation, offenders would reflect on their transgressions and repent.
4. Solitary confinement would be economical because prisoners would not need long periods of time to repent, and therefore fewer keepers would be needed and the costs of clothing would be lower.[4]

The New York (Auburn) System that was established in 1821 was based on the congregate system. Under this system, inmates worked in shops during the day and they were kept apart at nighttime. At Auburn, inmates were subjected to a reign of discipline that included floggings, the lockstep and wearing stripped uniforms.

Reformatory Period (1870s-1890s)

The Reformatory Movement emphasized indeterminate sentencing, parole, classification by degree of individual reform, rehabilitative programs and separate treatment for juveniles. The first young men's reformatory opened in Elmira, New York in 1876, followed by the creation of 20 other reformatories throughout the United States. The first reformatory for women opened in Indianapolis, Indiana and the first women's prison was established in Ossining, New York. The philosophy of this period was founded on the NPA's (National Prison Association, now known as the American Correctional Association) Declaration of Principles, the view that crime was a moral disease and the belief that criminals were "victims of social disorder."[5]

Progressive Period (1890s-1930s)

The Progressives, who were members of the positivist school, believed that the application of the scientific method would yield the causes of individual behavior. This movement featured an individual case approach, broader probation and parole, administrative discretion and the juvenile courts. Their philosophy was based on three assumptions: criminal behavior is not the result of free will but stems from factors over which the individual has no control (biological, psychological and sociological conditions); criminals can be successfully treated so that they can lead crime-free lives; and treatment must be focused on the individual and the individual's problem(s). In 1841, John Augustus, who is considered the "father of probation," acted as the nation's first probation officer, providing bail for the accused under the Boston Police Court's authority. Massachusetts passed a probation law in 1878. By 1930, thirty-six states and the federal government incorporated probation into their law books.

Medical Period (1930s — 1960s)

The medical model of corrections was based on the belief that criminal behavior is caused by social, psychological or biological deficiencies that require treatment.[6] The medical model, which was also based on progressive movement ideology, was implemented in the 1930s. Prisons were staffed with educators, psychologists and social workers whose function was to provide individualized treatment to inmates. In 1929, Congress authorized the new Federal Bureau of Prisons to develop institutions with treatment as the main goal. Punishment was no longer considered an effective means to deal with offenders and treatment took a central role in penology. In the late 1940s and early 1950s, psychiatry was used as a tool to rehabilitate offenders, utilizing group counseling, behavior modification techniques, psychotherapy and individual counseling to treat inmates. Maryland's Patuxent Institution was one of the best examples of a prison built according to the principles of the medical model.

Community Period (1960s-1970s)

During this period, the goal of the criminal justice system was redefined to be one of reintegration of the offender into the community. Prisons were to be avoided because they represented an artificial environment, thereby frustrating a crime-free lifestyle. The major objective of corrections was to focus not merely on psychological treatment but on the offender's readjustment into society. This philosophy relied heavily on probation, intermediate sanctions, parole and other alternatives to incarceration. Those alternatives included community service work, restitution, fine options, electronic monitoring and community-based centers.

Crime Control Period (1970s to Present)

The Crime Control model is essentially a rejection of the medical model as being unrealistic and overly ambitious in its approach. Concerns over rising crime in the 1960s and disillusionment with the promise of rehabilitation through treatment resulted in calls for longer sentences and distrust of the broad discretion given to correctional and parole authorities. This period relied on incapacitation rather than rehabilitation and determinate sentences as well as restrictions on the discretion of parole boards.[7]

Contemporary Corrections

The four major areas of correctional supervision are prisons, jails, probation and parole. The number of people under correctional supervision has risen continuously over the past three decades. Most notably, the number of persons incarcerated has soared to levels unknown in American history, as illustrated by the table on the following page.

Table 8-1
Number of Persons Under Correctional Supervision

Year	Probation	Jail	Prison	Parole	Total
1980	1,118,097	182,288	319,598	220,438	1,840,400
1985	1,968,712	254,986	487,593	300,203	3,011,500
1990	2,670,234	403,019	743,382	531,407	4,348,000
1995	3,077,861	499,300	1,078,542	679,421	5,335,100
2000	3,826,209	613,534	1,316,333	723,898	6,437,400
2005	4,166,757	740,770	1,448,344	780,616	7,045,100
2009	4,203,967	760,400	1,524,513	819,308	7,225,800

Bureau of Justice Statistics—Retrieved from:
http://bjs.ojp.usdoj.gov/content/glance/tables/corr2tab.cfm

Prisons and Jails

The terms "prison" and "jail" are sometimes improperly used interchangeably, however,they are actually incarceration facilities used for different purposes. Those who are convicted of felonies (crimes that carry a penalty of incarceration for one year or more) are housed in prisons. Jails are used for defendants while awaiting trial and those convicted of misdemeanors (a crime punishable by less than one year of incarceration).

Although the incidents of reported crime have steadily decreased since the early 1990s, the incarceration rate has steadily increased. The incarceration rate in 1980 was 138 per 100,000, a figure that represented a historic high.[8] With 715 per 100,000 people in prison, as of 2010, the United States ranks highest of all other countries. Russia is in second place with 584 per 100,000.[9] These figures do not include those on probation, parole, in jail or under other correctional supervision. According to the Bureau of Justice Statistics (BJS), the number of inmates held in custody in state and federal correctional facilities increased 10% from 1,316,333 in 2000 to 1,448,344 in 2005. During the same period, the number of correctional employees rose only 3%, resulting in a higher inmate-to-staff ratio in 2005.[10] However, during 2005, there were approximately 14 million arrests affected across the country.[11] With less than 5%

of the world's population, the United States has almost a quarter of the world's inmates.[12] Even considering that the United States incarcerates more people than any other country, those numbers are not nearly as high as they could be because they are limited by the capacity of prisons.

In New York State, for example, there were over 584,000 total arrests effected during 2010, 160,000 of which were felony arrests, slightly less than previous years. According to the New York State Department of Corrections, the capacity of New York State prisons is slightly less than 60,000.[13] Applying a conservative estimate of 90% plea bargains leaves approximately 144,000 convictions. Even if there were wholesale release of every prisoner in New York, including murderers, rapists and robbers, there would still be room for less than half of those convicted. Further, in New York City alone, there were about 50,000 arrests for marijuana in 2010.[14] The capacity of New York City jails (used for misdemeanors arrests) is slightly over 24,000. Again, applying 90% plea bargain rate leaves 45,000 convictions, over twice the capacity that the City's correctional system could hold. These figures do not include all the other misdemeanor arrests for that year.

Similar situations exist in other states. For example, according to a 2011 ruling by the U.S. Supreme Court, California must reduce its state prison population by over 30,000 inmates (from 143,435 to 109,805) by 2013.[15] Notwithstanding the reduction mandate, according to the California Department of Justice (DOJ), felony arrest rates are nearly four times the revised capacity of the state prisons. In 2009, there were a total of 407,000 felony arrests. While there was slightly over 1,600 for murder and 1,800 for rape, over 120,000, (25%+) were for felony sex and drug charges.[16] Prison overcrowding has reached a level that can only be alleviated by early release of inmates. Early release programs traditionally involve non-violent criminals, however, that non-violent status is based on the crime for which the person was convicted; which, because of plea bargaining is not necessarily the crime for which the person was arrested. It is likely, therefore that even persons who were initially arrested for violent crimes could be released with those who were truly non-violent.

Prison Gangs

During the 1920s and 1930s prisons were known for being breeding grounds for gangs. Today gangs flourish and grow stronger both inside and outside of prison.[17] Over 33,000 violent street gangs, motorcycle gangs and prison gangs with about 1.4 million members are criminally active in the U.S.[18] Considering the violent nature of crimes committed by members of those gangs it is not surprising that gang violence takes place in prisons as well. According to the Bureau of Justice Statistics (BJS) for example, there were an estimated 7,374 allegations of sexual victimization involving incarcerated men and women in 2007 and 7,444 in 2008.[19] People who are sentenced to prison are faced with the dilemma of either choosing to join a gang or to remain unaffiliated. Membership in prison gangs serves two purposes. First, inmates are afforded a certain level of protection from violence perpetrated by other inmates, and second, members can dominate other inmates, forcing them to submit to extortion, sexual acts or other favors by intimidation, the threat or actual use of force, offers of protection or other forms of pressure. Many predatory offenders have been sentenced to long prison terms and have little to lose. They typically target vulnerable inmates who are young and scared or mentally or physically weak.

Further, gang culture transcends prison boundaries, facilitated by the premature return of inmates to society together with high rates of recidivism. Gang members who are released from prison typically return to gang activities, eventually get arrested again and simply to return to prison gang activities: a cycle of violence that continues virtually uninterrupted by the criminal justice process. While in prison, gangs routinely recruit other unaffiliated inmates who share the same identifying characteristics. According to a 2004 survey of prison wardens and staff members from each of the 50 states, 94.2 percent reported that inmates were routinely being recruited into a gang while incarcerated. They further reported that sending a gang leader to prison simply provides the leader with a new arena in which to conduct recruiting efforts.[20]

Gangs typically attract people with similar gender, racial, ethnic or national-origin characteristics. For example, the *Neta* gang is made up of males of Puerto Rican-American or Hispanic origin; the *Aryan Brotherhood* are white males; the *Black Guerrilla Family* consists of black males; and the *Mexican Mafia*, *La Nuestra Familia* and the *Texas Syndicate* each consists of Mexican-American or Hispanic males. Others include the Los Angeles-based gangs, the Crips, the Bloods and Mara Salvatrucha (MS-13). Each of these gangs has distinctive identifiers or symbols, colors and tattoos. There are various initiations including taking a "Blood-in, Blood-out" oath which includes life-long allegiance and making a "hit" or other significant act of violence. The required violence ensures that the potential member is not an undercover officer or an informant assigned to infiltrate the gang. Gangs form alliances or working relationships with certain other gangs as well as maintain deep hatred for rival gangs. In many prisons gangs run much of inmate life. They determine which inmates eat at particular times, where they sit in the dining hall, desirable or undesirable work assignments, and ultimately, who lives and who dies.[21]

Infectious Diseases

Prisons and jails are particularly suitable for the spread of many infectious diseases, including Tuberculosis (TB), viral hepatitis (A, B, C, and D) and sexually transmitted diseases (STDs) and HIV infections.[22] The spread of these diseases is facilitated by the close proximity of prisoners as well as intimate relations between inmates. TB is a bacterial infection that destroys patients' lung tissue, making them cough and sneeze, and spread germs through the air. The risk of TB is higher in the prisons than in the general population; however, the spread of TB within prisons can ultimately increase the incidence in the general population.[23]

Of particular concern is that the spread of TB among prisoners can substantially increase the risk of mutated strains to the public at large. These risks are facilitated by shortened incarceration sentences, particularly in jails. Normally, TB is curable with about six months of antibiotic drug treatment. If an infected person begins to receive the necessary drugs they must finish the treatment course or the bacteria may mutate into a strain that is resistant to that particular antibiotic drug. Therefore, if an inmate is released prior to completing the treatment and without continued treatment, the disease can become drug resistant. These drug-resistant strains of TB can spread to others and can eventually develop into multi-drug resistant TB (MDR-TB) that requires the patient to be isolated for months on a regimen of antibiotics to which the TB bacteria is not resistant. The more treatment courses patients are given and fail to complete, the stronger and more widespread the resistance becomes. The World Health Organization (WHO) is currently concerned with the emergence of a new, totally drug-resistant TB.[24]

Probation and Parole

Early release and alternatives to incarceration traditionally involve probation, parole, community-based programs or release with no supervision. Although the terms "parole" and "probation" are often used interchangeably, they are two very different concepts based in the same idea, a supervised alternative to incarceration. The differences lie in the circumstances under which the person reenters society.

Although probation varies according to jurisdiction, in general, probation either follows completion of a fixed prison sentence or a person may be sentenced to probation only. There are strict conditions that must be complied with by the offender during the period of probation. Probationers must report to their probation officer on a regularly scheduled basis, attend drug or alcohol rehabilitation where applicable, attend counseling or therapy sessions, and apply for employment or keep their current job. Violation of these conditions can result in sanctions, including incarceration. Many judges sentence offenders to community service while on probation. With community service, the offender must complete a certain number of hours to satisfy the sentence.

Parole is the conditional release from prison. With parole, the offender has already served some time in a correctional facility and depending on the conditions of their sentence, may request early release. Upon this request, inmates may appear before a parole board to plead their case and convince the board that they have complied with prison rules while incarcerated and that they are not a threat to society. Similar to probation, there are certain conditions attached to parole. They must meet with their parole officer, hold down a job, attend counseling or substance rehabilitation as needed and not associate with other convicted criminals.

Although the number of people in prison is staggering, it is substantially less than the number under probation or parole supervision. The number of probationers has risen dramatically from 1.1 million in 1980, to over 4 million in 2008.[25] While probationers have risen in number, probation spending has generally failed to keep up with rising probationer populations.[26] Individual probation officer caseloads vary according to jurisdiction and the degree of risk of the probationers. Those probationers who are considered high risk require intensive supervision and are normally included in smaller caseloads than other offenders. Nevertheless, increases in probationers without commensurate increases in resources would necessarily result in increases of probation officer (PO) caseloads.[27] Increased caseloads are of concern primarily because POs are likely to be less able to detect violations of probation and to intervene effectively with offenders, thereby compromising public safety.

The increase in the prison population has understandably led to substantial increases in the parole population, resulting in larger caseloads for parole officers. In the 1970s, the average parole officer supervised a caseload of 45 parolees.[28] By 1999, most parole officers had caseloads of about 70 parolees, nearly twice as high, and substantially higher than what would be considered ideal.[29] In 2009, the total number under parole supervision reached over 800,000.[30]

Recidivism

One test of the effectiveness of a correctional process is the rate of recidivism, or the re-arrest of former inmates after release. According to the latest Bureau of Justice Statistics (BJS) study of over 270,000 prisoners released in 1994, 67.5% were re-arrested for a new offense within a three-year period after release. Almost all were re-arrested for a felony or serious misdemeanor.[31]

Summary

Corrections is the third part of the criminal justice system. As with the judiciary and law enforcement, corrections in the United States has its roots in Europe, particularly England. With independence from England and the U.S. Constitution, our system of corrections evolved through several periods of reform and sophistication, adding provisions for juveniles, rehabilitation, psychological counseling, and reentry programs, including alternatives to incarceration.

Current challenges to the correctional process are linked to overall problems facing the entire criminal justice system, specifically, the lack of sufficient resources to meet ever increasing demands. Increases in arrests by law enforcement have resulted in a volume of convicted criminals that corrections are not equipped to adequately supervise. Because of strict limitations on the capacity of incarceration facilities, there is an ever-increasing reliance on supervision outside of jails and prisons, particularly probation.

Corrections officials must also deal with problems of prison (and jail) gangs that wield extraordinary control over other inmates, through sexual assaults, intimidation and extortion and also use those correctional facilities to recruit new members. Additional challenges include the transmission of a variety of serious and sometimes fatal diseases. Treatment of inmates with these conditions further adds to the drain on already limited correctional resources.

Even with the limited capacity of detention facilities, the United States imprisons a higher percentage of its population than any other country and with current trends of annual increases of arrests the pressure on corrections to expedite reentry into society is expected to increase proportionately. The ideal of orderly rehabilitation and assimilation into society is severely inhibited. The efforts of probation and parole officers, those entrusted with the responsibility of overseeing reentry, are also thwarted by overly burdensome caseloads. Although detention facilities are limited by housing capacity, there are virtually no limits on the caseloads of probation and parole officers.

Commentary

There is no question that the correctional resources in America are woefully inadequate considering the current number of arrests and convictions, numbers that by all indications will continue in an upward trend. Initially, it may be considered a problem of supply and demand. There is an insufficient supply of available space in correctional facilities to meet the arrest and conviction demands of the rest of the criminal justice system. Although logical at first blush, the problem is much more complex than the law of supply and demand might explain.

The question is, at what point do we realize that we have an ever-increasing level of criminality in our country? Even though reported crime may be decreasing or leveling off, we must remember that unlike *mala en se* violations such as murder, robbery and burglary, regulatory law violations are not typically reported. The only official indication that these laws are violated is the arrests that law enforcement effect for these crimes. Arrests for regulatory law violations, for the most part, are the result of agency policy. Crackdowns on such offenses as illegal drugs or prostitution are usually initiated at the direction of mayors or police administrators. During the 1980s, for example, at the mayor's direction the New York City police unleashed a TNT (Tactical Narcotic Team) program that resulted in so many drug-related arrests as to virtually cripple the justice system. Because of overcrowding in the courts, police typically waited days to arraign their prisoners and the City had to find alternative facilities to house the overflow from municipal jails.

Someone once commented that we won the war on crime; we arrested all the criminals. This statement only illustrates, albeit sarcastically, the frustration with a criminal justice system that prematurely releases criminals back into society only to continue their criminal activities. Most people arrested for crimes are quickly released back into society, either immediately or after only a relatively short period of incarceration. It's a process similar to the catch and release practiced by fishermen. Throw the small ones back until they grow large enough to keep. Judges, who often find themselves in the middle of a mounting volume of arrestees and precious few places to put them, must make similar decisions. Those with few arrests or no arrest record at all or who committed minor offenses are thrown back into society with the warning that another appearance before that judge will result in jail time (an empty warning that is often repeated to the same individual). The keepers are the criminals who committed particularly serious crimes or who have extensive records of convictions.

The true level of regulatory law violation can only be estimated but is nearly impossible to know. We must keep in mind that it is the law that defines crime and criminals. Enacting more laws will result in more criminals, a situation that ultimately leads to more arrests, thereby exerting greater demands on the criminal justice system, particularly corrections. These increased demands result in a rapid turnover of prisoners, unrealistically high probation and parole caseloads, and accelerated return to society. This situation renders the mission of corrections, namely, retribution, deterrence, incapacitation and rehabilitation, nearly impossible to attain at a level sufficient enough to reduce the rate of recidivism. The first and fourth principles seem appropriate to this situation. They are: 1. *The enactment of a law requires a commitment to provide the resources and the will to enforce that law, and 4. Part of the legislative process should include input from those criminal justice elements most affected by that legislation.*

The return of convicts to society without the likelihood of rehabilitation only destines them to a return to the behaviors that resulted in their arrests in the first place. This problem is only worsened by the activity of prison gangs and their recruitment practices in jails and prisons. Young, first-time inmates are particularly vulnerable and must often choose between being victimized and joining a gang for protection. Because of the lifelong commitment they must make in order to join, their gang involvement does not end with their release. The gang's criminal activity only increases the likelihood of recidivism and traps them in a criminal lifestyle. This topic, along with infectious diseases related to incarceration will be discussed in Chapter Eleven (Societal Consequences).

High rates of released prisoners re-arrested within a few years coupled with general increases in arrests can only result in a catastrophic impact on society. Greater numbers of Americans arrested, resulting in broken homes, reduced likelihood of career opportunities, and loss of hope, can only lead to social decay and a growing underclass in society, and a class of people who are lost, homeless and friendless, plagued with diseases, outcasts from their families who live day-to-day existences surviving in the only way they know, crime. The remaining chapters in Part Three will explore this dilemma in greater detail.

Discussion Questions

1. Explain the connection and interaction of gangs in prison with those in society.

2. Discuss the similarities and differences between prisons and jails.

3. How do prisons affect the spread and severity of infectious diseases such as tuberculosis?

4. Is the answer to the increase in crime to build more jails and prisons or is the answer to this problem to take some other form of action? Explain.

5. What measures could be taken to address the problem of prison overcrowding that would not put the public in danger?

6. Discuss some of the problems that prisoners face during the process of re-entry into society.

7. What can be done to address the problem of prison gangs?

8. Some people have said that only violent offenders should be incarcerated. Do you agree or disagree with this statement? Why?

9. Discuss the similarities and differences between probation and parole.

10. Discuss the impact of mandatory minimums on the problem of prison overcrowding.

Notes

1. *United States v. LaBonte*, 117 S.Ct. 1673, 1687 (1997).

2. Lewis, D. W. (1965). *From Newgate to Dannemora*: Ithaca: Cornell University Press.

3. Clear, T. R., Cole, G. F., & Reisig, M. D. (2006). *American corrections* (7th edition). Tampa, FL: Thomson Publishing Co.

4. Takagi, P. (n.d.), The Walnut Street Jail: A Penal Reform to Centralize The Powers of the State, Retrieved from: www.socialjusticejournal.org/pdf_free/ Takagi-Walnut_Street_Jail.pdf.

5. American Correctional Association. (2011). *Prison policy initiative.* Northhampton, MA. Retrieved from American Correctional Association Website: http://www.prisonpolicy.org/aca.html.

6. Lehman, P. E. (1972). The medical model of treatment: Historical development of an archaic standard. *Crime & Delinquency, 18* (2), 204-12.

7. Ortmeier, P.J. (2006). *Introduction to law enforcement and criminal justice* (2nd. Ed.). Upper Saddle River, N.J.: Pearson Prentice Hall.

8. Maguire, K., & Flanagan, T. J. (1991). *Criminal justice newsletter.* Washington, D.C: United States Department of Justice.

9. International Centre for Prison Studies. (n.d.). *World prison brief.* Retrieved from: http://www.nationmaster.com/graph/cri_pri_per_cap-crime-prisoners-per-capita.

10. Bureau of Justice Statistics. (2011). Retrieved from http://bjs.ojp.usdoj. gov/index.cfm?ty=pbdetail&iid=530.

11. Snyder, H. N. (2011). *Arrest in the United States, 1980-2009.* Washington, DC: Bureau of Justice Statistics.

12. Liptak, A. (2008, April 23). U.S. prison population dwarfs that of other nations. *New York Times.* Retrieved from http://www.nytimes.com /2008/04/23/ world/americas/23iht-23prison.12253738.html?pagewanted=all.

13. New York State Department of Corrections. (n.d.). Retrieved from http://www.docs.state.ny.us/.

14. Long, C., & Peltz, J. (2011, November 5). At 50,000 pot busts lead arrests in NYC. *New York Newsday.* Retrieved from http://www.newsday.com/long-island/crime/at-50-000-pot-busts-lead-arrests-in-nyc-1.3299297.

15. Biskupic, J. (2011, May 24). Supreme court stands firm on prison overcrowding. *USA Today.* Retrieved from http://www.usatoday.com/news/ washington/judicial/2011-05-24-Supreme-court-prisons_n.htm.

16. California Department of Justice. (n.d.). Retrieved from http://stats.doj. ca.gov/cjsc_stats/prof09/00/15.htm.

17. Compton, T., & Meacham, M. (2005). Prison gangs: descriptions and selected intervention. *Forensic Examiner.*

18. Knox, G. W. (2005). *The problem of gangs and security threat groups (STG's) in American prisons today.* National Gang Crime Research Center.

19. Guerino, P., & Beck, A. J. (2011). Sexual victimization reported by adult correctional authorities, 2007-2008 *(NCJ 231172)*. Retrieved from: http://bjs.ojp.usdoj.gov/content/pub/press/svraca0708pr.cfm.

20. Knox, G. W. (2005). *The problem of gangs and security threat groups (STG's) in American prisons today.* National Gang Crime Research Center.

21. Gaes, G. G., Wallace, S., Gilman, E., et al (2002). *The influence of prison gang affiliation on violence and other prison misconduct. Prison Journal, 82* (3), 359-85.

22. (2000). *Federal Bureau of Prisons report on infectious disease management.* Retrieved from www.bop.gov/news/PDFs/report.pdf.

23. (2010). *Infectious diseases in prisons: spread of tuberculosis in prisons increases the incidence of TB in the general population.Science Daily.* Retrieved from http://www.sciencedaily.com/releases/2010/12/1012211 72250.htm.

24. Kelland, K. (2012, March 20). Drug-resistant "white plague" lurks among rich and poor. *Reuters.* Retrieved from: http://news.yahoo.com/drug-resistant-white-plague-lurks-among-rich-poor-113851688.html.

25. Bonczar, T. P. & Glaze, L. E. (2009). *Probation and parole in the United States, statistical tables* No. NCJ 231674). Washington, DC: Bureau of Justice Statistics, Office of Justice Programs, U.S. Department of Justice.

26. Scott-Hayward, C. (2009). *The fiscal crisis in corrections: Rethinking policies and practices.* New York, NY: Vera Institute of Justice, Center of Sentencing and Corrections.

27. Bonczar, T. P. & Glaze, L. E. (2009). *Probation and parole in the United States, statistical tables* No. NCJ 231674). Washington, DC: Bureau of Justice Statistics, Office of Justice Programs, U.S. Department of Justice.

28. Petersilia, J. (2000). *When prisoners return to the community: Political, economic, and social consequences.* Washington, DC: US Department of Justice, National Institute of Justice, Sentencing & Corrections.

29. Travis, J., Solomon, A. L., & Waul, M. (2001). *From prison to home: The dimensions and consequences of prisoner reentry.* Washington, DC: Urban Institute.

30. Bureau of Justice Statistics. (2011). Retrieved from http://bjs.ojp.usdoj.gov/index.cfm?ty=pbdetail&iid=530.

31. Langan, P. A., & Levin, D. J. (2002). *Bureau of Justice Statistics special report: recidivism of prisoners.*

Bibliography

American Correctional Association. (2011). *Prison policy initiative.* Northhampton, MA. Retrieved from American Correctional Association Website: http://www.prisonpolicy.org/aca.html.

Biskupic, J. (2011, May 24). Supreme court stands firm on prison overcrowding. *USA Today.* Retrieved form http://www.usatoday.com/news/washington/judicial/2011-05-24-Supreme-court-prisons_n.htm.

Bonczar, T. P. & Glaze, L. E. (2009). *Probation and parole in the United States, statistical tables* No. NCJ 231674). Washington, DC: Bureau of Justice Statistics, Office of Justice Programs, U.S. Department of Justice.

Bureau of Justice Statistics. (2011). Retrieved from http://bjs.ojp. usdoj.gov/index.cfm?ty=pbdetail&iid=530.

California Department of Justice. (n.d.). Retrieved from http://stats.doj.ca.gov/cjsc_stats/prof09/00/15.htm.

Clear, T. R., Cole, G. F., & Reisig, M. D. (2006). *American corrections* (7th edition). Tampa, FL: Thomson Publishing Co.

Compton, T., & Meacham, M. (2005). Prison gangs: descriptions and selected intervention. *Forensic Examiner.*

(2000). *Federal Bureau of Prisons report on infectious disease management.* Retrieved from www.bop.gov/news/PDFs/report.pdf.

Florida Department of Corrections. (n.d.). *Gang and security threat group awareness.* Retrieved from: http://www.dc.state.fl.us/pub/gangs/index.html.

Gaes, G. G., Wallace, S., Gilman, E., et al (2002). *The influence of prison gang affiliation on violence and other prison misconduct. Prison Journal, 82* (3), 359-85.

Guerino, P., & Beck, A. J. (2011). Sexual victimization reported by adult correctional authorities, 2007-2008 *(NCJ 231172).* Retrieved from: http://bjs.ojp.usdoj.gov/content/pub/press/svraca0708pr.cfm.

(2010). *Infectious diseases in prisons: spread of tuberculosis in prisons increases the incidence of TB in the general population.Science Daily.* Retrieved from http://www.sciencedaily.com/releases/2010/12/1012211 72250.htm.

International Centre for Prison Studies. (n.d.). *World prison brief.* Retrieved from http://www.nationmaster.com/graph/cri_pri_per_cap-crime-prisoners-per-capita.

Kelland, K. (2012, March 20). Drug-resistant "white plague" lurks among rich and poor. *Reuters.* Retrieved from: http://news.yahoo.com/drug-resistant-white-plague-lurks-among-rich-poor-113851688.html.

Knox, G. W., (n.d.) "A national assessment of gangs and security threat groups (STGs)" in Adult Correctional Institutions: Results of the 1999 Adult Corrections Survey. *Journal of Gang Re-*

search, 7, (3), 1-45, 2000, as reviewed in *Criminal Justice Abstracts*, Abstract Number 0715-32, June, 2000, p. 330.

Knox, G. W. (2005). *The problem of gangs and security threat groups (STG's) in American prisons today.* National Gang Crime Research Center.

Langan, P. A., & Levin, D. J. (2002). *Bureau of Justice Statistics special report: recidivism of prisoners.*

Lehman, P. E. (1972). The medical model of treatment: Historical development of an archaic standard. *Crime & Delinquency, 18* (2), 204-12.

Lewis, D. W. (1965). *From Newgate to Dannemora*: Ithaca: Cornell University Press.

Liptak, A. (2008, April 23). U.S. prison population dwarfs that of other nations. *New York Times.* Retrieved from http://www.nytimes.com/2008/04/23/world/americas/23iht-23prison.12253738.html?pagewanted=all.

Long, C., & Peltz, J. (2011, November 5). At 50,000 pot busts lead arrests in NYC. *New York Newsday.* Retrieved from http://www.newsday.com/long-island/crime/at-50-000-pot-busts-lead-arrests-in-nyc-1.3299297.

Maguire, K., & Flanagan, T. J. (1991). *Criminal justice newsletter.* Washington, D.C: United States Department of Justice.

National Gang Intelligence Center. (2009). *The national gang threat assessment 2009.*Retrieved from: http://www.fbi.gov/stats-services/publications/national-gang-threat-assessment-2009-pdf.

New York State Department of Corrections. (n.d.). Retrieved from http://www.docs.state.ny.us/.

Ortmeier, P.J. (2006). *Introduction to law enforcement and criminal justice* (2nd. Ed.). Upper Saddle River, N.J.: Pearson Prentice Hall.

Petersilia, J. (2000). *When prisoners return to the community: Political, economic, and social consequences.* Washington, DC: US Department of Justice, National Institute of Justice, Sentencing & Corrections.

Scott-Hayward, C. (2009). *The fiscal crisis in corrections: Rethinking policies and practices.* New York, NY: Vera Institute of Justice, Center of Sentencing and Corrections.

Snyder, H. N. (2011). *Arrest in the United States, 1980-2009*. Washington, DC: Bureau of Justice Statistics.

Takagi, P. (n.d.), The Walnut Street Jail: A Penal Reform to Centralize The Powers of the State, Retrieved from: www.socialjusticejournal.org/pdf_free/Takagi-Walnut_Street_Jail.pdf.

Travis, J., Solomon, A. L., & Waul, M. (2001). *From prison to home: The dimensions and consequences of prisoner reentry*. Washington, DC: Urban Institute.

U.S. Department of Justice. (1990). *Sourcebook of criminal justice statistics*.

United States v. LaBonte, 117 S.Ct. 1673, 1687 (1997).

PART THREE

Consequences for Society

American society relies on the government to provide a variety of services, including public protection from crime and disorder. The government seeks to fulfill this mandate primarily through law enforcement and also by relying on the public's cooperation and compliance with the law. When governmental efforts fall short of achieving the desired level of protection, society suffers the consequences. Those consequences take the form of lawlessness as well as a lack of respect for and confidence in the system of justice designed to accomplish those goals.

The reasons for government's failure to provide adequate protection to the public are many and varied and have been reviewed in the two previous parts of this book. Most notable is the inadequate resources of the criminal justice system to apprehend, process and incarcerate all those who violate the law. This problem of scarce resources has resulted in a need to prioritize.

Government's failure to properly safeguard the public is most notable in its premature release of dangerous criminals into society. The following three chapters will examine the societal effects of the criminal justice system's inadequacies. Chapter Nine will examine the role of government and its citizens in complying with the social contract as well as the government's responsibilities in applying the rule of law. In Chapter Ten, the issues of race and ethnicity will be examined from the perspective of law enforcement and the criminal justice system. Chapter Eleven will explore the effects of regulatory law on families, public health and the economy. Finally, Chapter 12 will summarize the book and provide concluding remarks.

CHAPTER NINE

The Social Contract and the Rule of Law

Introduction

American society relies on the support and cooperation of its citizens in accomplishing the Constitutional goals of domestic tranquility and the establishment of justice through the concepts of a social contract and the rule of law. The mechanism for achieving this purpose is the criminal justice system. Its primary function is to provide safety and security to the public through the prevention of crime and the apprehension, prosecution, and in particular, the incarceration of criminals for durations commensurate with their offense.

This chapter will demonstrate how the government has failed to uphold the rule of law and the social contract with its citizens by maintaining a criminal justice system that allows dangerous felons to avoid the incarceration they lawfully deserve. Also explored will be the growing lack of respect and compliance with the law by both the government and a large proportion of otherwise law-abiding people and the resulting loss of confidence in the criminal justice system. Various theories of criminality will also be reviewed in order to better understand those factors that underlie criminal behavior. Labeling theory in particular will demonstrate the ways in which the proliferation of laws actually contributes to criminality.

The Social Contract

Why do we have a government? Why do we have laws? These are questions that are seldom asked. We simply accept that there has always been a government and laws and we must obey those laws or suffer the consequences. Implicit in this arrangement of people, their government and laws is an unspoken agreement. An agreement, or contract, that is not signed or even formally acknowledged, but an agreement that, nonetheless, has consequences if violated.

This social contract is a concept in which people have a pact with each other and with their government, whereby the government and the people have distinct roles and responsibilities. This concept is based on the idea that people give up their free and ungoverned condition in favor of a society that provides them with order, structure and protection. Although not a physical, signed contract, it is still an implicit agreement that we enter into when we willingly involve ourselves in society and enjoy its benefits. The social contract in America is consistent with the Declaration of Independence, which states, "Governments are instituted among Men, deriving their just powers from the consent of the governed ..."

Accordingly, each person agrees to follow the laws of the government on the condition that everyone else does the same. That way, we are all relatively safe from each other and we all share in the social benefit that will result. We can reasonably be expected to follow the laws because, on the whole, they are to our own advantage. Breaking the laws tends to undermine them and thereby endangers our own wellbeing.

The concept of a social contract is not new. Plato provided its underlying philosophy in Book II of *Republic* in which Plato's elder brother, Glaucon, puts forth the following rationale:

> They say that to do injustice is naturally good and to suffer injustice bad, but that the badness of suffering it so far exceeds the goodness of doing it that those who have done and suffered injustice and tasted both, but who lack the power to do it and avoid suffering it, decide that it is profitable to come to an agreement with each other neither to do injustice nor to suffer it. As a result, they begin to make laws and covenants, and what the law commands they call lawful and just. This, they say, is the origin and

essence of justice. It is intermediate between the best and the worst. The best is to do injustice without paying the penalty; the worst is to suffer it without being able to take revenge. Justice is a mean between these two extremes. People value it not because it is a good but because they are too weak to do injustice with impunity.[1]

In other words, laws protect us from harming each other and provide a lawful environment in which our individual right to a peaceful existence is respected. Implementation of a social contract relies on laws to protect life and property and generally to prevent the strong from harming the weak.

What is law? According to Bastiat, law "is the collective organization of the individual right to lawful defense."[2] He further explains:

Each of us has a natural right—from God—to defend his person, his liberty, and his property. These are the three basic requirements of life, and the preservation of any one of them is completely dependent upon the preservation of the other two ... If every person has the right to defend even by force—his person, his liberty, and his property, then it follows that a group of men have the right to organize and support a common force to protect these rights constantly. Thus the principle of collective right ... The law is the organization of the natural right of lawful defense.[3]

Causes of Criminal Behavior

According to the social contract the government's primary responsibility is to enact the criminal laws necessary for the protection of life, liberty, property and social order and to enforce those laws by holding people accountable for their behavior. In order for the contract to best achieve its aims, it is important that everyone, or nearly everyone, be party to the contract. Even under the best of circumstances, it is expected that a small minority of people will choose to violate criminal laws. There are a number of criminological theories as to why people commit crime. These theories can be divided into two groups: Classical and Deterministic.

Classical Theory

The oldest of these criminological theories is the Classical Theory of Criminality, commonly known as Choice Theory, developed by Cesare Beccaria in the late 1700s. This theory posits that people choose to commit crime through a rational decision making process.[4] According to the theory, people weigh the possible gain and consequences of the act and choose to either commit the crime or not based on the possible outcomes.[5] It is important to note that the possible advantages and disadvantages of a criminal act are highly subjective and are determined primarily by individual circumstances rather than by the act itself. For example, a person who has never been arrested would consider being arrested a far more serious consequence than someone with an extensive criminal record. Similarly, the gain of stealing a few dollars would be more tempting to an impoverished person than to a wealthy person. Also, the consequences need not be limited to the arrest itself, but can include other things such as violation of sel-imposed standards of morality, religious consequences, damage/loss of reputation in the community, family reaction, and so on.

Deterministic Theories

In addition to Classical Theory, a number of deterministic theories have emerged. These theories can be grouped into three broad categories: biological, psychological and sociological. Each of these theories examines the underlying factors that predispose a person to criminal behavior. Biological theories of criminality generally focus on physiological characteristics such as hereditary, genetic predisposition to violence, diet and in rare cases, brain tumors.[6] Psychological theories are based primarily on the work of Sigmund Freud and focus on the critical first six years of life when such traits as ego, personality, conscience and values are imprinted. Accordingly, criminal behavior may be the result of damaged egos that lead to feelings of worthlessness and alienation, lowering a person's ability to control their urges.[7]

For a time, during the mid-1900s hereditary-based theories lost popular appeal in favor of psychological theories that argued that people are born with a clean slate and personality results from nurture rather than nature. Studies of identical twins separated at birth, who developed many similar traits in choices of occupations, spouses, habits, dress, and other life preferences, revealed the role that genetics plays in personality development, thereby resulting in greater acceptance of heredity as a significant determinant.

Sociological theories argue that such forces, as affiliations, peer pressure, neighborhood and life style are major determinants of criminality. Perhaps the best known is Edwin Sutherland's differential association theory. Sutherland posits that behaviors and attitudes that underlie criminal activity are learned from close relationships with significant others.[8] Perhaps the best example of this process is the influence that gangs have on their members. Youths in particular are attracted to gangs to fulfill a need for acceptance. That need together with their desire to learn is a strong motivator for the youth to do whatever is required to fit in with the other gang members. If the gang is involved in criminal activity then the new member will likely commit crimes in order to maintain affiliation with the gang.

Labeling Theory

Labeling theorists note that most people commit crimes at some time during their lives, particularly during their adolescent years; however, not everyone becomes defined as deviant or criminal. Youths who commit undetected crimes tend to mature without their early criminal behavior having any significant impact on the lifestyle. The President's Commission on Law Enforcement and Administration of Justice's report of 1967 contained the results of a self-report survey of 1,020 males and 670 females.[9] The study found that about 91% of the respondents admitted to having committed one or more crimes for which they could have been arrested.[10] Of those, approximately half were not apprehended and most did not continue committing offenses.[11]

Labeling theory proponents argue that being caught in a criminal act stigmatizes a person, particularly an adolescent with the label of deviant, troublemaker or criminal. Their peers' parents may not permit them to associate with the labeled youth, leaving only other similarly labeled youngsters as potential companions. Further, a record of criminal behavior can have an adverse affect on a person's educational and career opportunities. The ability to work in certain governmental positions, positions of trust and even being bonded may be denied to people with a criminal background. With the barring of opportunities for a normal lifestyle, the person is at a higher risk of falling into a life of crime.

Becker (1963) says that deviance is a normal part of adolescent life.[12] When such behavior is labeled deviant the adolescent sees himself as a "deviant," which encourages him to continue his deviant behavior into adulthood.[13] The primary deviant behavior might involve some minor theft, but this experience, through labeling, turns into more serious crime.[14] Secondary deviance is when the adolescent accepts the label and follows the deviant lifestyle.[15]

More recent labeling theorists came to recognize that societies "create" crime by passing laws. An unanticipated consequence of the proliferation of laws is an increase in the likelihood of new criminal behavior.[16] More laws mean more opportunities for youths and others to engage in criminal behavior that heretofore was not prohibited. This behavior leads to an increase in first-time offenders, a portion of whom, if caught, will likely continue a life of crime.

There are also numerous explanations based on combinations of the theories just mentioned. None actually predict criminality; however, they identify underlying risk factors that may predispose persons to engage in criminal behavior. In the final analysis, regardless of a person's predisposition to commit a crime, the ultimate decision is still a matter of choice. Albeit, the choice may be more difficult for some due to a variety of childhood and adolescent developmental circumstances previously discussed, as well as diminished capacity.

Criminal Justice and the Social Contract

Does the government, through the existing criminal justice system, uphold its responsibilities with regard to the social contract? A review of the previous chapters will help address this question, beginning with various alternatives to a trial because of a heavily ladened court system.

Prosecutors have the option of declining to prosecute a case even if the arrest is legitimate and there is ample evidence for a finding of guilt. The prosecutor's discretion in these matters is absolute, even over the objections of the arresting officer or the victim of the crime. Defendants may also be diverted to a community agency such as detoxification centers, psychiatric facilities or other suitable alternative facilities. There are other legitimate reasons for alternatives to trial. Some persons without a history of criminal behavior act while under the influence of drugs or alcohol and who are not likely to repeat their crimes, for example. Likewise, there are first-time offenders who commit a minor offense under extenuating circumstances and also are not expected to commit any future crimes. However, the vast majority of trial alternatives are engaged in for the sole purpose of reducing an excessive caseload.

Plea bargaining is perhaps the most frequently used alternatives to a trial, accounting for over 90% of cases. In order to encourage defendants to plead guilty and avoid a trial, the prosecutor will offer a variety of incentives. If a number of charges have been filed, the defendant can plead guilty to just one and the other charges will be dismissed. If there was only one charge the prosecutor could reduce it to a lesser offense. For example, a charge of robbery might be reduced to a larceny that carries a lower penalty. If the crime carries a mandatory sentence the prosecutor could change the charge to one that provides a lower period of incarceration, or none at all.

The social contract is compromised when criminals routinely receive lesser sentences than their crimes should warrant. Recall that there are four major goals of punishment in the American criminal justice system: retribution, deterrence, incapacitation and rehabilitation (*United States v. LaBonte*, 117 S.Ct. 1673, 1687 (1997).[17] Because those goals are not fully met when pleabargaining is employed, the public is placed at greater risk of victimization. If sentences are reduced there is less opportunity for treatment of the offender and adequate preparation for orderly reentry into society. The punishment and deterrence value of the sentence is also diminished. Most important, however, are the prevention of future crimes and the protection of the public through the control and detention of dangerous persons. Whether rehabilitation is successful or not, the longer a criminal is incarcerated the less opportunity that person has to victimize the public.

Conversely, the less time a criminal is behind bars, the more opportunity that criminal has to commit additional crimes against the public. As indicated in the previous chapter, the rate of recidivism is over 65% within three years release from prison.[18] Even sentences to periods of probation in lieu of incarceration because of prison overcrowding exposes the public to unnecessary risk of victimization from violent criminals. A recent study found that about one-quarter of offenders were re-arrested for a serious offense within three years of beginning their probationary term.[19]

The Rule of Law

The rule of law is also a concept that is subject to a variety of interpretations. Although there is no universally agreed upon definition, there are basic principles underlying this concept. The United Nations Secretary General's Report on rule of law formulates the rule of law in terms of end goals:

> A principle of governance in which all persons, institutions and entities, public and private, including the State itself, are accountable to laws that are publicly promulgated, equally enforced and independently adjudicated, and which are consistent with international human rights norms and standards. It requires, as well, measures to ensure adherence to the principles of supremacy of law,

equality before the law, accountability to the law, fairness in the application of the law, separation of powers, participation in decision-making, legal certainty, avoidance of arbitrariness, and procedural and legal transparency.[20]

Belton also identifies end goals for which the rule of law should strive:

> ... a government bound by and ruled by law;
> equality before the law;
> the establishment of law and order;
> the efficient and predictable application of justice; and
> the protection of human rights.[21]
> One might add that the Western concept of the rule of law should also include the separation of religion and state as a basic constitutional principle, since the influence of both state and religious institutions in the application of the law could lead to arbitrary interpretations. Even in Western countries with a strong religious presence, the policies of organized religion are separate from those of the government.[22]

In order to achieve these ends, Belton identifies three essential instruments:

> ... the existence of comprehensive laws or a constitution based on popular consent; a functioning judicial system; and established law enforcement agencies with well-trained officers.
> Absent any of these features, the rule of law may arguably break down. A constitution without legitimacy will not be respected by the people, and thus its principles cannot be upheld. If there is no constitutional check on the misuse of power, a corrupt judiciary or police force can manipulate the laws to their advantage, incompetent lawyers cannot adequately represent their clients, and so on.[23]

Binding the government to the law is something absolutely essential to the rule of law. It is important to make the distinction between the rule *of* law and rule *by* law. Rule by law implies a government that focuses on published and enforceable law but the government is not subject to the law. Therefore, a dictatorship or monarchy would qualify as ruling by law if some form of policing agency enforces the law and a judiciary rules on those who violate the law.

The government's role in upholding the rule of law is first and foremost to subordinate itself to the law in order to prevent arbitrariness. The government's responsibility also includes the defense of people from evil, to prevent people from acting on their natural desire to take revenge for actual or perceived wrongs that they have suffered at other people's hands and generally to resolve disputes (McBride, 2012).[24] Another factor is necessary to achieve the rule of law, namely the will of society to enforce basic principles of equality, fairness and justice.

An earlier expectation for the law was to encourage people to do the right thing, that is, to behave morally. In order to achieve this purpose, laws were enacted that made it illegal for people to engage in immoral behavior that would harm themselves or offend others. It was argued that law should enforce morality so as to preserve the cohesiveness of society. This effort gave way to the concept that laws should not sanction people for acting immorally unless their conduct involves harm to others. Consequently, many *moral laws,* particularly those involving consensual sexual relations, were eventually repealed and some others were found to be unconstitutional by the U.S. Supreme Court.

It is important to emphasize the importance of Belton's three instruments to achieve rule of law end results: laws based on popular consent, a functional judicial system and professional law enforcement.

Laws Based on Popular Consent

As indicated previously, it is expected that a small percentage of people will violate laws and that the police can adequately manage those violators. However, as the percentage of offenders increases, the ability of the police to enforce laws isdiminished, leading to chaos and ultimately, anarchy. The current state of traffic law enforcement exemplifies the problem of increased disobedience. It is apparently beyond the ability of police in most jurisdictions to fully enforce existing traffic laws, particularly in maintaining legal highway and parkway speeds. As cited in Chapter Five (traffic), over half of the teenage drivers reported using cell phones while driving, almost half text and about 40% report exceeding speed limits by 10 miles per hour (mph) or more.[25] Another survey of drivers found that nearly half of the drivers reported exceeding highway speed limits by 15mph and over 65% reported talking on cell phones while driving.[26] The rule of law works when most people agree on the importance of observing the law, even if police are not present. This is best achieved when the laws reflect the standards of the community affected by those laws. An essential component of the social contract is the public's agreement to maintain social order by obeying the law.

A Functional Judicial System

Previous chapters have also demonstrated the inadequacies of the judicial systems across the country. The courts find themselves in the middle of an impractical situation. Police, on the one hand, effect many more arrests than the courts have the capacity to properly adjudicate and correctional facilities cannot accommodate the numbers of guilty offenders. The judicial system must, of necessity, find alternatives. Those alternatives take two major forms: alternatives to trials and alternatives to incarceration. The primary alternative to trial is the plea bargaining process, a practice that has been amply covered in Chapter Seven (courts) and results in defendants being charged with lesser offenses and given lesser penalties than their original crimes would deserve. Probation is the primary alternative to incarceration, but other alternatives include suspended sentences, community service and adjournments pending dismissal of charges. Considering that the courts are where offenders must answer for their crimes, these practices tend to dilute not only the effectiveness of the courts but also the deterrent effect of law enforcement by the police.

Professional Law Enforcement

Considering the inadequate resources of the courts and corrections, police are left to deal with criminals that in many cases should have been incarcerated. Because of the high rate of recidivism, over 65% in a three-year period, police and the courts as well must expend valuable resources arresting and processing criminals who, in most cases, should have been behind bars.[27] Also, because of expected judicial responses to certain law violations, prostitution, for example, police must choose between expending scarce resources arresting violators that they know will be released by the courts without the imposition of any jail time or devote those resources to more productive crime prevention activities. It is a situation that further weakens the rule of law.

The public's respect for the rule of law is also diminished by the exercise of police discretion and the imposition of arrest and summons quotas on police officers. Officer discretion in the enforcement of certain laws leads to an uneven application of law. If the law is not fully enforced then each officer is left to decide at what level of disobedience he or she will take action. Again, with respect to speeders, some officers may choose to summons a driver who exceeds the speed limit by five mph others might wait until ten or fifteen mph, still others might only summons speeders who weave in and out of traffic. Adding to the arbitrariness of officer discretion is the issue of quotas. Will an officer who has achieved the quota be less apt to issue a summons than an officer who still needs additional summonses?

The principle that everyone is equally subject to the same law is violated, or at least is perceived as being violated, when people who are summonsed or arrested see others violate the same laws in full view of police officers with impunity. Because they know that police have the power to exercise discretion, particularly with regard to traffic offences, the imposition of sanctions has the appearance of a personal, arbitrary act rather than the objective enforcement of law. The efficacy of the rule of law is also impacted when bias in enforcement practices is perceived among members of racial and ethnic minorities.

Does the Government Subordinate Itself to the Law?

According to the first principle of this book: *The enactment of a law requires a commitment to provide the resources and the will to enforce that law.* When the government enacts laws, that act binds the government to fulfilling the intent of the law, that is, arresting and punishing those who violate those laws according to the provisions of those laws. If the government fails to commit itself to achieving the objectives of those laws through the criminal justice process then it has violated the intent of its own laws.

Traditionally, the concept of law enforcement is limited to the functions of law enforcement agencies such as the police. However, within the context of the rule of law, the government's lawful responsibility of law enforcement cannot be limited to policing agencies only but rather to the entire criminal justice system. Within this context, law enforcement does not end with an arrest. It is a process as well as a function. The law defines crimes and prescribes punishment for those crimes. For example, the crime of robbery is defined as the taking of property by the use of force or fear. It is a felony punishable by a term of incarceration of at least three years in prison, depending on individual state law. The government's responsibility is to enforce the entire law, to arrest and try the robber and, if convicted, to sentence that person according to the prescribed penalty. When, for reasons of expediency, the robber is allowed to plead guilty to a lesser offence with a lesser penalty and is prematurely released to the public to further victimize citizens, the government has violated the intent of its own criminal law.

Encouraging Criminal Behavior

Laws are intended to discourage criminal behavior. The threat of an arrest and the penalties associated with violating a law should dissuade a person from engaging in the prohibited behavior. However, laws that are not fully enforced lead to a lack of respect for the law and encourage further lawlessness. Perhaps the most visible example of encouraging illegal behavior is found on the streets and highways. The widespread disregard for traffic laws is obvious and has been well documented in previous chapters. Observing people driving in excess of speed limits and ignoring other traffic laws with little fear of police intervention simply encourages other drivers to do the same.

Prostitution is another example of how criminal behavior is encouraged by criminal justice practices. As indicated in previous chapters, arrested prostitutes are usually fined and are rarely sentenced to jail or prison for any appreciable amount of time. Such lenient treatment has failed to deter prostitutes from practicing their trade. Because prostitution is a business, those fines are simply written off as part of the cost of doing business. Further, except for times of major events such as conventions, enforcement of prostitution laws is a low priority among most police departments. The apparent lack of seriousness with which most jurisdictions enforce laws against prostitution, together with the low priority given prostitution by the judiciary, tends to encourage rather than discourage such behavior. In fact, although it was once considered a crime engaged in only by females, past decades have witnessed increasingly more males, particularly young males under the age of 16, engaged in prostitution.[28] Also, according to Schetky, about 60% of underage prostitutes are recruited by peers.[29]

Public Perceptions of the Criminal Justice System

It is very difficult to maintain the rule of law if citizens do not respect the law and the system of justice charged with enforcing the law. According to Sherman (2000), public confidence in the criminal justice system was rated at 23%.[30] Skovron, et al (1988) found high levels of public disapproval for shortening prison sentences.[31] According to the Bureau of Justice Statistics (BJS), about 67% of respondents believed that courts in their area did not deal harshly enough with criminals.[32]

With regard to drug enforcement, the BJS reported that over 65% believed that the government either made no progress or actually lost ground in coping with the problem of illegal drugs.[33] Also, according to high school seniors, over 85% reported that getting marijuana was easy, over 55% reported that it was also easy to get MDMA (ecstasy) or amphetamines, and 40% or more reported that they could easily obtain other narcotics including hallucinogens.[34]

Lack of confidence in the government's ability to protect the public may also be manifested in the perceived need to protect one's self from criminal victimization. Attitudes about gun ownership tend to reflect those concerns. For example, according to the BJS in 1993, about 34% of respondents believed it was important to protect the rights of Americans to own guns. By 2011, that figure rose to 48%.[35] In another study (Saad, 2012) 47% of American adults reported in 2011 that they owned a gun. This is up from 41% from the previous year and is the highest Gallup has recorded since 1993. Spain (2011) commenting on the same survey added that the poll also found that public support for gun rights was at an all-time high.[36]

Summary

We are a nation of laws and freedoms. Laws are organized to protect collective rights and freedoms of the people. They are intended to deter people from causing harm to others. An implied social contract exists between the people and their government. The government agrees to provide protection through the enactment and enforcement of laws. People agree to adhere to those laws or face the consequences provided for in those laws.

Nevertheless, people do violate laws. Social scientists have, over the years, developed a number of criminological theories in an attempt to explain the underlying conditions and reasons why people choose to commit crimes. These theoretical explanations fall into two general categories: choice and deterministic theories. None of those theories fully explain criminality but do shed some light on those conditions that may motivate or predispose people to commit crimes against each other.

Laws define crimes and the more behaviors prohibited by law, the more violations that can be committed. Adolescents are more likely to commit crimes than adults. Those who commit undetected crimes tend to mature into law-abiding adults. However, according to labeling theory, those who get caught face social, educational and career obstacles that hinder their ability to live normal, productive lives thus leaving them at greater risk of continuing a life of crime.

The government's responsibility in upholding the social contract is further hindered by practices within the criminal justice system. Plea bargaining and other practices that reduce or eliminate just punishment for those who violate the law place society at greater risk of criminal victimization. When criminals are sentenced to periods of incarceration that are shorter than their crimes would require they are simply given more opportunity to commit crimes. Additionally, shorter sentences prevent prisoners from receiving the treatment and rehabilitation necessary to become productive, law-abiding members of society.

Although there are a number of interpretations, the rule of law is a concept that fundamentally holds the government and its citizens subject to the same law. According to that concept, laws should be based on popular consent and enforced by professional law enforcement and a functional judiciary. Rule of law objectives are to achieve law and order and the protection of human rights by the predictable application of justice.

Essential to the precepts of the rule of law is the government's obligation to uphold the law. This is accomplished through a criminal justice process that follows the law and holds criminals accountable for their actions by applying sanctions that are consistent with the laws that were violated.

When the government fails to follow its own laws and allows criminals to prematurely reenter society the result is a breakdown in the rule of law, and loss of respect for the law and the institutions responsible for its enforcement. The inability to hold criminals fully responsible for their crimes provides them with the opportunity to commit additional crimes. The resulting diluted deterrent effect ultimately leads to the encouragement of additional criminal behavior. Such failure also manifests itself in diminished confidence in our justice system's ability to protect and the perceived need for self-protection.

Commentary

Although most people don't think in terms of a social contract, we do accept the basic premise that we have an obligation to obey laws. It is to our advantage to comply with laws because violating laws tends to undermine them and thereby endangers our own wellbeing. This is valid even if the laws are not popular or are not fully enforced. The government's role in this contract is to protect us from victimizing each other and also to create a system of justice that ensures that laws are enforced and those who violate those laws receive the punishment and treatment commensurate with their violations. But, there is an apparent breakdown in the execution of this contract by both the government and members of society.

A significant segment of the population believes that people have a duty to obey only certain laws, those designed to protect life and property, and that as long as they are not harming others they should not be prevented from engaging in activities that are private in nature. Those activities include the use of drugs, particularly marijuana, prostitution, gambling and other behaviors prohibited by regulatory law. Violators of such activities tend to rationalize their behavior arguing that marijuana is no worse than alcohol; prostitution is a relationship between two consenting adults, etc. They, of course, realize that these activities are illegal but do not accept the premise that such behavior is wrong.

Unfortunately, the violation of any law, whether just or not, tends to add to the burdens of the criminal justice system. Police are obligated to objectively enforce all laws, even those that may not be popular. Resources of the courts must be expended processing arrests regardless of the offenders' lack of intent to do harm. Sentences to correctional supervision must still be carried out even if those correctional resources are diverted from predatory criminals to violators of regulatory law.

The government's role in the breakdown of the social contract is twofold. Firstly, the government is complicit through the proliferation of regulatory law, which itself places additional burdens on the criminal justice system and also creates crime by providing additional laws that can be violated. These supplementary laws increase the opportunities for first-time offenders to engage in criminal behavior that in the past was not prohibited thereby resulting in the labeling process and the creation of additional criminals.

Secondly, in its refusal to provide the resources to adequately enforce laws and process offenders the government contributes to the problem. The first principle of this book addresses this issue: *The enactment of a law requires a commitment to provide the resources and the will to enforce that law.* The government's failure to protect is also evident. That failure is not necessarily on the part of the police only but by the criminal justice system as a whole. There is a general lack of confidence in the system. National victimization studies have consistently shown that about half of the crimes go unreported. The most typical reason given was that the victim believed that nothing would be done.[37]

Even witnesses are reluctant to cooperate in the prosecution of criminals. Some are fearful, with good reason. Witnesses are often confronted and intimidated by criminals who were released pending trial. Some witnesses are concerned about social pressures against "snitching." Other witnesses face the frustration of missing work because of seemingly endless postponements, only to see the defendant receive a less than adequate penalty for the crime. Some are reluctant to face cross-examination and others simply do not want to get involved.

There is no question that the government has failed to adhere to a commitment to support the enforcement of laws that it has enacted. But, what is the government? We refer to government as though it is a single entity, and from one perspective, it is. However, American government, either federal or state, is segmented and compartmentalized, consisting of separated legislative, judicial and executive branches, and these branches are not always motivated by the same priorities or focused on the same outcomes. Legislators enact laws and when they run for reelection, they point to the laws they sponsored and/or supported as evidence of their commitment to their constituents. Often those laws portray a commitment to being tough on crime. Rarely, however, do they seek input from representatives of the criminal justice system regarding the efficacy of those laws. The executive branch of government is charged with the responsibility of carrying out and enforcing the law. They must also deal with budgetary pressures and priorities. Every agency within the executive branch is in competition for finite resources and present annual requests for an ever-increasing share of the budget to meet their responsibilities. Within the criminal justice system, a disproportionate share of those resources is usually directed to the police. For example, in 2007 police agencies in America received about $104 billion, about twice the amount given to the judiciary and about 50% more than corrections. After all, politicians understand that the public automatically associates more police with increased safety.

The criminal justice system is also composed of separate agencies, each with its own unique functions and priorities. Police, of course, are focused on law enforcement, but which laws? As indicated in Chapter Six (police) the police effectiveness is evaluated on the amount of Uniform Crime Report (UCR) crime that is reported in their jurisdiction. UCR crimes are those that are referred to when police announce that crime has increased or decreased. These are crimes against persons and property such as murder, rape, robbery, burglary and arson. Violations of regulatory laws are seldom reported unless an arrest is made. If a citizen calls with a complaint of prostitution or drug dealing in their neighborhood, it is usually handled as a call for services. If the responding officer does not make an arrest no crime report will normally be prepared.

The judiciary is concerned primarily with processing. Fixed between the police with the potential of arresting more people than the courts have the capacity to try and correctional institutions with resources that are not sufficient to accommodate those arrested by the police, the courts must establish a system that devotes their scarce resources to those cases with the highest priority. Priority is usually given to the most serious crimes and also to those cases that receive media attention either because of the circumstances of the crime itself or because the offender or victim is well known to the public.

Corrections is also concerned with processing, or moving inmates through and out of the correctional facilities at about the same rate that they entered. Often, when backlogs occur and the number of inmates exceeds the legal capacity of the institution, prisoners must be released prematurely. Priority for release is generally given to non-violent prisoners.

Given the fragmented structure of both government and the criminal justice system, it is difficult, as a practical matter, to hold any one entity responsible for the dysfunction that is all too apparent. However, where else should we look? We elect politicians to lead and take responsibility but the targets are elusive. Frustrated with the apparent hopelessness of the state of criminal justice, those involved simply continue to work hard, giving the appearance of progress while actually falling behind. Perhaps we need a better-informed electorate who will demand the reforms needed to bring meaningful change.

Discussion Questions

1. It has been argued that the United States is a rule of law society. Provide several examples from the criminal justice system to support this notion.

2. Discuss the pros and cons associated with the practice of plea bargaining. Also discuss what might happen if this practice were to be banned.

3. Is the incarceration of individuals for longer periods of time to simply keep the public safe a viable solution to the crime problem? Provide support for your answer.

4. Is there any way that police discretion and rule of law can exist simultaneously? If not, what changes need to be made to police discretion for this to happen?

5. Provide an example of a law that encourages criminal behavior and explain how that law encourages criminal behavior.

6. Provide reasons why the public may not trust or respect the criminal justice system.

7. If more laws create more crime, than should we consider decreasing the number of laws to decrease crime? Provide support for your answer.

8. In this chapter, the argument was made that the violation of any law burdens the criminal justice system. Are there any cases or times when a violation of law may not burden the criminal justice system?

9. It is estimated that two out of three people will recidivate within three years of their release from prison. Is this evidence that the system itself is not working, that we just don't understand why people commit crime, or both? Explain.

10. Rule of law seems to support the notion of sending more criminals to prison, however, the corrections system is already overburdened and is not doing a good job of rehabilitating those already in it. Explain how the practice of imprisoning more people may only compound the crime problem and not resolve it as this concept argues.

Notes

1. (1992). *Plato's Republic (Book II), G.M.A. Grube and C.D.C. Reeve's translation.* Indianapolis: Hackett Publishing Co. 358 e-359 b.

2. Bastiat, F. (1850). *The law.* Retrieved from: http://bastiat.org/en/the_law.html#SECTION_G004.

3. Ibid.

4. Beccaria, C. (1977). *On crimes and punishment* (6th ed.). Indianapolis, IA: Bobbs-Merrill Co.

5. Ibid.

6. D'Asaro, B., Grossback, C., and Nigro, C. (1975). Polyamine levels in jail inmates. *Journal of Orthomolecular Psychiatry,* 4, 149-52.

7. Aichorn, A. (1965). *Wayward youth.* New York: Viking.

8. Sutherland, E., and Cressey, D. (1970). *Criminology.* Philadelphia: J.B. Lippincott. 71-91.

9. President's Commission on Law Enforcement and Administration of Justice.(1967). *The challenge of crime in a free society.* Washington, D.C.

10. Ibid.

11. Ibid.

12. Becker, H.S. (1963). *Outsiders: Studies in the sociology of deviance.* New York: The Free Press of Glencoe.

13. Ibid.

14. Ibid.

15. Lemert, E. (1951). *Social Pathology.* NY: McGraw-Hill.

16. Hartjen, C. (1974). *Crime and Criminalization*. New York: Praeger.

17. United States v. LaBonte, 117 S.Ct. 1673, 1687 (1997).

18. Langan, P. A., & Levin, D. J. (2002). *Bureau of Justice Statistics special report: recidivism of prisoners.*

19. Baber, L. (2010). Federal probation, 74, (3), Retrieved from: http://www.uscourts.gov/uscourts/FederalCourts/PPS/Fedprob/2010-12/results.html#4.

20. Secretary General. (2004). The rule of law and transitional justice in conflict and post-conflict societies. Report of the Secretary-General, S/2004/616, August, paragraph 6.

21. Belton, R. K. (2005, January). Competing definitions of the rule of law: Implications for practitioners. Rule of Law Series Number 55. Carnegie Papers.

22. Ibid.

23. Ibid.

24. McBride, N.J. (2010). *Letters to a law student* (2nd. Ed.). Pearson Education.

25. Van Tassel, W. (2007, August). 17 Experts: Manager of the American Automobile Association driver improvement programs. *Seventeen Magazine.*

26. AAA. (2010). Traffic safety culture index.

27. Langan, P. A., & Levin, D. J. (2002). *Bureau of Justice Statistics special report: recidivism of prisoners.*

28. Schetky, D, H. (1988). Child pornography and prostitution. *Child Sexual Abuse.* Brunner/Mazel.

29. Ibid.

30. Sherman, L. W. (2000). Trust and confidence in criminal justice.

31. Skovron, S. E., Scott, J. E., and Cullen, F. (1988). Prison crowding: Public attitudes toward strategies of population control. Journal of Research in Crime and Delinquency,25 (2), 150-69.

32. Bureau of Justice Statistics (2012).

33. Ibid.

34. Ibid.

35. Ibid.

36. Spain, W. (2011, October 27). Gun ownership in U.S. soars: Gallup. *Market Pulse Archives.* Retrieved from: http://www.marketwatch.com/story/gun-ownership-in-us-soars-gallup-2011-10-27.

37. Truman, J. L. (2010). 2010 National Crime Victimization Survey bulletin. U.S. Department of Justice.

Bibliography

AAA. (2010). Traffic safety culture index.

Aichorn, A. (1965). *Wayward youth*. New York: Viking.

Baber, L. (2010). Federal probation, 74, (3), Retrieved from: http://www.uscourts.gov/uscourts/FederalCourts/PPS/Fedprob/2010-12/results.html#4.

Bastiat, F. (1850). *The law*. Retrieved from: http://bastiat.org/en/the_law.html#SECTION_G004.

Beccaria, C. (1977). *On crimes and punishment* (6th ed.). Indianapolis, IA: Bobbs-Merrill Co.

Becker, H.S. (1963). *Outsiders: Studies in the sociology of deviance.* New York: The Free Press of Glencoe.

Belton, R. K. (2005, January). Competing definitions of the rule of law: Implications for practitioners. Rule of Law Series Number 55. Carnegie Papers.

Bureau of Justice Statistics. (2012). Table 2.0018.2011. Retrieved from http://www.albany.edu/sourcebook/index.html.

Bureau of Justice Statistics (2012). Table 2.44. Retrieved from http://www.albany.edu/sourcebook/index.html.

Bureau of Justice Statistics. (2012). Table 2.47. Retrieved from http://www.albany.edu/sourcebook/index.html.

Bureau of Justice Statistics (2012). Table 2.83. Retrieved from http://www.albany.edu/sourcebook/index.html.

D'Asaro, B., Grossback, C., and Nigro, C. (1975). Polyamine levels in jail inmates. *Journal of Orthomolecular Psychiatry,* 4, 149-52.

Duhaime, L. (2007). Hammurabi's code of laws (circa 1780 B.C.). Retrieved from http://www.duhaime.org/LawMuseum/LawArticle-105/1760-BC—Hammurabis-Code-of-Laws.aspx.

Gallup Politics. (2012, February 7). Self-reported gun ownership in U.S. is highest since 1993. Retrieved from *Gallop* Website: http://www.gallup.com/poll/150353/self-reported-gun-ownership-highest-1993.aspx.

Hartjen, C. (1974). *Crime and Criminalization*. New York: Praeger.

Langan, P. A., & Levin, D. J. (2002). *Bureau of Justice Statistics special report: recidivism of prisoners.*

Lemert, E. (1951). *Social Pathology*. NY: McGraw-Hill.

McBride, N.J. (2010). *Letters to a law student* (2nd. Ed.). Pearson Education.

(1992). *Plato's Republic (Book II), G.M.A. Grube and C.D.C. Reeve's translation.* Indianapolis: Hackett Publishing Co.

President's Commission on Law Enforcement and Administration of Justice. (1967). *The challenge of crime in a free society.* Washington, D.C.

Schetky, D, H. (1988). Child pornography and prostitution. *Child Sexual Abuse.* Brunner/Mazel.

Secretary General. (2004). The rule of law and transitional justice in conflict and post-conflict societies. Report of the Secretary-General, S/2004/616, August, paragraph 6.

Sherman, L. W. (2000). Trust and confidence in criminal justice.

Skovron, S. E., Scott, J. E., and Cullen, F. (1988). Prison crowding: Public attitudes toward strategies of population control. *Journal of Research in Crime and Delinquency, 25* (2), 150-69.

Spain, W. (2011, October 27). Gun ownership in U.S. soars: Gallup. *Market Pulse Archives.* Retrieved from: http://www.marketwatch.com/story/gun-ownership-in-us-soars-gallup-2011-10-27.

Sutherland, E., and Cressey, D. (1970). *Criminology.* Philadelphia: J.B. Lippincott. 71-91.

Truman, J. L. (2010). 2010 National Crime Victimization Survey bulletin. U.S. Department of Justice.

United States v. LaBonte, 117 S.Ct. 1673, 1687 (1997).

Van Tassel, W. (2007, August). 17 Experts: Manager of the American Automobile Association driver improvement programs. *Seventeen Magazine.*

CHAPTER TEN

Race Relations

Introduction

This chapter will explore the issue of race relations and the various ways regulatory laws contribute to strained relations between police and minority communities. Minority recruitment into police departments as a means of alleviating some of those issues will also be reviewed. Particular attention will be given to the practice of police discretion, racial profiling, stop and frisk, and the vulnerability of inner city residents to opportunistic regulatory law enforcement.

Background

Racial disparity in the United States can be traced back to the establishment of the country. The acceptance of slavery by the founders and the continuance of the practice was a direct contradiction to the spirit of the Declaration of Independence, particularly the conviction that all men are created equal. Although many of the founders were against slavery, the issue became subordinate to the need to establish a union that could withstand the possible return of the British army.

The practice of slavery was not unique to America, however; throughout history conquering nation's enslaved people to serve in a variety of capacities, from domestic servants to agricultural and construction laborers. The perception that racial differences equaled inferiority only served to justify the practice. However, the idea of racial inferiority was inconsistent with the principles under which America was founded and there were continual efforts to resolve this disparity. Nevertheless, fiscal differences among the states exacerbated the controversy over slavery, leaving no amicable resolution to the problem. The agricultural southern states relied on slavery out of economic necessity while the northern states depended more heavily on industries where slavery was not particularly suitable. The issue of slavery continued to divide the country until its abolition following the Civil War.

The abolishment of slavery did not resolve the problems associated with race relations, however. Blacks were still considered socially inferior to whites, particularly in the South. Racial segregation was practiced openly and unabashedly in virtually every segment of society, including in churches, schools, restaurants and public transportation. These practices continued until the 1950s, when incidents of resistance began to gain national prominence. For example, in 1955, a woman by the name of Rosa Parks was arrested for refusing to sit in the "colored section" of a bus in Montgomery, Alabama.[1] Also, in a landmark case (*Brown v. Board of Education of Topeka Kansas*) the Supreme Court unanimously ruled that segregation in public schools was unconstitutional. Finally, in 1964, President Lyndon Johnson signed the Civil Rights Act that prohibited any kind of discrimination based on race, color, religion or national origin.[2] The 1960s also witnessed the Voting Rights Act of 1965 and an executive order by President Johnson requiring government contractors to take *affirmative action* in all aspects of hiring and employment. That is, to give preferential consideration to minorities in order to compensate for past discrimination in hiring.

The 1960s was also an era of civil unrest across the country. Demonstrations for racial equality occurred simultaneously with protests by anti-Vietnam War sympathizers and frequently devolved into riots. Most police officers in the 1960s had never experienced a riot or angry demonstration and most departments did not include riot control in their academy training. Therefore, police, who were not prepared to control large-scale demonstrations, often precipitated riots by their over-reaction to the behavior of the demonstrators. For example, in Selma, Alabama, in 1965, civil rights marchers led by the Reverend Martin Luther King were set upon by police wielding clubs and cattle prods. In 1967, one of the worst riots took place in Detroit. It took five days to restore order and only after 43 people died, about 7,000 were arrested, 1,300 buildings were destroyed and 2,700 businesses were looted. After the Reverend Martin Luther King was assassinated in 1968, rioting, looting and burning erupted in over one hundred cities across the country. Many spontaneous riots also erupted over police actions that resulted in the death or serious injury of a member of the black community. One of the incidents that achieved national prominence involved the video taping of several Los Angeles police officers beating a black motorist, Rodney King, who apparently offered little resistance. Six days of rioting broke out in 1992 after four of those officers were acquitted of all charges, including assault. In the wake of those riots, over 50 people had died, 2,383 injuries were reported, over 13,000 people were arrested and over $700 million in property damage was reported.[3]

Race and Class

The relationships between the police and ethnic and racial minorities present some of the more challenging problems to law enforcement. The blending or confusion of race and class further serves to complicate that relationship. This is particularly evident in inner city, economically depressed neighborhoods. According to the U.S. Census Bureau, the poverty level for blacks and Hispanics is about 27%, compared to about 10% for non-Hispanic whites.[4] Because inner city depressed neighborhoods are inhabited by economically disadvantaged people, it is more probable that they will be minorities. This phenomenon tends to feed the stereotype that minorities, blacks in particular, are a homogenous, economically downtrodden group. Other views, however, point to a stratified model whose members range from the prosperous to the destitute. It is further argued that an increasing black middle class migrated out of the inner cities to suburban life, leaving an underclass isolated from middle class life and influence.[5]

These neighborhoods also have a disproportionately high level of violent street crime, extreme poverty, unemployment, low rates of education and welfare-dependent single mothers that further serve to shape a stereotypical view of blacks and Hispanics. According to the Bureau of Justice Statistics (BJS), blacks were more likely than whites to be victims of violent crime, including robbery and aggravated assault, and somewhat more likely than whites to be victims of rape or sexual assault.[6] Additionally, Hispanics were victims of robbery at rates higher than those of non-Hispanics.[7] Murders are also higher in depressed neighborhoods and are most frequently intra-racial in nature. BJS statistics show that from 1976 through 2005, 94% of black homicide victims were killed by other blacks.[8] The same report also found that homicide victimization rates for blacks were six times higher than for whites and offender rates were more than seven times higher than the rates for whites.[9]

Statistics like these, which are based primarily on class, tend to reinforce racial stereotypes, particularly by white Americans. Because mostly white officers staff police departments, and because primarily people of color inhabit these neighborhoods, there is a tendency to associate race rather than class with crime.

Police Deployment

Police deployment strategies include a number of considerations, including calls for service, rush hour traffic conditions, schools, special events, and crime. However, the bulk of police resources are assigned according to reported crime. Because of the higher incidence of crime in poorer neighborhoods, there is a higher concentration of police assignments in these neighborhoods. Although necessary to address serious crime problems, the presence of police in large numbers carries with it several problematic outcomes.

Due to their economic status poor people are more likely to come in contact with the police. Many are homeless, resulting in minor offenses such as loitering, sleeping on park benches or public transportation, panhandling and various other disorderly acts. If a poor person owns a car it usually needs repair for such problems as cracked windshields or broken lights that can result in summonses by the police. Regulatory law enforcement such as this tends to be resented by members of the community. From their perspective, the police, who are there to protect them from violent crime, are instead harassing them by focusing on petty violations of laws. Activity quotas, particularly for traffic and other regulatory law offenses, only serve to exacerbate the resentment. The police image is one of being prejudiced, unfairly targeting minorities and applying a different set of enforcement standards on the basis of race.

Arrests for Regulatory Law Violations

Government statistics show that blacks experience a disproportionately high rate of arrests for violating regulatory laws. According to the 2010 Census, 14% of all people in the United States identified themselves as black, either alone, or in combination with one or more other races, while 75% of all people in the United States were identified as white, either alone, or in combination with one or more other races.[10] Additionally, data show that the rate of drug use among blacks and whites is comparable.[11] In a 2005 national survey on drug use by the Substance Abuse and Mental Health Services Administrations (SAMHSA) the percentage of whites who reported using drugs in the past month was 8.6% as compared with 9.7% of blacks.[12] Marijuana use was also comparable with 6.7% of whites and 7.9% of blacks having used marijuana over the past month.[13] Yet, according to FBI statistics, blacks accounted for 41% of arrests for weapons possession, 40.7% for prostitution, 33.6% for drug abuse and 68.6% for gambling.[14]

The large number of mostly Hispanic illegal immigrants has skewed arrest statistics for Hispanics. For example, in 2007, Hispanics accounted for about 40% of sentenced federal offenders as compared to about 27% white and 23% black. About 75% of Hispanics sentenced for immigration crimes were convicted of entering the U.S. illegally and 19% were convicted of smuggling, transporting or harboring an unlawful alien.[15] However, after discounting the 29% of Hispanics who were non-U.S. citizens, the percentage of Hispanics was reduced to about 11%.[16] About 56% of sentenced Hispanic citizens were convicted of drug offenses, 14% for immigration offenses and 30% for all other crimes.[17]

One of the explanations for the disparity in arrests of blacks and Hispanics, as indicated above, is the high concentration of police in minority neighborhoods, resulting in increased opportunities for observation. Another, more widely held explanation is that minorities are treated differently by police due to their broad discretion in the enforcement of regulatory law. As noted in previous chapters, because regulatory law offenses rarely have victims or complaining witnesses, the decision to arrest is solely at the discretion of the police officer.

Racial Profiling

The idea of criminal profiling has been the subject of several movies, books, and at least one television series, although in theory, profiling is not a new concept. It gained prominence as a forensic tool when the Federal Bureau of Investigation established a profiling unit primarily for the purpose of tracking and identifying serial killers. Traveling from place to place to commit their crimes, serial killers often leave a trail of unsolved murders because in each city or town that they kill someone the murder is considered a single incident and often goes unsolved. By debriefing serial killers, F.B.I. profilers assigned to the Bureau's Behavioral Analysis Unit-2 (BAU-2) are able to identify certain personal characteristics of those killers that might relate to others who commit similar crimes. For example, Ted Bundy was responsible for assaulting and killing at least 36 women in several states across the country at the rate of about one victim each month. Following his arrest, the profilers sought to understand how he became a serial killer. After a number of debriefings, they determined that the answer could be found in his development from birth to adulthood. Specifically, his behavior was influenced by his life experiences.[18]

The term "profiling" took on a different, more negative connotation when in the late nineties accusations were made against the

New Jersey State Police for race-based profiling; the idea that certain racial or ethnic groups are likely to be engaged in criminal activity and by stopping and searching cars operated by members of those groups the officers would probably find sufficient evidence to make an arrest. The controversy reached media prominence when a van operated and occupied by black and Hispanic men was stopped and during the process, after the van moved in what was perceived to be a threatening gesture, the officers fired 11 shots into the van. The police reported that as they approached the van from behind it lurched backwards in their direction. They later admitted that they stopped the van because of the race of the occupants. After an investigation by the New Jersey Senate Judiciary Committee, a consent decree was signed in which the state agreed to allow the U.S. Department of Justice to oversee State Police activities, including how traffic stops are conducted.[19]

The problem is not limited to New Jersey, however. Ample evidence shows that nationally, police stop black drivers at a higher rate than whites. During 1999, BJS estimates that as a percentage of licensed drivers, over 12% of African Americans were stopped compared with 10.4% of white drivers.[20] Although the percentage differences are not dramatic, when put in the context that blacks drive over 2,000 fewer miles per year than white drivers and black households are likely to own fewer cars than white households or none at all, the differences in rates take on greater significance.[21] It should be emphasized that virtually all of the racial profiling issues are associated with regulatory law violations. For example, if a robbery victim reports to a police officer that they were just robbed and point out the assailant, the police have little choice but to stop the suspect and conduct an investigation. However, with regard to regulatory laws, police can choose when, where, and with whom those laws may be enforced.

Stop and Frisk

Traffic stops are not the only situations that lend themselves to accusations of racial profiling. Police may also stop, frisk and question a person under certain circumstances. This authority emanated from the U.S. Supreme Court's opinion in the 1968 case, *Terry v. Ohio*. The case involved a police officer who observed three men who were engaged in conduct which, based on the officer's training and experience, appeared to be consistent with casing a store in preparation for a robbery. The officer approached the men, identified himself and began to question them. After not receiving prompt identification he patted the exterior clothes of one of the men and discovered a gun that led to the arrest of that man (Terry). The Court ruled that the conduct observed by the officer reasonably led him to believe that an armed robbery was about to be committed and he was therefore justified under the fourth amendment.

Since the Terry case, police have used the stop and frisk process as a tool to intercept criminals, thus preventing crimes from occurring. Also, by identifying suspicious persons the police are able to gather intelligence that might later be used in follow-up investigations. Unfortunately, because this practice is used primarily in high crime neighborhoods, the subjects of these stops are more likely to be minorities. Nevertheless, stops involving a disproportionate number of minorities have resulted in mostly negative public reactions across the country.

New York City Police stop and arrest data reveal that they stopped 684,330 people in 2011, a 14% increase over 2010, and a 100% increase over 2004. Of that number, about 12% were arrested or received summonses. About 87% were black or Hispanic and whites made up only about 9% of the total. Those percentages were consistent with previous years. The City's racial composition is about 25% black, 29% Hispanic, and 33% white. In defense of the practice, New York's Mayor Bloomberg pointed to a reduction of over 5,600 homicides compared to the previous decade. It was also reported that over 8,000 weapons were recovered, including 819 guns.[22]

Even where stop and frisk practices receive a good deal of community support, police are still criticized for their decision-making. A recent survey by the Pew Institute found that about 65% of Philadelphia residents support their Mayor's stop and frisk policy. However, 44% of black respondents, compared with 15%

of whites, did not believe that police used good judgment in executing the policy.[23]

Minority Officers

Over the past decades, police departments across the country have made concerted efforts to attract minorities and women into policing. Although there are many reasons for these efforts, including equal opportunity legislation, it was also envisioned that departments representing communities that they serve would gain greater respect and cooperation from members of those communities. Minority officers often possess particular qualities that help facilitate the police mission. For example, bilingual officers have a distinct advantage in not only interviewing witnesses and victims of crime but they can also function as undercover officers to infiltrate gangs and other criminal enterprises.

Efforts to integrate police departments were not without unique challenges, however. Minority and women officers often had to deal with resentment from fellow officers, especially if they were hired under affirmative action mandates. Some residents of the communities that they served also resented minority officers. Some expected the officers to give them special breaks and others treated the officers as traitors, having "sold out." Some minority officers, in responding to those pressures, found themselves treating minority offenders more harshly than whites in an effort to gain acceptance by their fellow officers.

Minorities and women also found difficulty in attaining upper supervisory and command positions within their departments. A number of legal actions brought by minority and women officers resulted in federal, state and local court-ordered promotions so that the racial and gender makeup of departments' management achieved consistency with the proportions of minorities and women officers.

Another area of contention is in the deployment of minority officers. In order to provide communities with a better-represented cadre of officers, some departments assign minority officers to patrol neighborhoods with people of the same race or ethnicity as the officer. Legal actions taken by those officers resulted in an order of the U.S. Fifth Circuit Court of Appeals (*Allen v. City of Mobile*, 331, 1971) that deemed this practice to be discriminatory and ordered the departments to cease engaging in this practice.

Problems associated with the integration of minority officers have diminished somewhat with the appointment of minority and women police chiefs and commissioners as well as increased integration of police departments in general. This trend is having some positive results in public confidence in the police, particularly in minority communities served by these departments.[24]

Summary

America was founded upon principles of human equality and yet tolerated slavery for nearly one hundred years. Even after the abolishment of slavery, many areas of the country forcibly separated blacks from whites in almost every societal setting. Eventually, this practice, too, was legislatively abolished. Although slavery and racial segregation are no longer contemporary issues, there continues to be a perception of inferiority associated with people of different races and ethnicities. Often, fear and distrust are associated with racial and ethnic differences as well. Those differences are most visible in the enforcement of law, particularly regulatory law. Because of the disproportionate economic deprivation of minorities, a large proportion tends to live in poorer inner city neighborhoods, places where the incidents of violent crime are common. Although those neighborhoods, with their accompanying crime problems, are typically identified by race or ethnicity they are more correctly related to class.

These neighborhoods, because of a higher rate of crime, necessitate a higher concentration of police patrols. While there, police are in a position of observe regulatory law violations and because of activity quota mandates must take action, limiting their exercise of discretion. Historical racial differences between police and inner city communities contribute to the specter of racial bias into the situation. Additionally, the prevalence of summons and arrest activity involving minorities raised claims of racial profiling. Crime and summons statistics showing that a disproportionate number of minorities are subjects of police enforcement including stop and frisk activity, tend to support those claims. Because there are seldom any complaining witnesses or victims of these crimes police have wide discretion in their enforcement policies and practices.

One of the measures to alleviate the tension between police and inner city communities has been the recruitment of minorities by police departments. These efforts were not without problems, however. Initially, minority officers experienced resentment from fellow officers and from members of the community, as well. However, with the advancement of minorities and women to higher levels of authority within police departments many of those initial problems were resolved.

Commentary

Nowhere are the consequences of regulatory law more evident than in poor neighborhoods. Police and minorities are pitted against one another in an inner city arena with both sides being victims of circumstances that are beyond their control. Police are sworn to enforce regulatory laws and are often mandated to meet specific quotas of enforcement. Community members, themselves frequent victims of violent crimes, are victimized anew by a system designed to protect them. As a result they are stigmatized as criminals and the police labeled as bigoted persecutors. The victimization does not end there, however. Family members, particularly children, suffer when parents and loved ones are imprisoned. The police image is tarnished and people who are distrustful of the police and fearful of the violent criminals find themselves in the middle of a helpless and hopeless circumstance.

One of the book's principles seems appropriate here, that is: *Because police service is qualitative in nature, measures of that service should be expressed in qualitative rather than quantitative terms.* This principle is consistent with the concept of problem solving policing that was discussed in Chapter Six. Police, together with the rest of the criminal justice system and appropriate social service efforts, should be directed to solving underlying community problems rather than attacking the more obvious symptomatic manifestations of those problems, such as gambling, prostitution and drug abuse. Besides the wasteful expenditure of valuable criminal justice resources, the disproportionately high arrest and incarceration of minorities serves to perpetuate a racial and ethnic underclass.

Discussion Questions

1. If more minority police officers worked in the areas where there is a high concentration of minorities living how might this impact minority's view of the police as a whole?

2. If police officers had been better trained to handle large-scale riots in the pre-1960s era, how might this have had an impact on the communities' perception of the police during the riots of the 1960s and 1970s?

3. Discuss the fundamental tenets of affirmative action and what affirmative action seeks to accomplish.

4. Discuss the advantages and disadvantages of the stop and frisk policy.

5. Identify several reasons why minority and women police officers have a hard time integrating into the police sub-culture.

6. You have been hired to create a police department for a very poor town. Describe the qualities you would look for in the officers you will hire to staff this department.

7. When policing a poor community, should police overlook more regulatory law violations than they would in a richer community, since the offenders cannot really afford the monetary cost of the fines? Provide support for you answer.

8. Provide several examples of how the members of a poor offender's family can be negatively impacted by their arrest.

9. Would it help or hinder policing efforts if police departments mandated that in order to be a police officer you must live within that department's jurisdiction? Explain your answer.

10. Identify several qualitative methods that could be used to evaluate the performance of the police.

Notes

1. Brunner, B., and Haney, E. (n.d.). Civil rights timeline: Milestones in the modern civil rights movement. Retrieved from http://www.infoplease.com /spot/civilrightstimeline1.html.

2. Ibid.

3. Harden, T. (2001, April). America's long list of race riots. *The Telegraph.* Retrieved from: http://www.telegraph.co.uk/news/worldnews/northamerica/ usa/1316209/Americas-long-list-of-race-riots.html.

4. United States Census Bureau. (2011). *Poverty.*

5. Wilson, W. J. (1987). *The Truly Disadvantaged.* University of Chicago Press.

6. Bureau of Justice Statistics (2012). *Homicide trends in the U.S.* Retrieved from: http://bjs.ojp.usdoj.gov/content/homicide/race.cfm.

7. Truman, J. L., and Rand, M. R. (2009). *Criminal victimization.* United States Department of Justice.

8. Bureau of Justice Statistics (2012). *Homicide trends in the U.S.* Retrieved from: http://bjs.ojp.usdoj.gov/content/homicide/race.cfm.

9. Ibid.

10. United States Census Bureau. (2010). *2010 Census data.* Retrieved from: http://2010.census.gov/2010census/data/index.php.

11. Ibid.

12. SAMHSA. (2007). *2004 And 2005 national surveys on drug use and health.*

13. Ibid.

14. Federal Bureau of Investigation. (n.d.). *Crime in the United States.* Retrieved from: http://www2.fbi.gov/ucr/cius2009/data/table_43.html.

15. Lopez, M. H., and Light, M. (2009). *A rising share: Hispanics and federal crime.* Pew Research Center.

16. Ibid.

17. Ibid.

18. Morton, R. J. (2005). *Serial murder: Multi-disciplinary perspectives for investigators.* United States Department of Justice.

19. (2001). *Report of the New Jersey Senate Judiciary Committee's investigation of racial profiling and the New Jersey State Police.*

20. Schmitt, E. L., Langan, P. A., and Durose, M. R. (2002). *Character-*

istics of drivers stopped by police, 1999. Bureau of Justice Statistics.

21. Raphael, S. and Stoll, M. A. (2001). Can boosting minority car-ownership rates narrow inter-racial employment gaps? In W. G. Gale and J. Rothenberg Pack (n.d.). *The Brookings–Wharton Papers on Urban Affairs, 2.* Washington, DC: The Brookings Institution, 99–145.

22. Gardiner, S. (2012, February 14). Stop-and-frisks hit record in 2011. *Wall Street Journal.*

23. Lin, J., and Clark, V. (n.d.). The pew charitable trusts, public opinion poll. *Philadelphian Research Initiative.* Retrieved from http://www.pewtrusts. org/resource_library_search.aspx?keyword=stop%20and%20frisk.

24. Frank, J. et al.(1996). Reassessing the impact of citizens' attitudes toward the police: A research note. *Justice Quarterly, 13,* 321-34.

Bibliography

Brunner, B., and Haney, E. (n.d.). Civil rights timeline: Milestones in the modern civil rights movement. Retrieved from http://www.infoplease.com/spot /civilrightstimeline1.html

Bureau of Justice Statistics (2012). *Homicide trends in the U.S.* Retrieved from: http://bjs.ojp.usdoj.gov/content/homicide/race. cfm

Fagan, J. and Davies, G. (2000). Street stops and broken windows: Terry, race, and disorder in New York City. *Fordham Urban Law Journal, 28,* 457.

Federal Bureau of Investigation. (n.d.). *Crime in the United States.* Retrieved from: http://www2.fbi.gov/ucr/cius2009/data/table_ 43.html

Frank, J. et al.(1996). Reassessing the impact of citizens' attitudes toward the police: A research note. *Justice Quarterly, 13,* 321-34.

Gardiner, S. (2012, February 14). Stop-and-frisks hit record in 2011. *Wall Street Journal.*

Harden, T. (2001, April). America's long list of race riots. *The Telegraph.* Retrieved from: http://www.telegraph.co.uk/news/ worldnews/northamerica /usa/1316209/Americas-long-list-of-race-riots.html.

Lin, J., and Clark, V. (n.d.). The pew charitable trusts, public opinion poll. *Philadelphian Research Initiative.* Retrieved

from http://www.pewtrusts.org/resource_library_search.aspx?
keyword=stop%20and%20frisk.

Lopez, M. H., and Light, M. (2009). *A rising share: Hispanics and
federal crime.* Pew Research Center

Morton, R. J. (2005). *Serial murder: Multi-disciplinary perspectives
for investigators.* United States Department of Justice.

Raphael, S. and Stoll, M. A. (2001). Can boosting minority car-
ownership rates narrow inter-racial employment gaps? In W.
G. Gale and J. Rothenberg Pack (n.d.). *The Brookings–
Wharton Papers on Urban Affairs, 2.* Washington, DC: The
Brookings Institution, 99–145.

(2001). *Report of the New Jersey Senate Judiciary Committee's investigation of racial profiling and the New Jersey State Police.*

SAMHSA. (2007). *2004 And 2005 national surveys on drug use and
health.*

Schmitt, E. L., Langan, P. A., and Durose, M. R. (2002). *Characteristics of drivers stopped by police, 1999.* Bureau of Justice
Statistics.

Truman, J. L., and Rand, M. R. (2009). *Criminal victimization.* ,
United States Department of Justice.

United States Census Bureau. (2010). *2010 Census data.* Retrieved
from: http://2010.census.gov/2010census/data/index.php.

United States Census Bureau. (2011). *Poverty.*

Wilson, W. J. (1987). *The Truly Disadvantaged.* University of
Chicago Press.

CHAPTER ELEVEN

Societal Consequences

Introduction

Previous chapters revealed how regulatory laws impact the criminal justice system and contribute to the erosion of public respect for the law. In this chapter we will review the effects that regulatory law has on society as a whole as well as particular segments of society most directly affected. The manner in which regulatory law contributes to criminality will be discussed as well as the effects of incarceration on minorities and the perpetuation of an underclass in America. The costs of regulatory laws, both in economic and the human terms of unemployment, broken families and public health will also be presented.

The Facilitation of Crime

There is no question that the enactment of many regulatory laws were based on noble ideals, a society free of socially and morally objectionable behavior. Unfortunately, the law of unintended consequences is also in effect. Take the Harrison Act of 1914, for example. It was ostensibly enacted to bring the United States into compliance with the Hague Convention Treaty of 1912 and to regulate the production, importation, sale and distribution of opium or coca leaves or their derivatives. It prohibited doctors from prescribing opiates to patients with addictions to the drugs.[1] This was apparently in response to the high rate of addiction, particularly among women. Opiates had been available by prescription from doctors or in the form of tonics and elixirs from pharmacies. Notwithstanding the intent of the law to curb the problem of drug addiction, in practice it had the opposite effect. Instead of legal sources of the drugs, those with addictions were forced to find alternative providers.

Enter the criminals. Unlike the passive practice of prescribing opiates to addicted patients, criminals continually endeavor to increase profits by using more aggressive methods. There are always those who are willing to take the risks associated with providing unlawful goods or services in order to receive the attendant rewards. Not unlike legitimate businesses, these criminal enterprises seek to increase their profits by expanding their market base and by diversification. Drug dealers typically increase their sales revenues by seeking new customers, including the enlistment of addicts to entice their friends and acquaintances into drug use in order to afford to feed their own habit. Addicts typically resort to crimes of burglary, larceny, prostitution and robbery in order to pay for drugs.

Dealers also expand into new territories. If rival gangs are servicing those territories then street violence usually determines who will dominate the area. Turf wars often result in the death or injury of innocent bystanders, including children. In order to increase revenues, dealers also introduce new products, such as illegally obtained prescription drugs, as well as synthesized substances such as LSD and Methamphetamine. The marijuana laws of 1937 simply added a new product to an already growing illegal market.

Additionally, as seen with prohibition, gangs must establish working arrangements with international criminal cartels and transportation networks to ensure sufficient sources of their merchandise. Providing illegal products also depends on the cooperation of corrupt government officials, including law enforcement. Through bribes, intimidation and assassinations violent gangs are able to operate with little interference. Such violence is not limited only to the United States. The chaos and state of near anarchy in Mexico must be taken into consideration as we calculate the cost of the war on drugs. Such costs must also consider the tens of thousands of people who were murdered and others living in fear and still others forced to smuggle drugs into the U.S. or be killed. In addition to the carnage and the enormous amounts of money expended on drug enforcement is the cost in human potential. The millions of people who have been arrested, imprisoned or otherwise impacted by the arrest of a parent or family member must also be added to the cost of the war on drugs. This will be addressed later in this chapter.

When comparing the state of drug use and addiction prior to the Harrison Act and the Marijuana Tax Act with the current situation, one can only wonder which is more socially acceptable.

As indicated in the 4th principle of this book: *Part of the legislative process should include input from members of the criminal justice system most affected by that legislation.* Legislative failure to consult with police, prosecutors and judges often results in laws that are ill conceived or virtually unenforceable. A quote that appeared in Chapter 3 of this book bears repeating. It was made by August Vollmer in 1936, after the Harrison Act and failure of Prohibition but prior to the Marijuana Tax Act. Vollmer was perhaps the most prominent figure in law enforcement of that time, having served as a police chief, an author of several books on police administration, a college professor and president of the International Association of Chiefs of Police. He warned against regulatory laws in the following statement:

> Stringent laws, spectacular police drives, vigorous prosecution, and imprisonment of addicts and peddlers have proved not only useless and enormously expensive as means of correcting this evil, but they are also unjustifiably and unbelievably cruel in their application to the unfortunate drug victims. Repression has driven this vice underground and produced the narcotic smugglers and supply agents, who have grown wealthy out of this evil practice and who, by devious methods, have stimulated traffic in drugs. Finally, and not the least of the evils associated with repression, the helpless addict has been forced to resort to crime in order to get money for the drug which is absolutely indispensable for his comfortable existence.... Drug addiction, like prostitution and like

liquor, is not a police problem; it never has been and never can be solved by policemen. It is first and last a medical problem, and if there is a solution it will be discovered not by policemen, but by scientific and competently trained medical experts whose sole objective will be the reduction and possible eradication of this devastating appetite. There should be intelligent treatment of the incurables in outpatient clinics, hospitalization of those not too far gone to respond to therapeutic measures, and application of the prophylactic principles which medicine applies to all scourges of mankind.[2]

Eroding the Rule of Law

A free society relies heavily on people's willingness to comply with the law. Law enforcement, along with the rest of the criminal justice system, does not have the resources to deal effectively with more than a small percentage of law violators. Therefore, when large numbers of people refuse to comply with laws the criminal justice system becomes overwhelmed and must compensate by establishing priorities. Police focus on the more serious violent crimes, prosecutors rely on plea bargaining to manage their caseloads, and judges explore alternatives to incarceration in order to ease jail and prison overcrowding. These practices demonstrate to the public that certain offenses are not taken seriously by the justice system and are therefore not particularly important. The public, in response, is conditioned to accept these illegal practices as simply a fact of life. Such is the case with most regulatory laws, particularly those dealing with drugs, prostitution and traffic.

Despite the enormous money and resources devoted to stopping the importation, manufacture, distribution, sale and use of illegal drugs, reports have shown that they are nevertheless readily available and widely used by adults and children alike. Large-scale arrests of high-profile drug smugglers together with the confiscation of tons of contraband have had little impact on the supply of drugs. Further, the efforts at decriminalization have certainly not discouraged the demand for drugs. Law enforcement officers and prison guards are often bribed into cooperating and facilitating illegal drug operations. Drug use among prisoners is well known and prison officials are apparently unable to control the problem even in a highly controlled environment. Moreover, there has been a widespread liberalization in public attitudes toward the use of drugs. People in the entertainment media who openly brag and joke about their use of drugs tend to make the practice even more tolerable.

The entertainment media has also promoted the practice of prostitution. The image of a "happy hooker" has been used in movies and television shows for decades. Detective shows in particular depict a professional familiarity between the investigator and the neighborhood prostitute who is a source of information about local crime. The suggestion is that the detective will overlook her criminal activities in return for her information. As indicated in previous chapters, despite periodic roundups by police and the breaking up of high-profile prostitution operations, the criminal justice system has proved ineffective in controlling street prostitution.

Traffic laws are perhaps the most visible and widely violated laws. Drivers routinely exceed speed limits, talk on hand held phones and text while driving. Self-report studies by the American Automobile Association (AAA) found that about half of the drivers report exceeding highway speed limits by 15 mph, talking on cell phones, and texting while driving.[3] Additionally, over 65% of drivers often feel pressured from other drivers to drive faster than they would prefer.[4] Compounding the problem is the fact that police in marked cars frequently drive along with the speeding traffic, giving tacit approval of their behavior. People tend to justify their violations of law with the excuses that *everyone else is doing it* and *the police don't care*. With the exception of drunk driving, most traffic offenses are not handled through the arrest process but drivers are summonsed to appear in a traffic court. In addition to the disregard for traffic laws themselves is the number of people who neglect to pay traffic fines. Many large cities in particular lack the resources to aggressively collect fines and are left with millions of dollars of unpaid driving and parking summonses.[5]

Incarceration

Over the past decades the incarceration population in the U.S. has grown substantially. Previous chapters have shown that over 2.3 million American adults are currently behind bars compared with about 500,000 in 1980. The United States leads the world in the percent of its population in prison with the next closest country being Russia with about two thirds proportionately. In fact, about 25% of the prisoners in the entire world are behind bars in the United States. Why are U.S. rates of incarceration so much higher? The most logical response is that the increase is merely a reflection of an increase in crime. However, there has been only slightly more reported crime over the past three decades thus explaining only a small part of the increase. The major increase can be attributed to stricter sentencing policies, especially for those convicted of drug-related crimes.[6]

Although incarceration rates are based on a percentage of the entire population, the racial and ethnic makeup of prisoners shows a disproportionately higher percentage of minorities. According to the BJS over 8.3% of blacks between 18 and 64 years of age are incarcerated as compared with 2.7% of Hispanics and 1.1% of whites.[7] Of course, not all prisoners were convicted of regulatory law offenses, and it should be emphasized that violent and career criminals should be put behind bars for significant terms. However, slightly more than half of all those behind bars in federal prisons during 2010 were convicted of drug offenses.[8]

Moreover, families with a parent in prison are more likely to experience a reduction in household income to the poverty level.[9] Over 65% of prisoners were employed prior to being incarcerated and over half were the primary wage earner for their family. Additionally, former inmates earn less money and have fewer opportunities for advancement.[10,11] Family incomes, along with education, are major indicators of a child's future economic achievement.[12]

Being convicted of any crime tends to lead to future criminal behavior. Inmates are pressured into joining prison gangs for protection and tend to build relationships with criminally active peers.

Because their potential for gainful employment is diminished after release, many turn to criminality for their livelihood and increase their risk of becoming career criminals. With so many people and families affected, and with such concentration of the impacts among young, poorly educated men from disadvantaged neighborhoods, the costs of incarceration in terms of its impact on the social structure of this country are incalculable.

Perpetuating an Underclass

Over half, about 54%, of inmates are parents with children under the age of 17 years and about 3.6% of children in America have a parent behind bars. The greatest impact is on black children, with about 11.4% having a parent in prison compared with 1.8% of white children and 3.5% of Hispanic children. Children with fathers in prison are six times more likely to be expelled or suspended from school than other children.[13] In addition to academic challenges, children of inmates are also at higher risk for a variety of social problems including early sexual behavior, substance abuse, antisocial behavior and ultimately, criminality.[14] It is not clear, however, if these risks are due exclusively to the incarceration of a parent or to the general family environment of law violating parents.

Children of inmates are unintended victims of their parents' crimes. They suffer from a variety of consequences, including the emotional and psychological trauma of separation from their parent. Often deprived of a wage earner, these children are more likely to fall into poverty and are at an increased risk of juvenile delinquency.[15] These children may also be placed in foster homes or even worse, they may wind up homeless and living in shelters or on the streets.

With over 2.5 million children with a mother or father in prison, the impact on their prospects for economic achievement is substantial. Research suggests that there are two factors that are influenced by parental incarceration: family income and children's educational advancement. Both have a bearing on a child's future economic achievement.[16] According to the Pew's Economic Mobility Project, parental income is one of the strongest indicators of one's own chances for upward economic mobility.[17] Many children of parents who begin at lower income levels are themselves at that level later in life, including a disproportionate number of black children and those without a college degree.[18]

With the relatively high rate of minority incarceration it is not surprising that black and Hispanic children under 18 years old make up a disproportionate share of the low-income population in the country. As of 2010, 64% of black children and 63% of Hispanic children live in low-income families as compared with 31% of white children.[19] Moreover, according to the U.S. Government Accountability Office (GAO), children living in poverty face an increased risk of adverse outcomes including poor health and criminal activity.[20] In addition to poor health, growing up in poverty also has an adverse impact on the quality and quantity of labor that a person is able to perform.[21]

Children thus trapped in a cycle of broken homes, convict parents, poverty, poor health, educational deprivation and juvenile crime are bound to continue that life style later in life. Early sexual activity leading to children whom they are ill prepared to raise simply adds to the risk that they will also become inmate parents, leaving that legacy to their family's future generations.

Infectious Diseases

Maintaining their health is a particular challenge to people who live in poverty. They have a greater risk of becoming ill and die at younger ages than those with higher income levels. They are also more likely to live in neighborhoods with limited health care resources as well as environmental and social conditions that are conducive to the spread of disease. Over the past century, deadly infectious diseases such as polio, malaria and typhoid fever declined in America and no longer pose a serious threat. However, diseases that are common in Africa and South America are likely to afflict millions of Americans particularly in poorer neighborhoods or poorer regions of the country. Such diseases as Chagas, a leading cause of heart failure and stroke among Latinos, cysticercosis, a cause of convulsions and ascariasis, which leads to abdominal pain and fever are rapidly being introduced into this country. These diseases are spread by such means as parasites in insects, tapeworms and roundworms in the soil.[22]

The U.S. Centers for Disease Control and Prevention (CDC) estimates that 300,000 Americans are afflicted with Chagas, and that between 60 and 300 babies are born with the disease in the U.S every year. Another study found that almost 900,000 black women in the South and impoverished inner cities in the North are infected with the parasite that causes trichomoniasis (trich). People infected with trich are more susceptible to HIV (Hotez, 2009).[23] The same study by Hotez estimates that about 10,000 infants annually are infected with cytomegalovirus (CMV) a congenital virus that leads to hearing and vision loss sometimes years after infection (2009).[24] Also, up to an estimated 200,000 people living in poverty may be infected annually with dengue fever, a viral disease transmitted by mosquitoes that can lead to the failure of the circulatory system.[25] Finally, according to Hotez, " ... we don't know the full extent of their impact, how they are transmitted, or how they contribute to disability. We do not have good diagnostic methods. We can't even begin to think about controlling these diseases."[26]

These health hazards, together with the conditions of poverty, inadequate educational opportunities and other social problems previously cited all function to maintain people in underclass conditions.

Minority Relations

Although the topic of race relations was reviewed in the previous chapter, it should be emphasized again. Developing positive race and minority community interactions rates high on the list of major issues faced by police executives. The historical frictions between police and those communities have long been problematic. The fact that police who are mostly white arrest a disproportionate number of minorities has led to distrust and resentment by community members and an "us versus them" mentality on the part of police officers. Exacerbating the already strained relationship have been recent claims of racial profiling. Whether well founded or not, claims of discriminatory stops and arrests have been almost exclusively for regulatory law violations.

Misdirection of Criminal Justice Resources

Also as indicated previously, the primary responsibility of the criminal justice system is the protection of life and property. People expect police to protect them from violence and theft, depend on police to safeguard their homes and vehicles and provide public facilities that are free from danger of victimization. Further, if they are victimized and the culprit caught, they expect that person to pay an appropriate price for their crime. Unfortunately, such is not the case. Although the police often arrest perpetrators of crime the ideals of justice usually end there. Previous chapters have demonstrated how prosecutors employ the pleabargaining process in order to expedite the adjudication process. The results, although advantageous to the prosecutor, defense attorney, defendant and the court calendar nevertheless leave the victim with little satisfaction that justice has been served. Even when criminal trials are conducted, because of prison overcrowding judges tend to impose lighter sentences or seek alternatives to incarceration, leaving victims and witnesses to worry about retribution from the criminal.

The costs of enforcing regulatory laws, processing defendants and incarcerating those convicted are enormous. Drugs, in particular, account for a significant number of arrests. For example, according to the BJS, in 2007, over 1.6 million adults and over 195,000 juveniles were arrested for drug abuse violations.[27] Considering not only the law enforcement costs of effecting an arrest but also the lost patrol time in processing the defendant, the impact on police ability to protect life and property is severely diminished.

Even if the majority of defendants agree to a plea bargain, thus saving trial resources, they still must be presented at arraignment utilizing prosecutorial and other court resources. Judges must still preside over and agree to the plea agreement, review the defendant's criminal record and pass sentence.

As was cited earlier in this chapter, over half of all prisoners in federal facilities have been convicted for drug crimes. Without even considering the economic costs of incarceration, which will be reviewed in the following section, those inmates are occupying cells that could have been used for more violent criminals.

National and Local Economy

The enforcement of regulatory laws has taken its toll on the country's economy. Police costs related to the arrest process, lost patrol time, prosecutors, judges and court personnel expenses account for only part of the total regulatory law drain on the economy. Perhaps the most direct economic impact is the actual expense of incarceration and/or probation or parole supervision. According to 2008 statistics, federal, state and local governments spent nearly $75 billion on corrections, primarily on incarceration. State correctional costs alone are more than $50 billion, accounting for about 1 out of 15 dollars of states' budgets. One day in state prison costs about $80 per inmate. Considering the current state of the economy, with federal and state budget shortfalls the strain on states' ability to provide other essential services will, of necessity, be adversely impacted. Federal costs per inmate at about $68 are somewhat less than what the states expend but are, nevertheless, substantial, adding to the already skyrocketing budget deficit. Additionally, due to the steady increases in incarcerations and the need for more prisons, the state and federal governments have borne enormous expenses in construction and staffing costs. Consequently, more than half of the states are now seeking alternative sentencing and corrections strategies that cost less than prison, but can still protect public safety and hold offenders accountable.[28]

The less obvious economic impact of the high prison rate, as suggested earlier, involves federal and state welfare and other public assistance programs for needy families of inmates, such as food stamps, Medicaid, Temporary Assistance for Needy Families

(TANF), energy or utility assistance programs and vocational rehabilitation services, as well as a variety of assistance programs for
women, infants and children. When public assistance is added to
the traditional costs of incarcerating regulatory law offenders, the
economic impact is even greater and will obviously rise commensurate with growing prison populations. Also incalculable is the lost
tax potential from wages of otherwise incarcerated offenders. The
likelihood that a criminal record will adversely impact a convict's
future earnings potential will also add to the loss of tax revenue.

Summary

This chapter explored the various effects of regulatory laws and
their enforcement on society, beginning with the way in which regulatory law tends to lead to more crime rather than control targeted behaviors. There are always people who are willing to risk
criminal sanctions for the opportunity to make large amounts of
money or in order to have access to the products or services they
desire. The question is whether the criminal sanctions are sufficient enough to be a deterrent. If not, then the law will not achieve
its purpose but simply encourage people to commit crimes and
contribute to an already burdened criminal justice system. The arrest of violators of regulatory laws, in addition to falling short of
providing a meaningful deterrence, has other social consequences.
Inmates with families can no longer support their spouses and
children, leaving them in impoverished conditions. Children in
those conditions are often relegated to a cycle of poverty, poor
health, unemployment and crime and are destined to remain in a
social underclass.

Conditions of poverty, in addition to the obvious consequences,
also contribute to the spread of infectious diseases. Despite the decline of many serious and fatal diseases of the 20th century, new
contagions from other continents have begun to spread, primarily
in underprivileged communities. Poor health resources result in a
failure to identify and treat these diseases in a timely manner, thus
contributing to their spread.

Regulatory law enforcement also utilizes criminal justice resources that might otherwise be available for those who commit more serious crimes, particularly those who victimize people and their property. Because of the strain on those resources, particularly prison capacity, there is not enough to incapacitate predatory criminals for sufficient periods of time in order to prevent them from further victimizing.

Finally, those criminal justice resources devoted to regulatory law offenses add substantially to the cost of government. States, in particular, that are experiencing economic short falls must divert monies from such essential services as education to the incarceration of regulatory law offenders.

Commentary

The consequences of regulatory laws are many and profound. Despite warnings from such prominent figures as Abraham Lincoln, Fiorello LaGuardia, and August Vollmer, legislators continued to enact such laws. In all fairness, however, they were responding to serious social problems. Yet, without practical input from representatives of the various criminal justice services, potentially foreseeable outcomes could not be taken into consideration. Once committed, however, federal and state governments were obligated to continually appropriate more and more resources to support futile enforcement efforts. Burgeoning correctional populations increased the need for additional prisons and jails. Likewise, the various wars on drugs and crime accompanied commensurate increases in law enforcement personnel. The connection of those efforts with some of the consequences that plagued society apparently went unnoticed.

Perhaps the most serious consequence of regulatory law is the loss of human potential, particularly among minorities. People of color have been particularly hard hit, primarily by prejudicial treatment that relegated many of them to a cycle of poverty, inadequate education and crime, both as victims and perpetrators. The association of criminal and minority evinced a stereotypical image that tended to validate existing racial prejudices. The existence of serious crimes in minority communities also resulted in greater concentrations of police that in turn led to opportunistic observations of regulatory law offenses. These observations, together with the prompting of activity quotas, had the effect of further victimizing those who were in fear of predatory criminals, ultimately resulting in enmity between minority communities and the police.

Still to be determined are the effects of serious and deadly communicable diseases that are beginning to appear in poorer minority communities. Illness is perhaps one of the major contributors to a cycle of poverty. It puts a strain on family relationships, interferes with educational achievement and employment opportunities and further relegates those who are disadvantaged to a continued life of poverty.

Discussion Questions

1. Discuss some of the unintended consequences of the enactment of regulatory style laws.

2. Outright prohibitions of certain behaviors such as drug use or consumption of alcohol have tended to backfire in the past. Provide several possible explanations as to why those problems occurred.

3. Discuss the advantages and disadvantages of the war on drugs.

4. Discuss the impact that the war on drugs has had upon the criminal justice system and provide some possible methods to curb this negative impact.

5. Do you think media representation of crime has an impact on whether or not people will engage in those crimes? Why?

6. Discuss several ways to help children who have one or both parents currently incarcerated so that they do not fall into this "cycle of crime."

7. Discuss how the presence of an infectious disease in a community might spawn an increase in criminal behavior.

8. If regulatory laws are costing so much to enforce and the community doesn't see them as major problems, should the police just stop enforcing these laws altogether? Explain your answer.

9. Discuss some feasible ways to decrease the cost of incarceration without decreasing the number of inmates in the system.

10. Pick a criminological theory and use that theory to explain how living in poverty can lead to crime.

Notes

1. Brecher, E. M. (1972). *Licit and illicit drugs: The Consumers Union Report on Narcotics, Stimulants, Depressants, Inhalants, Hallucinogens, and Marijuana—Including Caffeine, Nicotine, and Alcohol.* Boston, MA: Little Brown.

2. Vollmer A. *The Police and Modern Society,* (Berkeley, 1936), pp. 117-18.

3. AAA. (2010). Traffic Safety Culture Index. Retrieved from: http://www.aaafoundation.org/resources/index.cfm?button=research.

4. Ibid.

5. Beltzer, Y. (2011, April 26).Controller issues audit on unpaid parking tickets. Retrieved from http://www.q13fox.com/news/kcpq-parking-ticket-scofflaws-cost-city-of-seattle-millions-20110206,0,5922128.story.

6. Abramsky, S. (2007). *American furies.* Boston, MA: Beacon Press.

7. Bureau of Justice Statistics (2010). *Correctional Populations.* Retrieved from: http://bjs.ojp.usdoj.gov/content/glance/tables/corr2tab.cfm.

8. Guerino, P., Harrison, P. M., and Sabol, W. J. (2010). *Prisoners in 2010.* United States Department of Justice

9. Johnson, R. C. (2009). "Ever-increasing levels of parental incarceration and the consequences for children." In *Do prisons make us safer? The benefits and costs of the prison boom.* Steven Raphael and Michael Stoll, 177–206. New York: Russell Sage Foundation.

10. Western, B. (2006). *Punishment and inequality in America.* New York: Russell Sage Foundation.

11. Glaze, L., and Maruschak, L. (2010). *Parents in prison and their minor children.* United States Department of Justice.

12. Isaacs, J., Sawhill, I., and Haskins, R. (2008). *Getting ahead or losing ground: Economic mobility in America.* Economic Mobility Project. Washington, DC: The Pew Charitable Trusts.

13. Johnson, R. C. (2009). "Ever-increasing levels of parental incarceration and the consequences for children." In *Do prisons make us safer? The benefits and costs of the prison boom.* Steven Raphael and Michael Stoll, 177–206. New York: Russell Sage Foundation.

14. Hawkins, J. D. (1995). Controlling crime before it happens: Risk-focused prevention. National Institute of Justice Journal, 10-18.

15. Johnson, R. C. (2009). "Ever-increasing levels of parental incarceration and the consequences for children." In *Do prisons make us safer? The ben-*

efits and costs of the prison boom. Steven Raphael and Michael Stoll, 177–206. New York: Russell Sage Foundation.

16. Butler, S. M., Beach, W. W., and Winfree, P. L. (2008). *Pathways to economic mobility: Key indicators.* The Economic Mobility Project.

17. Pew Charitable Trusts. (2010). *Collateral costs: Incarceration's effect on economic mobility.*

18. Ibid.

19. Addy, S., and Wight, V. R. (2012).*Basic facts about low-income children, 2010 children under age 18.* National Center for Children in Poverty.

20. United States Government Accountability Office. (2007). *GAO-07-344 poverty in America economic research shows adverse impacts on health status and other social conditions as well as the economic growth rate.*

21. Ibid.

22. Burns, M. (2009). America's hidden diseases. Miller-McCune. Retrieved from: http://www.miller-mccune.com/health/americas-hidden-diseases-25138/Hotez PJ (2009) One World Health: Neglected Tropical Diseases in a Flat World. PLoS Negl Trop Dis 3(4): e405. doi:10.1371/journal.pntd.0000405.

23. Ibid.

24. Ibid.

25. Ibid.

26. Ibid.

27. Bureau of Justice Statistics (2010). *Correctional Populations.* Retrieved from: http://bjs.ojp.usdoj.gov/content/glance/tables/corr2tab.cfm.

28. Lambert, L. (2009, March 2). Cost of locking up Americans too high: Pew study. *Reuters.* Retrieved from: http://www.reuters.com/article/2009/03/02/us-usa-prisons-idUSTRE5215TW20090302.

Bibliography

AAA. (2010). Traffic Safety Culture Index. Retrieved from: http://www.aaafoundation.org/resources/index.cfm?button=research.

Abramsky, S. (2007). *American furies.* Boston, MA: Beacon Press.

Addy, S., and Wight, V. R. (2012).*Basic facts about low-income children, 2010 children under age 18. National Center for Children in Poverty.*

Bassuk, E.L. et al. (1996). The characteristics and needs of sheltered homeless and low-income housed mothers. Journal of the American Medical Association, 276 (8): 640-46.

Beltzer, Y. (2011, April 26).Controller issues audit on unpaid parking tickets. Retrieved fromhttp://www.q13fox.com/news/kcpq-parking-ticket-scofflaws-cost-city-of-seattle-millions-20110206,0,5922128.story.

Brecher, E. M. (1972). *Licit and illicit drugs: The Consumers Union Report on Narcotics, Stimulants, Depressants, Inhalants, Hallucinogens, and Marijuana—Including Caffeine, Nicotine, and Alcohol.* Boston, MA: Little Brown.

Bureau of Justice Statistics (2010). *Correctional Populations.* Retrieved from: http://bjs.ojp.usdoj.gov/content/glance/tables/corr2tab.cfm.

Burns, M. (2009). America's hidden diseases. Miller-McCune. Retrieved from: http://www.miller-mccune.com/health/americas-hidden-diseases-25138/Hotez PJ (2009) One World Health: Neglected Tropical Diseases in a Flat World. PLoS Negl Trop Dis 3(4): e405. doi:10.1371/journal.pntd.0000405.

Butler, S. M., Beach, W. W., and Winfree, P. L. (2008). *Pathways to economic mobility: Key indicators.* The Economic Mobility Project.

Glaze, L., and Maruschak, L. (2010). *Parents in prison and their minor children.* United States Department of Justice.

Guerino, P., Harrison, P. M., and Sabol, W. J. (2010). *Prisoners in 2010.* United States Department of Justice.

Hawkins, J. D. (1995). Controlling crime before it happens: Risk-focused prevention. National Institute of Justice Journal, 10-18.

Isaacs, J., Sawhill, I., and Haskins, R. (2008). *Getting ahead or losing ground: Economic mobility in America.* Economic Mobility Project. Washington, DC: The Pew Charitable Trusts.

Johnson, R. C. (2009). "Ever-increasing levels of parental incarceration and the consequences for children." In *Do prisons make us safer? The benefits and costs of the prison boom.* Steven Raphael and Michael Stoll, 177–206. New York: Russell Sage Foundation.

Lambert, L. (2009, March 2). Cost of locking up Americans too high: Pew study. *Reuters.* Retrieved from: http://www.reuters.com/article/2009/03/02/us-usa-prisons-idUSTRE5215TW20090302.

Pew Charitable Trusts. (2010). *Collateral costs: Incarceration's effect on economic mobility.*

United States Government Accountability Office. (2007). *GAO-07-344 poverty in America economic research shows adverse impacts on health status and other social conditions as well as the economic growth rate.*

Vollmer A. *The Police and Modern Society,* (Berkeley, 1936), pp. 117-18.

Western, B. (2006). *Punishment and inequality in America.* New York: Russell Sage Foundation.

CHAPTER TWELVE

Summary and Conclusions

Introduction

There are generally two categories of criminal laws. One category, *malum en se* is necessary and the other, *malum prohibitum*, or regulatory law, is optional. In a free society, the government has a fundamental responsibility to protect the life, property and rights of its citizens. *Malum en se* laws together with a well functioning criminal justice system are necessary to meet that responsibility. Regulatory laws tend to be optional, depending on societal standards of acceptable behavior. But, whose standards should be considered? American society is diverse, with a variety of attitudes. Those differences are associated with race, religion, national origin, age, region of the country and political ideology. Nevertheless, there has been a century–long movement toward the federalism of criminal laws. Experience has shown that regulatory laws enacted at the national level are less likely to succeed because they lack broad-based support.

Laws define crimes. Behavior that is evil, wrong, immoral, indecent, harmful to others or otherwise socially unacceptable is lawful unless a law defines it as illegal. Likewise, laws define criminals. People who engage in those behaviors are only considered criminals after laws prohibiting those behaviors are enacted.

There is a mindset among many people, legislators included, who believe that in addition to laws that protect people from harm by others there should also be laws that protect people from themselves. This is a slippery slope that can eventually lead to ill-advised laws. The question is where to draw the line. People engage in a variety of self-destructive behaviors. Some overeat or eat the wrong kinds of food, leading to heart problems, diabetes and certain forms of cancer. Others take over-the-counter medications to excess, or smoke, or drink too much or engage in promiscuous and unprotected sex or other risky behaviors. The urge to do something about those problems is understandable, particularly with very real social consequences associated with those behaviors.

There are also those who naïvely believe that if some behavior is made illegal, people will stop doing it. This is based on their belief that the threat of being arrested is as foreboding to everyone else as it is for them. For someone who has never been arrested, the idea of being handcuffed, hauled into a police station and perhaps incarcerated could be terrifying; therefore, it should be as strong a deterrent for everyone else. However, the threat of being arrested is not the same for everyone, particularly for those who have an extensive criminal record. Being arrested for the tenth time does not hold the same dread as it might have the first time.

Perhaps the most visible accomplishment of legislators is their sponsorship or support for criminal laws. Because of the separation of powers, legislators are not directly responsible for the enforcement or outcomes of their laws. However, that does not negate the wisdom of coordination with criminal justice practitioners, particularly in the creation of new criminal laws and the resources necessary to their enforcement. A good deal of the problems raised in this book could be attributed to this omission.

Resources are critical to the enforcement of laws and if, as is the case, those resources are spread too thinly our system of justice begins to break down. If there are not enough police to enforce all the laws, not enough prosecutors and judges to try cases and not enough correctional resources to effectively incarcerate and rehabilitate inmates, then crime is bound to increase. Logically, the more of those finite resources that are devoted to regulatory law offenders the less that will be available to deal with *malum en se* law offenders, who commit crimes against persons and/or property. The main thrust of this book has been the effect that regulatory laws have had on the police as well as the criminal justice system and on American society.

Prohibition

We began with an examination of the Prohibition era as a case study of some of the problems associated with regulatory laws. The objective desired by the ratification of the 18th Amendment and the accompanying prohibition laws was to prevent alcohol consumption and the societal ills that result from drunkenness. After a little more than a decade, the futility of those attempts became apparent. Instead of eliminating or even reducing alcohol consumption and public intoxication, alcohol consumption actually increased. Prohibition also ushered in a wave of criminality, bribery and corruption of public officials as well as the concept of organized crime syndicates. The end of Prohibition did not end organized crime, however. They took on the appearance of legitimate businesses as a cover for their continued illegal practices that included smuggling, money laundering, gambling and a variety of other illegal enterprises.

Perhaps the most important lesson learned was not necessarily that prohibiting alcohol was not a viable or worthwhile pursuit, but that the nationalization of that ban did not take into account the diversity of public mores and values. For over a century various states banned alcohol, beginning with Tennessee in 1838 and Maine in 1846, and ending when Oklahoma, in 1959, repealed its prohibition laws. Citizens in those states were able to assert their standards and influence their legislators to enact laws that reflected their changing value systems. This practice of following the will of the people is consistent with the principle: *In order to gain maximum support and be most reflective of community standards, regulatory laws should be enacted at the lowest level of government that is practical.* When laws incorporate the values and standards of the community there is a greater probability of voluntary compliance with those laws.

Illegal Drugs

Unfortunately, such was not the case with national drug laws. Enacted during the same general period as alcohol prohibition, national efforts to control the distribution and use of drugs have failed to do either. Drugs use has permeated virtually every part of our society, including our schools. Despite the huge quantities of drugs intercepted by government officials there is still enough to supply the needs of anyone who wants them. Also, arrests and incarceration of those involved in drug distribution and use have seemingly had little effect on the problem. In fact, they only added to overall crime by limiting jail and prison space that could house those who commit crimes against persons and property. So devastating have been the results of drug laws that even repealing them would not eliminate the problems resulting from those laws.

Obviously there are outcomes to the enactment of any laws. Some are expected but others are unanticipated and undesirable. There is no question that regulatory laws, such as those dealing with drugs, are intended to improve society. However, the question of unforeseen consequences must be raised. All decisions are made with the intent of achieving certain results. Other results, or consequences may also occur; some may be expected and others might not be so apparent. The question is, were those results unforeseen because it was impossible to do so or because there was no reasonable effort made to discover those unintended outcomes? When regulatory laws are enacted with the advice and input of criminal justice practitioners, adverse outcomes might either be avoided or means of compensating for those results could be planned. Such was not the case when August Vollmer's warnings against drug laws were ignored. The resulting problems of increased addiction, increased criminality in terms of drug smuggling, and crimes by addicts to pay for their drugs, could have been anticipated and perhaps avoided, but were not.

Repealing those laws does not automatically reverse or nullify those undesired outcomes, however. Take for example a smoker with late stage lung cancer. The cancer will not go away if the person quits smoking. Similarly, when Prohibition laws were repealed, organized crime syndicates continued to operate and grow, infecting many aspects of society. Likewise, if drug laws are repealed, it is not likely that drug cartels will cease to exist.

Gun Control

Not all regulatory laws have had such negative outcomes. Although there are some national laws limiting who may purchase firearms, for the most part regulations regarding gun possession have remained under state and local control and have to a large degree reflected the values of each state's citizens. Because of the diversity of attitudes toward firearms there are significant differences in the degree of restrictiveness among the various states. Most states permit their citizens to own and carry handguns as long as they are not felons and they attend short gun safety classes. About nine states permit only those who can show a need to carry a handgun and two states refuse to allow their citizens to carry handguns at all. This diversity demonstrates the difficulty in attempting to apply national standards. They would either be too restrictive for most people or too liberal for others.

Prostitution

Unlike *malum en se* laws that seek to protect life and property, the purpose of regulatory law is to control and suppress behavior that is deemed by society to be unacceptable. By that standard, laws regulating prostitution have failed to achieve their purpose. Prostitution is an illegal business for which offenders are subject to fines, incarceration or both. Although numerous arrests are made by police the penalties imposed on prostitutes have failed to dissuade them from continuing their trade. Because of limited correctional resources, prostitutes seldom receive substantial jail time but usually receive a fine in exchange for a guilty plea. These fines as well as bribes to corrupt police officers are accepted as part of the cost of doing business and fall short of deterring women and men from participating in prostitution.

As described in Chapter Four, prostitution has contributed to the spread of sexually transmitted diseases including HIV/AIDS and has resulted in the brutalization, rape and murder, as well as virtual slavery of prostitutes, including those who are in the country illegally. Studies cited in Chapter Four suggest that many prostitutes feel trapped in their lifestyle and would welcome opportunities for alternatives. However, the current enforcement approach does little to provide those alternatives but merely leaves the prostitutes with nowhere else to go except back into the streets. The principle that states *If a law fails to achieve its intended purpose or if there are legitimate reasons why it should not be enforced as written then it should be revised or repealed*, would be applicable in this situation. Rather than enforcement only, diversion alternatives to arrests and prosecution should be explored.

Vehicle and Traffic

Vehicle and traffic laws present a unique challenge to the police. Although they are regulatory laws, with the exception of driving while intoxicated people who violate most of them are not considered to be criminals. Police efforts to enforce traffic regulations have not resulted in general conformity to those laws, however. Studies have found that compliance with traffic laws is eroding. There is widespread speeding, hand held cell phone use including texting, and driving under the influence of drugs or alcohol. With regard to speeding most drivers admit to feeling pressured by other drivers to drive faster than they would prefer. Although police resources are limited, the lack of compliance with those laws can be attributable in part to police departments' use of activity quotas as a means of reducing traffic violations. It is a matter of quality vs. quantity as illustrated by the principle, *because police service is qualitative in nature, measures of that service should be expressed in qualitative rather than quantitative terms.*

As explained earlier, summonses and arrests are means to accomplish the end result of achieving a high level of compliance with the law. Quotas tend to focus more on the means rather than the end result and ultimately become an end result unto itself. Police administrators often point to activity reports to show the department's response to particular crime problems. However, police officers seldom consider their activity in that context. The quota itself is their job assignment, not the outcomes that are expected to result from their enforcement. When an officer reaches his or her quota then that part of their job is done. Some officers reach their quota early while others wait until the last days of the period, be it by month or week. The results, in terms of effectiveness, are random. Unless consistent enforcement is applied to specific targeted areas the resulting sporadic, hit and miss enforcement will fail to achieve any meaningful results.

Conditioning is required in order to modify people's behavior. In its initial stages that conditioning needs constant reinforcement. When a driver realizes that the probability of being stopped and summonsed for speeding is rather high, he or she is more likely to obey speed limits. The likelihood of compliance diminishes as the probability of being caught is reduced. Attempts to instill that high a level of enforcement everywhere is not practical for most police departments. The personnel demands would be prohibitive. However, taking control of limited areas would be possible with little more than normally available resources. Once drivers accept that speeding in targeted areas will result in a summons then voluntary compliance will result and fewer police will be needed for the occasional speeder. Of course, increasing the speed limits might also be considered along with corresponding increases in levels of enforcement.

Police

Regulatory laws have taken their toll on police in a number of ways. Most regulatory laws, particularly those pertaining to drugs, prostitution and gambling sometimes involve significant sums of money. Because, as indicated frequently, violations of these laws are rarely reported to the police, there exists a fertile environment for bribery and police corruption. Very often the only ones who know of a potential arrest are the officer and the criminal. The temptation of the money in addition to the knowledge that in some cases the arrest will not result in a significant penalty is enough to lure some officers into corruption. Many officers who had noble reasons for wanting to join the police succumb to those temptations. Police departments have had a long history of individual incidents of corrupt officers as well as systemic corruption within entire departments. Various commissions that were created to investigate police corruption point to a gradual erosion of police officers' values together with the enforcement of regulatory law as contributing factors in corruption. Although there is no excuse for corrupt officers, as long as the conditions described above exist, it is reasonable to expect that officer corruption will continue.

Courts

Criminal courts face the challenge of insufficient resources to adequately adjudicate the volume of arrests made by police. Among the rights guaranteed by the U.S. Constitution to persons arrested for a crime is the right to a trial. Because the courts do not have adequate resources to try the majority of people accused of crime, some incentive is needed to induce a defendant to waive that right. Historically, plea agreements have provided those incentives. With very few exceptions, defendants are offered reduced sentences, reduced charges or both in exchange for a plea of guilty. Career criminals and their attorneys have become proficient at working the system, resulting in many of those criminals serving little or no jail or prison time as compared to the sentence consistent with the crime for which they were arrested. These criminals are soon released into society only to resume their criminal activities. In addition to the disillusionment experienced by victims of those crimes, this practice also results in cynicism among police, which is also a major contributor to police corruption.

Corrections

Increasing arrest and conviction rates have taken their toll on corrections as well. Prison overcrowding has become the norm and the burgeoning inmate population in America has reached proportions exceeding all other nations. Add to that the even larger numbers of people under correctional supervision on probation and parole and that still only shows part of the problem. There are also countless millions of convicted felons who have been released into society. A large proportion of them will recidivate and will eventually be back in prison. Their criminal activities do not cease while they are incarcerated, however. Prison gangs subject other inmates to harassment, intimidation, extortion and sexual as well as other forms of assault and murder. Those gangs also recruit new members who are required to make lifetime commitments to gang activity both in and out of prison, commitments that are destined to eventually return them to prison. Jails and prisons are also fertile ground for disease contagion, particularly sexually transmitted diseases and tuberculosis.

Social Contract and the Rule of Law

People place their confidence in the government to provide a variety of services and safeguards; not least among them is the protection of life and property. Laws and a criminal justice system exist to meet those expectations. Critical to this arrangement is confidence in adherence to the rule of law by citizens and the government alike. This arrangement begins to break down when citizens increasingly violate laws and the government fails to respond accordingly. The idea that it is acceptable to violate some *unimportant* laws, especially if nobody seems to care can easily infect society. Are there such things as unimportant laws? Of course some laws are more serious than others but if a law is enacted, the intent of the legislation is that the law should be enforced and criminal justice officials, including police, take an oath to enforce those laws.

Of course, not everyone chooses to violate laws. For some, it makes no difference how many others do something that is illegal, they will follow their own standards of morality. Those standards are founded on the belief that it is simply wrong to violate the law. Others, adolescents in particular, can be more easily influenced by what other people do, especially their peers. Many young people violate laws as a right of passage as they experiment with risky behavior. Most mature out of that stage in their development to live normal, mainstream lives. However, those who are caught face a more problematic future and the proliferation of regulatory laws only increases the chances of that first arrest. Having been labeled as a criminal or deviant brings with it a number of consequences that together may result in a higher probability of continued criminality.

Race Relations

The enforcement of regulatory laws has taken its toll on relations between the police and minority communities. For a variety of reasons, including high concentrations of police in high crime inner city disadvantaged communities, minorities (particularly black residents) are subject to a higher level of regulatory law enforcement than those in other neighborhoods. Although intentional racial profiling cannot be discounted, the mere presence of more officers presents greater opportunities to observe offenses, including regulatory laws violations. This is particularly unfortunate given the fact that those police are deployed primarily to protect the citizens from violent crimes. Those arrests have also taken their toll on families. A child's opportunity for economic achievement is negatively related to the incarceration of a parent. As indicated in previous chapters, incarceration often removes the major source of income for the family and can result in the placement of dependent children in foster care. This disruption can also interrupt the child's education and as previously explained can result in a continuation of a social underclass.

Societal Consequences

The previous chapter reviewed a number of adverse societal outcomes of regulatory law enforcement. The drug epidemic in this country is perhaps the most serious. Particularly disturbing is the high percentage of school children that admit to having easy access to drugs. The negative outcomes of increased incarceration have also had far reaching implications. Increases in criminal gangs due to prison recruitment also add to the overall crime problems of our country. Inmates join gangs for a variety of reasons, including the need for protection from other inmates. Once in the gang, their lifetime commitment follows them even after their release from prison into society, where their gang affiliation obligates them to continued criminal activity.

Besides the enormous impact on the national economy, the cost in human terms cannot be understated. Literally millions of people with criminal records will not be able to reach their full potential. As indicated previously, the perpetuation of a societal underclass is furthered by the arrest of already underprivileged inner city minority residents. People in this situation are also subject to poor health, education and services and increased susceptibility to infectious diseases. Many of those diseases are new to this country and, under conditions that exist in those neighborhoods, are difficult to diagnose and treat.

Conclusion

Regardless of category, all laws exact a cost to society. Most obvious are the resources needed to enforce, adjudicate and incarcerate those who violate laws. Not generally calculated are the costs in human terms. Offenders are labeled as criminals and as such experience a loss in earning potential and are blocked from a variety of life's opportunities. Regulatory laws have had a particularly devastating effect on the relations between police and minority communities. Already plagued by violent street crime, they are victimized again by a system of enforcement that imposes activity quotas on police, compelling police to enforce regulatory laws where serious victimization occurs. Disproportionately high numbers of police are assigned to those communities for the protection of the inhabitants. While there they are in a position to observe violations of regulatory laws resulting in more summonses and arrests than elsewhere. This disparity has led to claims of racial profiling and has perpetuated an image of racism among police.

Moreover, those arrests have consequences to an already fragile social structure. Those who are arrested may lose their jobs and the ability to support their families. If they are incarcerated the impact is even more profound and may result in children being forced into foster care and having even less potential than would ordinarily be the case. There are over 1.5 million children in the U.S. with an inmate parent. Their access to quality education, health care, and positive adult role models are very likely to be diminished, leading to a continued cycle of poverty and crime.

There are similar consequences of regulatory laws to society at large. More regulatory laws necessarily mean more people will be arrested and eventually incarcerated, adding to an already record volume of inmates and former inmates. Because of criminal gang involvement and reduced employment opportunities many of those who progress through the criminal justice system are destined to continue a life of crime. Most affected are racial and ethnic minorities, particularly blacks, whose incarceration rates are many times higher than whites. This disparity has contributed to a continued and deepening underclass.

In addition to those directly affected are their children, the future generation who are more likely to continue in a life of poverty than not. The underclass life consists of environmental and social conditions that contribute to the spread of disease that is further exacerbated by the lack of adequate health care and health education. A host of diseases continue to plague those communities and the threat is growing. This cycle of crime, poverty and disease is likely to continue for generations to come.

Discussion Questions

1. Discuss the purpose of laws. Why are laws enacted? What are they designed to do for society?

2. What are some possible explanations for why some people will continue to engage in a behavior even after that behavior has been deemed to be illegal?

3. Provide several reasons why the war on drugs failed to achieve its goals?

4. Some have made the argument that prostitution is a victimless crime and should thus be legalized. Do you agree or disagree with this statement? Why?

5. Provide an example of a traffic law that you think should be amended or repealed. Explain your answer.

6. Discuss possible measures that could be taken to address the problem of overcrowding in prisons or jails.

7. What are some steps/measures that police could take to better the level of service that they provide to inner-city areas populated predominately by minorities?

8. What were some of the unintended consequences of the war on drugs?

9. Discuss some measures that could be taken to prevent the children of incarcerated adults from falling into a life of crime.

10. Provide several examples of aspects of the U.S. judicial system that would support the claim that the United States is a rule of law society.

Index

18th Amendment, 29, 30, 32, 39, 40, 51, 57, 233

activity quotas, 91, 94, 117, 118, 124, 125, 201, 207, 226, 236, 241

American Automobile Association (AAA), 88, 89, 217

amphetamines, 48, 51, 187

Anti-Saloon League, 30, 31

August Vollmer, 49, 111, 215, 225, 234

Automated Enforcement, 93, 98

blue wall of silence, 128

bootlegging, 33, 38

bribes, 37, 38, 59, 121, 123, 125, 147, 214, 235

children, 12, 30, 109, 207, 214, 216, 219, 220, 224, 240–242

Children of inmates, 219

Choice Theory, 8, 176

Civil laws, 7

Classical Theory of Criminality, 8, 176

Cocaine, 47, 48, 50, 53, 54, 115

Code of Hammurabi, 6

common law, 133, 134

communicable diseases, 22, 75, 226

Community Era, 113

community service, 111, 155, 160, 183

community standards, 17–19, 41, 72, 183, 233

community support, 40, 41, 72, 204, 233

Correctional agencies, 9

Corrections, 5, 9, 54, 102, 147, 151, 152, 154, 155, 157, 162, 164, 184, 191, 193, 223, 238

corruption, 36–38, 56, 59, 78, 79, 110, 111, 116, 120–128 147, 153, 233, 237, 238

courts, 3, 5, 9, 11, 15, 18, 20, 22, 51, 56, 68, 78, 93, 102

courts, *continued*, 133–135,
137, 145, 151, 154, 163,
183, 184, 186, 189, 191,
238
Crack Cocaine, 48, 53
crime syndicates, 57, 124, 125,
233, 234
criminal behavior, 5, 8, 11, 20,
80, 109, 118, 154, 173,
175–179, 185, 186, 188,
190, 218
criminal court, 8, 53, 133,
134, 136, 144, 147, 238
criminal justice resources, 3,
10, 17, 19, 24, 56, 60, 80,
147, 151, 162, 171, 191,
208, 216, 222, 225
criminal justice system, 3–5,
9, 10, 12, 15, 17, 19, 21–25,
41, 42, 47, 54–57, 59, 65,
80, 101, 102, 104, 111, 118,
133, 135, 147, 151, 154,
162–164, 171, 173, 179,
185, 186, 188–193, 208,
213, 215–217, 222, 224,
231, 232, 239, 242
Criminal law(s), 3, 5, 7, 9, 10,
21, 142, 388, 120, 175, 185,
231 and 232
criminal trials, 9, 146, 222
criminal victimization, 3, 187,
188
criminals, 8, 11, 12, 33, 36, 39,
40, 58, 67, 102, 119, 121,
123, 127, 143, 144, 146,
152–154, 157, 161–164,
171, 173, 179, 180, 184,

186, 188–190, 193, 204,
207, 214, 218, 219, 223,
225, 226, 231, 236, 238, 241
criminological theories, 176,
187

Declaration of Independence,
174, 197
defense attorney, 36, 102, 136,
140, 141, 144, 145, 146,
222
defensive gun use, 69, 70
deterministic theories, 8, 176,
187
distilleries (stills), 33, 35, 38,
40
drug addiction, 49, 50, 52,
213, 214, 215, 234
drunkenness, 30, 31, 233
due process, 13, 128, 134

early release, 3, 11, 12, 22, 56,
144, 157, 160
false arrests, 123–125
free society, 10, 17, 41, 107,
216, 231

gambling, 7, 78, 110, 121,
189, 201, 208, 233, 237
grand jury, 135, 136, 138–140
grass eaters, 121
gun control, 5, 65, 67, 70–72,
235

hallucinogens, 187, 227, 229
Harrison Act, 32, 48–50, 52,
57, 213, 215

HIV, 23, 58, 74, 75, 159, 221, 235
human behavior(s), 29, 65

illegal drugs, 5, 14, 47, 51, 52, 55, 59–61, 72, 122, 163, 186, 216, 217, 233
illegal immigration, 15, 16
incarceration, 3, 9, 11, 12, 56, 133, 155, 156, 159, 160, 162–164, 173, 179, 180, 183, 185, 188, 208, 213, 216, 218–220, 222, 223, 225, 234, 235, 240–242
infectious diseases, 76, 159, 164, 220, 224, 241
inmate parent(s), 218, 219, 220, 242
Inmates, 11, 13, 58, 102, 152–154, 156–162, 164, 192, 218, 219, 223, 224, 227, 232, 239, 241, 242
internal affairs, 119, 121, 122

jail(s), 12, 15, 33, 37, 76, 78, 102, 135, 137, 144, 146, 151, 152, 155, 156, 157, 159, 162, 163, 164, 184, 186, 216, 225, 234, 235, 238, 269
Judge(s), 9, 11, 36, 78, 102, 108, 115–116, 133–146, 160, 163–164, 215–216, 222–223, 232
judicial process, 3, 9, 23, 133, 145

judicial system, 9, 56, 59, 121, 133, 134, 181–183
jurors, 138–140
juvenile delinquency, 135, 219

Knapp Commission, 121, 122, 128

Labeling theory, 173, 177, 178, 188
Law Enforcement, 13, 15, 17, 19, 20, 23, 24, 33, 34, 36–38, 41, 49, 51–54, 58, 60, 67, 77, 79, 80, 90–94, 107–109, 111–113, 119, 120, 123, 125, 135, 136, 147, 162, 163, 171, 177, 181–185, 188, 191, 197, 201, 202, 206, 214–217, 222, 224, 225, 238, 240
legislators, 12, 13, 24, 41, 67, 190, 225, 231–233
life and property, 3, 5, 9, 22, 107, 108, 175, 189, 222, 231, 235, 239
London Metropolitan Police, 109
LSD, 48, 51, 53, 214

Malum in se, 7, 231
Malum prohibitum, 7, 231
mandatory sentences (sentencing) 13, 22, 53, 144, 146, 179
Marijuana, 47–54, 57, 60, 115, 157, 187, 189, 201, 214, 215

Marijuana Tax Act, 50, 57, 215
meat eaters, 121
Methamphetamine (Crystal
    Meth), 47, 48, 214
minorities, 92, 112, 119, 120,
    184, 198, 199, 201, 202,
    204–208, 213, 218, 221,
    225, 240, 242
minority officers, 205–207
Mollen Commission, 121–123,
    127, 128

Narcoterrorism, 55, 56
New York Police Department,
    109, 121

opium /opiates, 47, 49, 52,
    213
Organized Crime, 14, 20, 38,
    39, 52, 55–57, 109, 233,
    234

parole, 9, 11, 103, 116, 151,
    153, 155, 156, 160–162,
    164, 223, 239
parole officer, 9, 11, 103, 116,
    151, 161, 162
Peterloo Massacre, 108
pimps, 74, 75, 80
plea negotiations/plea-
    bargaining, 11, 22, 102,
    142–146, 157, 179, 180,
    183, 188, 216, 222
Police agencies, departments, 9,
    10, 16, 34, 50, 76–77, 87,
    91–92, 107, 109–114,
    116–117, 119–121,

124–125, 142, 186, 191,
    197, 200, 205–209, 236–238
police corruption, 56, 59, 78,
    79, 110, 116, 120–125, 127,
    147, 237, 238
police cynicism, 147, 238
Police deployment, 92, 96,
    112, 119, 124, 200
police discretion, 10, 17, 23,
    76, 78, 79, 89, 90, 92, 102,
    112, 116, 117, 128, 184,
    197, 202, 206, 207
Political Era, 110
poverty, 12, 29, 47, 199,
    218–221, 224–227, 242
prison, 3, 9, 11, 12, 16, 22,
    36, 38, 58, 76, 79, 102, 135,
    144, 146, 151, 152–154,
    155, 156–158, 159,
    160–162, 164–169, 180,
    185, 186, 193, 216–219,
    222–225, 234, 238, 239,
    241
prison gangs, 158, 159, 162,
    164, 218, 239, 241
probable cause, 123, 138–140,
    142
probation, 9, 11, 15, 59, 102,
    116, 146, 151, 153–156,
    160–162, 164, 180, 183,
    223, 239
probation officer, 102
profiling, 10, 92, 94, 116, 118,
    119, 124, 197, 202, 203,
    207, 222, 240, 242
Prohibition, 5, 14, 20, 29–33,
    34–41, 47, 49, 51, 52, 56,

57, 59, 67, 72, 214, 215, 233, 234

prosecutor(s), 9, 11, 22, 24, 102, 121, 122, 133–136, 138, 140–142, 144–146, 179, 215, 216, 223, 232

prostitution, 5, 7, 15, 50, 65, 72–85, 101, 110, 121, 163, 184, 186, 189, 191, 201, 208, 214–217, 235, 237

race relations, 197, 198, 221, 240

racial profiling, 10, 92, 94, 116, 118, 119, 124, 197, 202, 203, 207, 222, 240, 242

Racial segregation, 198, 206

Reform Era, 110, 111

regulatory law(s), 3–5, 7, 13, 14, 18–21 29, 41, 65, 72, 94, 101–103 107, 114–116, 119–121, 124–128, 146, 147, 163, 164, 171, 189, 191, 197, 201–203, 206–207, 213, 215, 216, 218, 222–226, 231, 232, 234–237, 238, 240–242

revolving door justice, 11, 127, 143, 146

Rotten Apple Theory, 120, 126

rule by law, 181, 182

rule of law, 10, 12, 15, 17, 23, 128, 171, 173, 180–186, 188, 216, 239

Scofflaws, 93

Second Amendment, 66, 68, 71

selective enforcement, 10, 22, 23, 116

sexually transmitted diseases, 73, 75, 159, 235, 239

smuggling, 33, 34, 37, 52, 56, 72, 201, 233, 234

social contract, 171, 173–175, 179, 183, 187–189, 239

speakeasies, 35, 36

stare decisis, 133

stop and frisk, 197, 203, 204, 207

strict liability laws, 88

Sullivan Act, 67

temperance movement, 47

Terry v. Ohio, 204

The Untouchables, 38

Traffic enforcement, 23, 87, 90–94, 119, 183

Transit Police, 94–96, 124

Tuberculosis, 22, 76, 159, 239

U.S. Constitution, 7, 10, 29, 34, 66, 71, 74, 134, 162, 238

underclass, 208, 213, 219, 221, 224, 240–242

Uniform Crime Reports, 111

vehicular traffic, 5, 65, 87

victimization, 3, 70, 119, 144, 158, 180, 187, 188, 190, 200, 207, 222, 241

victimless crime, 73, 74, 79, 101, 120

Violent felons, 11, 22
Volstead Act, 32–37, 40, 57

Walnut Street Jail, 152
War on Drugs, 14, 47, 52, 53,
    56, 60–64, 214, 215, 225
Women's Christian Temper-
    ance Union, 30, 31